RECONCEPTUALIZING CURRICULUM DEVELOPMENT

"This book is a thoughtful reminder of what curriculum and teaching have meant in the past and could mean again in a brighter future."

Nel Noddings, author of *Education and Democracy in the 21st Century*

"Curriculum work really starts with people, not with theories. Professor Henderson understands this. This magisterial work offers a strong analytical focus on the pedagogical features of the curriculum—on the interactive life of the teacher and the student. The field of Curriculum Studies has long languished with a multiplicity of theories that has challenged its disciplinary integrity. Too many of its practitioners have pledged avoidance to institutional and normative concerns. Professor Henderson's work defies this trend and offers renewed promise to fulfill the historic involvement of curriculum professors in the work of the school. We have waited too long for this thoughtful and exciting line of inquiry."

Peter Hlebowitsh, Dean and Professor, University of Alabama

Reconceptualizing Curriculum Development provides accessible, clear guidance on curriculum problem solving and educational leadership through the practice of a synoptic curriculum study. This practice integrates three influential interpretations of curriculum—curriculum as deliberative artistry, curriculum as complicated conversation, and curriculum as *currere*—with John Dewey's lifetime work on reflective inquiry. At its heart, the book advances *a way of studying* as *a way of living* with reference to the question: How might I live as a democratic educator?

The study guidance is organized as an open-ended scaffolding of three embedded reflective inquiries informed by four deliberative conversations. Study recommendations are provided by a carefully selected team. The field-tested, study-based approach is illustrated through a multilayered, multivoiced narrative collage of four experienced teachers' personal journeys of understanding in a collegial study context. Applying William Pinar's argument that a 'conceptual montage' enabling teachers to lead complicated conversations should be the focus for curriculum development in the field's current 'post-reconceptualist' moment, the book moves forward the educational aim of facilitating a holistic subject/self/social understanding through the practice of a balanced hermeneutics of suspicion and trust. It closes with a discussion of cross-cultural collaboration and advocacy, reflecting the interest of curriculum scholars in a wide range of countries in this study-based, lead-learning approach to curriculum development.

James G. Henderson is Co-Coordinator, Teacher Leader Endorsement Program, Kent State University, USA.

Studies in Curriculum Theory

William F. Pinar, Series Editor

Reid • *Curriculum as Institution and Practice: Essays in the Deliberative Tradition*
Pinar (Ed.) • *Queer Theory in Education*
Huebner • *The Lure of the Transcendent: Collected Essays by Dwayne E. Huebner. Edited by Vikki Hillis. Collected and Introduced by William F. Pinar*

For additional information on titles in the Studies in Curriculum Theory series, visit
www.routledge.com/education

RECONCEPTUALIZING CURRICULUM DEVELOPMENT

Inspiring and Informing Action

James G.Henderson and Colleagues

Routledge
Taylor & Francis Group

NEW YORK AND LONDON

First published 2015
by Routledge
711 Third Avenue, New York, NY 10017

and by Routledge
2 Park Square, Milton Park, Abingdon, Oxon OX14 4RN

Routledge is an imprint of the Taylor & Francis Group, an Informa business

© 2015 Taylor & Francis

Library of Congress Cataloging-in-Publication Data
   Reconceptualizing curriculum development : inspiring and informing action / edited by James Henderson.
      pages cm — (Studies in curriculum theory series)
   Includes bibliographical references and index.
   1. Curriculum planning. I. Henderson, James, 1945-
   LB2806.15.R425 2014
   375'.001—dc23   2014017040

ISBN: 978-0-415-70427-4 (hbk)
ISBN: 978-1-315-76259-3 (ebk)

Typeset in 10/12 Bembo
by codeMantra

Printed and bound in the United States of America by Publishers Graphics, LLC on sustainably sourced paper.

Thanks, Janis, for your loving support and for your lessons in understanding and compassion for all forms of life.

CONTENTS

FOREWORD

William F. Pinar

The future is not in front of us; it's behind, concealed in the past, in the time before schooling as scores in a false international competition occurred to politicians determined to deflect blame for their own failures.[1] Curriculum development was one casualty of the manufactured crisis in the schools, curriculum development conceived as procedure.[2] Such proceduralism ensured standardization,[3] the anathema of education as critical thinking, creativity, and caring. As this volume testifies, these have been rescued in the reconceptualization of curriculum development that has now been achieved.[4]

Reactivating the past—through academic study[5]—reconfigures the present, restructuring it as a moment in time, not the illusory endless "now" created by our coincidence[6] with the screens at which we stare.[7] Presentism (in which time flat-lines), narcissism (in which alterity is effaced), exhibitionism (in which "communication" becomes compulsory): these are the present circumstances in which we work, in which James Henderson and his colleagues attempt to teach. In an era of tweeting not talking, celebrity not recognition, consumption not creativity, the challenges educators face seem insurmountable.[8] Non-coincidence with what is—indeed, intransigence—becomes in our time the core of a professional ethics[9] that positions our commitment to children as central.[10]

Against the continuing cultural collapse and reconstruction that consumer capitalism[11] compels, memory becomes primary. As it temporalizes, memory contextualizes what is in front of us, providing much maligned "content," knowledge even. In contrast to "information," *knowledge* contains the craft of its creator, bears the imprint of one's lived experience, one's reading, thinking, writing. Dated, it invites us to the distinctive moment of its creation, enabling us to notice what is unprecedented about the present. When the past becomes present, we can begin to work through present circumstances. The past Henderson reactivates in this resounding collection cannot be confined to be one era, as he returns us to Socrates as well as Dewey.[12]

There is an imprinting incident, one that informs—perhaps even animates—Henderson's exemplary commitment to curriculum as "inspired and informed action." He describes it in the preface: a long weekend with his wise mentor Normand Bernier, accompanied by James Macdonald and Bernice Wolfson.[13] An "inquiry experiment," Jim and several other students "engaged in Socratic dialogue on the cultural and philosophical study of education."[14] Without time or other constraints, the inquiry was "open." It was, he remembers, "my first powerful experience with the value of inspired lead learning." Inspiration and leadership[15]—aren't these reciprocally related?—inform educational experience, even as they cannot guarantee it.[16]

It is the temporal complexity of the present moment—once it is activated, alive, actual not virtual (displaced on a screen)—that requires our specification of what is at stake.[17] This intellectual obligation offers nothing less than "freedom-through-understanding."[18] Never only intellectual or final, such understanding represents a moment of working-through of what has been bequeathed to us, recognizing its "recursive" character, inviting "creative co-designing, pedagogical transacting, and evaluative deepening." Engaging in such complicated conversation[19] teaching is indeed an "art," inviting sometimes abstract expression of concrete incidents, sometimes simplification.[20] Judgment—reliant on knowledge and information, wisdom,[21] and savvy, structured by ethical ideals[22]—becomes an ongoing professional practice that inspires interlocutors through the eddies that sometimes stop the flow of conversation. Surely, professional judgment steadies[23] the "hermeneutic, holistic pedagogy [that] is at the heart of this new curriculum development." In the final chapter, Henderson presents an enactment of this cosmopolitan[24] conversation among educators from four continents, focused on "the worth and feasibility of the book's central ideas," among these "lead learning, caring pedagogical artistry, nuanced curriculum understanding, and responsible professional autonomy." Their worth is entirely obvious. Whatever their feasibility—present circumstances are infamously unfavorable, but never underestimate the power of human agency inspired by ethical ideals—James Henderson and his impressive colleagues have indeed reconceptualized curriculum development. They have done so in part by working through the past, enabling them to recast the present. The reconceptualization of curriculum development that James G. Henderson and his colleagues have accomplished here comforts us that the future we find may—miraculously—be the future for which we pray.[25]

Endnotes

1   For a history of this displacement—first blaming the schools for 1950s military failure, then for 1980s economic mismanagement—see Pinar, 2012; Berliner and Biddle, 1995.

2 Recently reviewed (see Jupp, 2014 for a succinct summary), the so-called (see Pinar, 2013a) Tyler Rationale (Tyler, 1949) was definitively critiqued by Kliebard (1970).

3 Citing Schwab, Henderson reminds us that "pedagogical artistry cannot be enacted through standardized, one-size-fits-all practices."

4 Repudiating its bureaucratic legacy—a form of "institutionalism" (Airton, 2013, p. 535; Pinar, 2011, 190, n. 3; see also p. 91 and 165, n. 36)—I offered a reconceptualization of curriculum development as primarily intellectual (see Pinar, 2006; for its contextualization, see Grimmett & Halverson, 2010). Here, Henderson and his colleagues recast curriculum development as "synoptic," enacting that canonical curriculum concept by incorporating the key concepts of (not only) contemporary curriculum studies. Both proposals share what Henderson characterizes as "an open synoptic design" that offers an indispensable "starting kit" to teachers and students alike.

5 Study, not teaching, is the site of education (Pinar, 2006). In chapter 5, Wendy Samford importantly associates study with reconceptualized curriculum development, inviting us "to embrace study as curriculum development." Solitary and social, study encourages agency—"dynamic, engaged student learning" in Henderson's fine phrasing—as it invites students to find their way through the material they must— want to—learn. Ethically engaged teachers and administrators—actually present (in more than one sense) persons, not online images—are indispensable, not only for young children, but also for inspired participation in the complicated conversation that is the curriculum.

6 "Coincidence" not as happening by chance (although there is that), but in its formal definition, e.g., as the condition of being identical, the collapsing of difference. Presentism and narcissism are among the cultural consequences of the omnipresence of technology.

7 "It is the social world turned into an interactive mirror," Mejias (2013) points out, "miniaturized and projected onto a screen for our pleasure ... a means for the masses to contemplate a simulation of themselves and express themselves through this simulation" (pp. 14–15). The public world—structured by difference—disappears.

8 While the assault on the teaching profession is unique—no other profession suffers the same obsession with "outcomes"—it is hardly the only profession to suffer. "The prevailing ideology," Kuklick (2002) summarizes, "seems to be that regulation of professional behavior is best left to the free play of market forces." She adds: "many professionals understand themselves as mere technicians, having abandoned the belief that their occupations are oral callings, which require that they both treat clients holistically and consider the social implications of professional decisions" (p. 141). The reconceptualization of curriculum development demonstrated in this text becomes central in the re-professionalization of the U.S. teaching force.

9 Referencing Dewey, Henderson reminds us that "education is a noble vocational calling and a vital public service." No mere "job," teaching compels us to study, to engage in ongoing, often complicated conversation with our students, our predecessors, and ourselves, for the sake of those present and those yet to come. Professional ethics, then, becomes a set of subjective and social intellectual practices— cooperative, yes, even "collaborative" (as this volumes testifies) undertakings—with "potential for the moral transformation of the self" (Bielskis, 2011, p. 303), the self of each concerned, children and teachers alike.

10 Even the American Medical Association felt it necessary to remind physicians that "a physician's paramount responsibility is to his or her patients." While the Association allowed that a doctor "owes a duty of loyalty to his or her employer," it acknowledged that "this divided loyalty can create conflicts of interest, such as financial incentives to over- or under-treat patients." AMA guidelines assert that "physicians should always make treatment and referral decisions based on the best interests of their patients"

(quoted in Pear, 2012, p. A16). The parallel with the profession of education is, I trust, obvious. In face of "school reform," intransigence is ethically advised, as Jen Griest, Jennifer L. Schneider, Susan School, and Konni Stagliano affirm in chapter 9: "We, teachers, do not need to let ourselves feel restricted by the forces around us; we can refuse to let others dictate the educational experiences we create for our students and ourselves." Guided by professional ethics, it is time, they note, "to turn inward."

11 Henderson quotes Dewey to remind us that the atomized (I'd say predatory) individualism that "pecuniary culture" (Dewey's phrase) constitutes "the deepest problem of our times" (Dewey again). Education is reduced to its economic impact—consider STEM and Common Core—and its democratic significance seems simply forgotten—except by courageous educators. "Since the beginnings of my teaching career," Daniel J. Castner testifies (in chapter 2), "I have maintained a commitment to consider myself *in the service of the public.*"

12 These two "bookends" hold up a long row of ancestors and contemporaries whom Henderson and his colleagues acknowledge. These authorities authorize us to participate in the conversation they themselves created and continued. Without memory—studious acknowledgement of intellectual histories—the conversation ends, chit-chat begins, as continuity, coherence, and community all fade in the false futurism of instrumentalism. The ends justifying the means are re-expressions of the present, anyway, not the future unfolding from the past that we reconstruct ethically for the sake of social justice and subjective excellence. These are reciprocally related, as Boni Wozolek appreciates in chapter 6, where she reminds us that "social justice is a deeply personal topic," requiring us "to position social justice in the intersection of how one knows, the epistemological, and one's way of being, the ontological."

13 These are among the most important curriculum scholars and leaders of that era, along with Dwayne Huebner (1999) and Maxine Greene, with whose work Henderson has engaged in the past (see Henderson et al., 1998) and continues to do so in this collection.

14 Unless otherwise indicated, all quoted passages are from this volume.

15 As Henderson and Kesson (2004) have long appreciated, there is an intimate connection between practical wisdom and inspired curriculum work.

16 The conceptualized curriculum development Henderson provides here is "designed to foster dynamic, engaged student learning." Countering the implied promises of "outcomes," Henderson's choice of verbs is crucial, as "foster" means: 1) to provide a child with care and upbringing, 2) to encourage the development of something, 3) to keep a feeling or thought alive. The manipulation of children that structures so-called "evidence-based" research on "what works" is conspicuously absent here. What is powerfully present is an articulation of our ethical commitment to children, requiring repudiation of "school reform," forefronting not tests but our relationships with the students with whom we work. These, Luxon (2013) points out, "are at their best when they draw on those 'practices of the self' that educate individuals in a self-authorship resistant to being overwritten by cultural narratives" (p. 8). One such "practice of the self" is autobiography, embedded in Henderson's invocation of a "new" and "integrated individualism," collaborative curriculum development ("development-from-within"), implying the formulation of a revitalized professional identity (see chapters 2–8). Another such "practice" is dialogical encounter, animated participation in complicated conversation—ethical, intellectual engagement—with others (see chapters 9 and 11). A third is reflection, evident throughout the collection but the point of chapter 10, where we are returned to Henderson's verb "foster," when Catherine Hackney concludes: "We, as teachers and principals, must muster up the courage to promote and 'protect our good work' (Schwartz & Sharpe, 2010, p. 287), for our profession, but most especially, for all of the students we serve."

17 What is at stake in every present moment is irrevocably concrete but also abstract, requiring a double consciousness that the concept of allegory invites (Pinar, 2012). The reverberating facticity of teaching in everyday life—and its symbolic significance—is evident in Petra Pienkosky Moran's affirmation of mythopoetics, a tradition that accentuates the specific—including what Moran affirms as "the deep, personal connections" among students and teachers—as well as the "archetypical," including the mythic figures of "the hero, the mother, the explorer." For me, threading the needle that is the present moment incorporates both what is perhaps unprecedented, and its resonance with what has preceded it, as well as what it portends.

18 As Jennifer L. Schneider elaborates in chapter 3, this ideal can be enacted in our daily lives through finding and creating "wiggle room." "Acting upon wiggle room," Schneider wisely counsels, "is a way for you to move forward with intention and thoughtful actions, making your teaching a mindful practice of holistic understanding."

19 For a conversation complicated by culture and location, see chapter 11, where Tero Autio, Aboudou Hamidou Berthé, Donna Adair Breault, Rosemary Gornik, Thomas E. Kelly, Kauko Komulainen, and Wen-Ling Lou reflect on challenges reconceptualized curriculum development faces and poses.

20 Erudition is the prerequisite to pedagogical participation in complicated conversation, as even "facilitation" requires not only academic expertise but interpersonal sensitivity, as well. The destruction of professional authority in "school reform"—in the name of "flexibility" and "student-centeredness"—spells the end of education. Replacing it will be, we are told by Ben Williamson (2013), "centrifugal schooling," a "vision of the future of education and learning that is decentered, distributed, and dispersed rather than narrowly centered, channeled, and canalized" (p. 17). Its "keywords," Williamson (2013) informs us, "are 'networks,' 'connections,' and 'decentralization,' as a family of related centrifugal terms. These key words articulate a shift from a centered tradition of thinking about schooling, as an institutional process that happens on school premises through formal pedagogical techniques of transmission, to an emerging, decentered vision where learning is continually dispersed and cybernetically distributed into society through new technologies, communications networks, the informal pedagogies of media, and emerging social practices of interest-based, peer-to-peer, just-in-time participatory learning" (p. 7). In this "vision"—I'd call it a nightmare—teachers are gone, as are schools, dismissed as antiquated "brick-and-mortar" impediments to online learning (see Pinar, 2013b, pp. 24–44). Clearing the way for Microsoft's marketing and profiteering, the Bill and Melinda Gates Foundation appears determined to bulldoze what remains of the infrastructure—tenure, union protection, faculty governance—of the profession of teaching in the United States (see, for example, Banchero, 2011; Dillon, 2010; *Los Angeles Times*, 2012; Rich, 2013). If there is ever a Nuremberg-style trial of those who have perpetrated the crimes against humanity that "school reform" represents, Bill Gates would be among the first to be indicted.

21 Henderson was early in realizing the relevance of this ancient concept to practice today (see Henderson & Kesson, 2004). Now it is acknowledged as central to understanding curriculum (see Smith, 2014; Wang, 2014).

22 Henderson invokes the notion of "virtue," recalling the important work of Alasdair MacIntyre. As Blackledge and Knight (2011) point out, "MacIntyre insists not only that virtue is predicated upon the existence of social practices through which people are able to make sense of their lives within particular traditions, but also that capitalist and state institutions undermine these practices, thus preventing us from actualizing our potential as social and rational animals" (pp. 1–2). While virtue-ethics suffers "defects" —see Callinicos, 2011, pp. 64–65—its very invocation helps shift the

emphasis of education back to "inputs" over "outcomes," on "ethics" over "politics." Reconceptualizing curriculum development, Christine Fishman reminds us in chapter 4, means emphasizing meaning as well as efficiency, "the distinctly moral nature of teachers' work."

23 "Less a problem of epistemological uncertainty," Luxon (2013) points out, discussing Foucault's sense of *parrhesia* (fearless speech), "the shakiness addressed by *parrhesia* is an inability to orient and steady oneself through one's relations to oneself, to others, and to truth-telling" (p. 177). Later, Luxon (2013) explains that "the practices of *parrhesia* thus educate individuals to what I term a 'disposition to steadiness.' As individuals improve their ability to manipulate their curiosity, they learn to forestall immediate reactions and instead to maintain a steady attitude toward themselves, to attend to changes and reactions, and to sift through a raft of information—some sensory, some analytic—before drawing a conclusion. Individuals must try to navigate the two extremes of unblinking fixity and mindless distraction" (p. 191). In this sense, professional judgment can correct subjective imbalances as it monitors internal information, enabling more precise—attuned—engagement with one's interlocutors. Teacher-proof programs—like interactive online curricula—substitute programmed formulae for dialogical encounter.

24 In chapter 7, Beth A. Bilek-Golias emphasizes the importance of breadth in curriculum, including knowledge of "the ways in which we are with one another as interconnected parts of the world." Such knowledge, she points out, challenges us "to embody an individual openness as a way of life in order to proceed to embrace *ecological cosmopolitanism.*"

25 The great James B. Macdonald (1995) appreciated that "prayer" is also a metaphor for yearning. In a moving and dramatic gesture, he characterized curriculum theory as a "prayerful act" (p. 11). Macdonald's son Bradley, a professor of political science at Colorado State University, kindly collected his father's works, canonical in U.S. curriculum studies. A former Ph.D. student of mine, Ashwani Kumar, completed a superb study of Krishnamurti and Macdonald, a copy of which I sent to Professor Macdonald, documenting our remembrance of and appreciation for his father's lasting importance.

PREFACE

Education … marks the most perfect and intimate union of science and art conceivable in human experience. The art of thus giving shape to human powers and adapting them to social service is the supreme art; one calling into its service the best of artists; that no insight, sympathy, tact, executive power, is too great for such service. Every teacher should realize the dignity of his [or her] calling; that he [or she] is a social servant set apart for the maintenance of proper social order and the securing of the right social growth. (Dewey, 1897/2013, pp. 39–40)

Teaching profits from—no, requires at its best—artistry. Artistry requires sensibility, imagination, technique, and the ability to make judgments about the feel and significance of the particular. … The creation of schools in which the growth of teachers is taken seriously will require evolution: it will take time to learn how to create them. To create such places a new kind of school culture will have to be crafted, a culture that cares as much about the growth of teachers as the growth of students. (Eisner, 2005a, pp. 201, 203)

This book introduces and illustrates a new curriculum development that is designed to foster dynamic, engaged student learning. Imagine highly motivated teachers and students. Envision them enthusiastically collaborating in critical thinking and creative problem-solving activities. This text advances an inspired curriculum development that is designed to turn this educational vision into a daily reality through disciplined professional study and practice.

Curriculum development is a key study topic in education since it touches on a host of essential practices—including program designing, lesson and unit planning, and student learning evaluation. The term 'curriculum' comes from the Latin *currere* which literally means "the course to be run" (Eisner, 1994, p. 25). The implication in this Latin phrase is that the educational course that the student will "run" will be *good* for him or her. It will provoke, energize, and sustain growth. Doll (2000) writes, "Curriculum is … a coursing, as in an electric current. The curriculum should tap this intense current within, that which courses through the inner person, that which electrifies or gives life to a person's energy source" (p. xii). This book advances a curricular 'development-from-within' pathway that is designed to electrify and liberate human potential in education.

This curriculum development approach was initially conceived in July 2009 and then piloted and refined over a six-year period in the context of two Kent State University (KSU) graduate courses (Henderson, 2010a). One course is entitled "Fundamentals of Curriculum" and is the introductory course in KSU's Curriculum and Instruction (C&I) M.Ed. and Ph.D. programs. Both beginning and experienced teachers enroll in this course. The other course is entitled "Curriculum Leadership" and is the keystone seminar in KSU's 12-credit-hour Teacher Leader Endorsement Program (TLEP). In Ohio, teachers must have a minimum of 10 years of professional experience before they can pursue the addition of this endorsement to their license.

Though this text's design was conceived in 2009 and then continuously revised in an action research context (Hackney & Henderson, 2014), there is a story behind this theoretical and empirical research that traces back to 1968; and sharing this story provides an autobiographical, collegial context for understanding the book's design. I begin with this narrative, which is organized around four interrelated motivational themes: *inspired lead learning, caring pedagogical artistry, nuanced curriculum understanding*, and *responsible professional autonomy*. The preface will then conclude with a concise overview of the book.

I graduated from college with a degree in History in June 1968 and immediately entered into the University of Wisconsin-Milwaukee's (UWM) Teacher Intern Program. This was a Master of Arts in Teaching (M.A.T.) program that combined teaching certification with a chosen master's degree specialization. I worked on attaining an Elementary Education license while pursuing a degree in the Cultural and Philosophical Foundations of Education. My first graduate course in this specialization was taught by Normand Bernier, and the first book I read in his seminar was John Dewey's *Individualism Old and New*, published in 1930. Dr. Bernier embodied the "Socratic love" that Phillips (2007) elegantly summarizes:

> To Socrates, the only life worth living was one permeated with honor and chivalry, idealism and *arête* [personal excellence]. He acted in and on behalf of the spirit of the world he envisioned and believed could be realized, if only he could capture the imaginations of enough fellow Athenians, speak to their better angels, and inspire them to join him in his quest and take it for their own. ... Socrates believed we must have vivid imaginative lenses, but he also filtered his vision through a healthy rationalist sensibility. (p. 311)

At the conclusion of his seminar, Dr. Bernier invited interested students to join him and two other UWM faculty members, James Macdonald and Bernice

Wolfson, in a Socratic inquiry experiment at a farm north of Milwaukee. We would begin an engaged Socratic dialogue on the cultural and philosophical study of education on Friday night and not worry about time constraints. As I best recall, I was one of seven students who volunteered to participate in this open-ended inquiry. Our conversation continued, with short sleeping timeouts, until Tuesday morning. It was my first powerful experience with the value of inspired lead learning, not only for the education profession but for the culture as a whole.

I began working on my doctoral degree in Curriculum and Teaching Studies in 1974 at Stanford University, and Elliot Eisner served as my doctoral advisor. As I initiated my doctoral studies, I received a very clear message from Dr. Eisner that meaningful educational inquiry required inspired, visionary imagination—a message that was ultimately refined and articulated in his 1979 book, entitled *The Educational Imagination*. My work with Dr. Eisner further reinforced my commitment to advance inspired lead learning in education. Eisner (1994) concludes the third edition of his 1979 text with this critical, visionary comment:

> It is the mark of a sophisticated educator … to avoid the panaceas, nostrums, oversimplifications, and slogans that are often found in the public press. We need to provide responsible leadership that embraces the possibilities of education and is willing to explore the alternative routes that can be traveled to achieve them. (p. 384)

I will be forever grateful to Drs. Bernier and Eisner for their insights into the vital importance of inspired lead learning in education.

The two KSU courses that served as the sites for piloting this text's curriculum development approach—"Fundamentals of Curriculum" and "Curriculum Leadership"—are both organized around the concept of *inspired lead learning*. Barth (2008) writes that, "In our [education] profession, especially, one is a learner and thereby a leader. The moral authority of the educational leader comes first and foremost from being a learner" (p. x). The purpose of the inspired lead learning in both courses is to formally and/or informally invite the collegial study and practice of *teaching* for Subject understandings embedded in democratic Self and Social understandings, abbreviated as *3S pedagogy*. This motivational and curricular aim serves as the organizing problem of this book, which I will discuss further later in this preface.

John Dewey's "My Pedagogic Creed" is required reading in both KSU courses, and a quotation from the conclusion of his 1897 essay opens this preface. Dewey envisions educators as lead professionals in their society, and this professional vision is a factual reality in Finland. Sahlberg (2011) writes:

> Dewey saw the pupil's own experience … as the critical path to understanding. Dewey also contended that democracy must be the main value in each school just as it is in any free society. The education system in

> Finland is ... shaped by these ideas of Dewey and flavored with the Finnish principles of practicality, creativity, and common sense. What the world can learn from educational change in Finland is that accomplishing the dream of a good and equitable education system for all children is possible. But it takes the right mix of ingenuity, time, patience, and determination. (p. 144)

Pink (2009) organizes current research on intrinsic motivation into three interrelated categories: purpose, autonomy, and mastery. He summarizes his first motive in this way:

> We know that the richest experiences in our lives aren't when we're clamoring for validation from others, but when we are listening to our own voice—doing something that matters, doing it well, and doing it in the service of a cause larger than ourselves. (p. 145)

When graduate students in the two KSU courses are introduced to the comprehensive, cultural purpose of serving as lead learners for 3S pedagogy, they respond enthusiastically and appreciate being treated in this professional way. I thank them for their passion. It has encouraged me to create this book.

Educators who engage in this text's inspired lead learning must necessarily address two key mastery challenges: *caring pedagogical artistry* and *nuanced curriculum understanding*. I began my doctoral studies as one of the graduate assistants for a national curriculum evaluation project headed by Elliot Eisner, Joseph Schwab, and Decker Walker. Schwab's (1969/2004) work on the "arts" of the eclectic and the practical, and Walker's (1971) application of these arts for "naturalistic" curriculum development, served as key frameworks for this evaluation work. Schwab argues that curriculum work requires an eclectic artistry that culminates in "arts of the practical," which are deliberative in nature and cannot be reduced to precise protocols. The arts involve contextually-based, case-by-case deliberations. In short, Schwab contends that pedagogical artistry cannot be enacted through standardized, one-size-fits-all practices.

Walker (2003) extends Schwab's argument when he writes, "Good deliberation is the main strategy for reaching better curriculum decisions, but deliberation is not a panacea. To do it well is an art that demands much study and long practice .... " (p. 226). Eisner (1994) adds further insight to this artistry with his explanation that teaching "is sensitive, intelligent, and creative—those qualities that confer on it the status of an art—it should, in my view, not be regarded as it so often is by some, as an expression of unfathomable talent or luck but as an example of humans exercising the highest levels of their intelligence" (p. 156).

As I concluded my doctoral studies, I was fortunate that Nel Noddings became a member of my dissertation committee. I experienced the artistry of her Socratic caring; and in a recent publication, I formally thanked her for her inspiring advising (Henderson, 2012). As Dr. Noddings (1984) argues and illustrates in her *Caring* text, a Socratic "ethic of caring" lies at the heart of pedagogical artistry. In short, at the heart of the art of teaching is the art of sustaining meaningful, affirming relationships. Noddings (1984) describes the three key components of her Socratic caring: confirmation, dialogue, and cooperative practice:

> When we attribute the best possible motive consonant with reality to the cared-for, we confirm him; that is, we reveal to him an attainable image of himself that is lovelier than that manifested in his present acts. ... Confirmation, the loveliest of human functions, depends upon and interacts with dialogue and practice. I cannot confirm a child unless I talk with him and engage in cooperative practice with him. (pp. 193, 196)

In her recent inquiry into democratic education in the twenty-first century, Noddings (2013) concludes with this expression of Socratic, holistic care: "Rejecting the notion that schooling should concentrate on intellectual development academically conceived, we should design programs that support satisfying ways of life for whole persons" (p. 157).

Collectively, Schwab's, Walker's, Eisner's, and Noddings's scholarship offers valuable perspectives on *caring pedagogical artistry*. The challenge of mastering this artistry is a compelling motivator for many educators; and as Pink (2009) notes, engaging in this quest for mastery requires a commitment to disciplined learning, to the enjoyment of the developmental pursuit, and to a balancing of work and play (pp. 118–128).

Because this book's curriculum development approach is grounded in *caring pedagogical artistry*, curriculum and instruction will not be treated as separate topics. When teachers are managed through top-down systems, 'curriculum' is generally viewed as separate from 'instruction.' This enables policy makers and administrators to control teachers through rewards and punishments, which Pink (2009) characterizes as "carrots and sticks." However, from a Socratic love of wisdom perspective, teaching lies at the heart of curriculum. In fact, pedagogy is treated as the core fundamental of curriculum, and this book is based on this organizing premise.

This quest for pedagogical mastery is tied 'hand-in-foot' to the quest for a *nuanced curriculum understanding*. 3S pedagogy requires the embrace of subtle, multilayered shades of grey. I received my doctoral degree in Curriculum and Teaching in 1981, and I attended the inaugural Bergamo Conference on Curriculum Theory and Classroom Practice, sponsored by the *Journal of Curriculum Theorizing (JCT)*, in 1983. This was an exciting time for curriculum studies since the "reconceptualization" of the field was in full bloom. Curriculum work, in both its study and practice manifestations, was being reconceived as an open-ended set of emancipatory, creative projects drawing on the critical social sciences, the arts, and the humanities. 'Curriculum' was being rethought in critical, fluid, and artistry terms and not as the production of standardized tools for the management of teachers.

Cherryholmes's (1988) notion of critical pragmatism touches on the spirit of this curriculum reconceptualization:

> If practical effects are determined by uncritically comparing what happens with conventional standards, pragmatism becomes vulgar and naïve, as vulgar and naïve as unreflective acceptance of conventional standards and structures. ... Critical pragmatism considers not only what we choose to say and do, along with their effects, but also what structures those choices. Critical pragmatism pursues the fundamental questions asked by poststructural analysis into the design as well as the operation of our social practices and institutions. (p. 14)

William Pinar and Janet Miller emerged as, arguably, the two most influential lead learners of reconceptualized curriculum studies; and in 1995, Pinar with three of his doctoral students (William Reynolds, Patrick Slattery, and Peter Taubman) published the signature, synoptic text of this reconceptualist phase of curriculum studies. Their book was entitled *Understanding Curriculum*; and in their final chapter, they summarize the "journey" of understanding curricular phenomena:

> Curriculum is intensely historical, political, racial, gendered, phenomenological, autobiographical, aesthetic, theological and international. Curriculum becomes the site on which the generations struggle to define themselves and the world. Curriculum is an extraordinarily complicated conversation. (pp. 847–848)

In her celebrated collection of autobiographical essays, Miller (2005) shares her perspective on this layered understanding of curriculum: "The field [has moved] away from its long-standing managerial, technocratic, and positivistic orientation, and toward multivocal, multiperspectival theorizings of curriculum ... [to] a riotous array of theoretical perspectives that point to expansive and complex conceptions of curriculum reconceptualized" (p. 28).

Thanks, Bill and Janet, for your Bergamo/*JCT* curriculum leadership. Your lead learning is an inspiration and a model for this book. Your inclusive 'big tent' approach to the study and practice of curriculum embodies the virtue of "practical wisdom" as conceived over two thousand years ago by Aristotle (2011). He argues that human happiness is realized through the wise balancing of diverse virtues, and Haidt (2006) provides a twenty-first century interpretation of Aristotle's practical wisdom:

> By drawing on wisdom that is balanced—ancient and new, Eastern and Western, even liberal and conservative—we can choose directions in life that will lead to satisfaction, happiness, and a sense of meaning. We can't simply select a destination and then walk there directly. ... But by drawing

> on humanity's greatest ideas and best science, we can … know our possibilities as well as our limits, and live wisely. (p. 243)

The mastery of *nuanced curriculum understanding* takes time. It is a circuitous journey of understanding, involving many twists and turns that are grounded in diverse, idiosyncratic self-insights and joys. This book has been designed to foster and celebrate this fluid, personal journey.

This book's curriculum development approach has an open synoptic design without ideological categories or enclosed traditions. There is only a 'starting kit' of seven interrelated study and practice topics that cut across a wide range of curriculum and teaching perspectives and virtues. The mastery of these seven topics is treated as an essential feature of 3S pedagogical artistry. After all, how can educators possibly teach for 3S understanding if they are not working on their own nuanced curriculum understanding?

Responsible professional autonomy completes the motivational framework that guides this book. The *inspired lead learning* that fosters the mastery of *caring pedagogical artistry* and *nuanced curriculum understanding* blossoms in an environment of what Dewey (1910/1933) calls "genuine freedom." He argues:

> Genuine freedom, in short, is intellectual; it rests in the trained power of thought, in ability to "turn things over," to look at matters deliberately, to judge whether the amount and kind of evidence requisite for decision is at hand, and if not, to tell where and how to seek such evidence. If a man's [or woman's] actions are not guided by thoughtful conclusions, then they are guided by inconsiderate impulse, unbalanced appetite, caprice, or the circumstances of the moment. To cultivate unhindered, unreflective external activity is to foster enslavement, for it leaves the person at the mercy of appetite, sense, and circumstance. (p. 90)

This sense of authentic freedom Pink (2009) argues is built into our evolutionary heritage: "We're born to be players, not pawns. We're meant to be autonomous individuals, not individual automatons" (p. 106).

The feel for autonomy underlying this book's design is based on a particular interpretation of professional responsibility. Though standardized management accountability—with its controlling, clunky, and rigid 'one-size-fits-all' logic—is currently dominant in most countries of the world, these systems are still exercises in problem solving. Establishing critical distance from these accountability systems must not lead to the rejection of intelligent curriculum and teaching problem solving. It is important to not throw the 'baby' out with the bath water! Instead, the focus needs to be on shifting the locus of control to frontline educators, particularly teachers, who are engaged in the continuous discipline of building their problem-solving capabilities.

This book challenges educators to recognize that, if they want to argue for professional autonomy for 3S pedagogy, they have the responsibility to develop their capacities to engage in sophisticated reflective inquiries informed by multilayered deliberative conversations. As Dewey (1910/1933) notes, reflective inquiry lies at the heart of responsible and responsive professional freedom. At the beginning of his book, Dewey argues that "reflective thinking impels to inquiry." He explains,

> beliefs ... demand our investigation to find out upon what grounds they rest. ... Active, persistent, and careful [inquiry-based] consideration of any belief or supposed form of knowledge in the light of the grounds that support it and the further conclusions to which it tends constitute reflective thought. (pp. 7–9)

Building peer and public trust through responsible problem solving is central to the emergence of professional autonomy in education; and though this theme pervades the entire text, it will be highlighted in chapter 4. I thank John Dewey for his prodigious and still current explorations of the disciplined 'logic of inquiry' that underlies professional freedom.

Now that the motivational framework for this book's curriculum development approach has been established, an overview of the text's design can be succinctly presented. Chapter 1 presents the book's rationale and design. It opens with four 'snapshots' of the inspired practice of 3S pedagogy written by a kindergarten, a fourth grade, a secondary, and a higher education teacher. Part I follows the introductory chapter. It contains an introductory essay and seven lead-learning invitations. These invitations, which constitute chapters 2–8, are written by seven educators who are excited about encouraging the collegial study of their chosen topic. Though at this point in their careers, they are not scholarly experts; they are exemplars of this book's curriculum leadership approach. Collectively, they demonstrate that educators are capable of working as dedicated, disciplined students of a sophisticated problem solving; and they illustrate the diversity of professional voices that lies at the heart of authentic lead learning. The seven educators composed their invitations in the context of six months of respectful collegial collaboration.

Chapters 2–8 are designed as an integrated problem-solving gestalt. They are seven invitations to study and practice three interrelated, reflective inquiries informed by four deliberative conversations. The reflective inquiries in chapters 2–4 address three dimensions of the book's organizing problem, which was introduced earlier in this preface. This overarching problem can be stated as a question: *How can the collegial study and practice of 3S pedagogy be introduced and sustained?* Three key facets to this question can be articulated as subquestions. *How to teach for 3S understanding? How to embody 3S understanding in classroom, school, and community contexts? How to build trust for 3S pedagogy through collegial study and practice?* These three questions organize the reflective inquiry invitations in chapters 2–4. Chapters 5–8 then invite deliberative conversations that inform these reflective inquiries. These four invitations address the curricular nuances of management-to-wisdom critique and negotiation, educational equity, democratic interdependence, and mythopoetic inspiration.

Part II contains a brief introductory essay and three chapters. Chapter 9 presents the lead-learning experiences of three graduates of KSU's TLEP. These dedicated teacher leaders share multilayered, critically insightful, and inspired stories that are organized in a narrative montage format. Their collegial accounts serve as personal embodiments of this text's reconceptualized curriculum development. Chapter 10 is written by an experienced educational administrator and scholar who will comment on the synergistic relationship between curriculum and leadership as advanced in this book. Chapter 11 is organized as a simulated panel discussion on the pragmatic feasibility of this new curriculum development. What are its promises and challenges? The panelists are an international group of teachers, teacher educators, educational administrators, and curriculum scholars who represent a diversity of North American, European, African, and Asian cultural contexts.

I want to conclude this preface by personally thanking all of this text's 18 coauthors. As this book project began, I referred to them as 'contributors'; but as we worked with one another in a spirit of responsible professional autonomy, the notion of 'coauthoring' emerged as the more appropriate collegial term. Though the book's argument and design is based on my many years of graduate study and scholarship, its content results from the reciprocal collaboration of autonomous professionals who respect personal "voice" (Miller, 1990) and idiosyncratic "lines of flight" (Deleuze & Guattari, 1987). In effect, the creation of the text has been an exercise in democratic "ethical fidelity" (Badiou, 2001): the collegial collaborations underlying the creation of this book have been guided by the challenge of 'walking' this text's new curriculum development 'talk.'

I want to thank the part I coauthors: Daniel Castner, Jennifer Schneider, Christine Fishman, Wendy Samford, Boni Wozolek, Beth Bilek-Golias, and Petra Pienkosky Moran for their thoughtful lead-learning invitations; and my special thanks to Jennifer Schneider for her assistance with the part I collaborations. I also appreciate Daniel Castner's, Christine Fishman's, Boni Wozolek's, and Beth Bilek-Golias's narrative contributions to chapter 1. The part II coauthors had unique coauthoring roles. My thanks to Jen Greist, Susan School, and Konni Stagliano for their inspiring contributions; and in particular, I want to highlight Jennifer Schneider's creative facilitation of the chapter 9 montage. I want to express a special word of gratitude to Catherine Hackney for her chapter 10 contribution. Cathy and I have had numerous conversations about the book, and I appreciate the insights she brings to the text's lead-learning advocacy.

The chapter 11 'panel discussion' was organized and facilitated by Tom Kelly. Tom had recommended the addition of this chapter 11 at the annual Bergamo Conference in October 2012, and Tom and I have been continuously discussing the pragmatic feasibility of this text's new curriculum development since that time. My special thanks to Tom for his many thoughtful contributions to the book's design and rationale and, in particular, for his inspiring and hopeful concluding words as the international panel's moderator. Tom's chapter 11 coauthors have busy professional lives, and I appreciate the time they took to contribute a wide range of international perspectives on this book's curriculum development and leadership. My thanks to Tero Autio, Aboudou Berthé, Donna Adair Breault, Rosemary Gornik, Kauko Komulainen, and Wen-Ling Lou.

Brief autobiographical sketches of the 19 coauthors (I include myself) are included at the end of the volume.

1

A NEW CURRICULUM DEVELOPMENT: INSPIRATION AND RATIONALE

Curriculum … emerges from an orientation and vision of who and what we are, where we come from, and where we are going. What is of the most extraordinary import, of course, is which particular vision we decide to choose, for the choosing of a vision allows us to become that vision. (Macdonald & Purpel, 1987, p. 192)

For the creation of a democratic society we need an educational system where the process of moral-intellectual development is in practice as in theory a cooperative transaction of inquiry engaged in by free, independent human beings who treat ideas and the heritage of the past as means and methods for the further enrichment of life, quantitatively and qualitatively, who use the good attained for the discovery and establishment of something better. (Dewey, 1952/2013a)[1]

Inspiration

This book advances a new conception and practice of curriculum development that is inspired by a powerful pedagogical artistry. The preface began by inviting you to imagine highly motivated teachers and students engaged in critical thinking and creative problem solving activities. This chapter begins with brief illustrations of this pedagogical artistry, written by four of the lead-learning authors in part I: a kindergarten teacher, a fourth grade teacher, a high school teacher, and a university professor. They present four snapshots of their holistic teaching, which they see as personalized embodiments of their institutions' mission statements and their country's democratic aspirations. They hope that their individualized snapshots are instructive and, possibly, inspirational. Collectively, these four narratives are reminders that many educators feel they have a noble vocational calling which they understand in their own terms. There are many educators who don't see themselves as bureaucratic functionaries, corporate employees, or compliant technocrats. They view themselves as lead professionals with important visionary, progressive responsibilities. In broader cultural and policy terms, countries that do not recognize such educators' vital role in the dynamic health of their societies may be condemning their current and future generations to stagnant, regressive, and rigid lives.

Dan's Pedagogical Snapshot: Two Oppositional Boys

Clark joined my kindergarten class one mid-fall day with a warning label: oppositional defiance disorder. A very intelligent and charming little boy, he shared many interests with his classmates. However, the explosive outbursts that brought this hideous label to this adorable little boy soon made themselves known to the entire hallway.

A confrontation would begin anytime an adult would say, "No Clark. Not like that, like this." And these confrontations seemed to escalate in a consistent manner. First, Clark would warn with a defiant verbal protest. Then, he would raise his volume and intensity, often using obscenities. If the demands placed on Clark persisted, he would become physically aggressive with anyone or anything that was in close proximity. After a few incidents, the principal made arrangements for a "specialist" to observe and create a behavior plan. This "plan" would also be used for data collection, necessary for documenting a student's need for an alternative placement in a "behavioral unit."

In the meantime, I independently worked to devise a plan for allaying Clark's challenges. Based upon the easily discernible provocations and predictable escalation I observed characterizing previous incidents, I made just one decision. Henceforth, Clark's participation would be invited, not directed, and never demanded. It went something like this.

"Story time, everyone, please join me at the carpet."

"No!" Clark shouted, "I'm drawing a picture! I won't do it!"

"That's fine, buddy. Take your time. Just know that you are welcome to join us over here."

I went about our planned classroom activities. I was pleased to see Clark listening to the story as he finished his drawing. Soon, Clark's listening from a distance progressed to participating from a distance and a gradual inching toward the group. Before I knew it, on his own terms, Clark became actively engaged in classroom activities, and now discussions are rarely protested.

When the 'behavior specialist' arrived to observe Clark's noncompliance and disruptive outbursts, she was not able to pick him out of the crowd. Indeed, in our classroom, he enjoyed new identities such as "dinosaur expert" and "Jacob's best friend." At my first free moment, the consultant and I conversed.

"Is Clark here today?"

"We have a plan in place that is working pretty well for Clark. A compliance-based sticker chart really sets him up to fail."

"Well, it really depends upon what the data indicate once we get this plan in place and you can begin to document his progress. Which one is he?"

"He's the child who's oppositional, defiant, and has explosive outbursts. You are a behavior consultant and you can't pick him out of a group of 25 children in a kindergarten classroom; please write that down. That's the most important data to report!"

"C'mon, Dan, just tell me who he is."

"No! I won't do it! This will be discussed at the IEP meeting, which should be about us restructuring to accommodate his needs, not documenting his inability or unwillingness to accommodate our structures."

Chris's Pedagogical Snapshot: Shining a Light into the Parental Communication Void

I'm teaching in the voids. My entry into this text's holistic pedagogy began a couple of years after the 9/11 disaster, and it was more like a festering hole than a blooming flower. Once the shock was absorbed, I became acutely aware of my own ignorance. Since I was in front of my students when I first heard of the horror, it seemed to me that my teaching was implicated. In my classroom of second graders, familiar practices just couldn't answer the abyss between what had happened, and my responsibilities to my students.

And that was how I commenced my doctoral studies. That I did it alongside of daily teaching duties has allowed a particular dialectic to emerge, one where the wisdom of professors, colleagues, texts, and theories found fertile fields in my classroom and life. Again, not like seeds of a well-sown crop, but more like soil amendments sifting into the hollows. My own journey of understanding about this way of being has opened my gaze regarding my role in a broader context. I've been able to continue lead learning as cofacilitator of an Educational Issues parent-teacher group. To my knowledge, there doesn't appear to be another initiative like the Educational Issues Book Club. But the conditions for it surely exist elsewhere. Let me explain.

A few years ago, the dilemmas of parent communication came up during a discussion with my colleagues. We complained that parents must have no clue about the content of our teaching work. Emails at the last minute about where to send kids at dismissal, conferences at which they insisted their children deserved more individualized instruction, expectations that homework would take a back seat to athletics—all concerns that led us to the conclusion that many parents did not understand what we did at school. We realized we probably had some of the same ignorance about parent and family life. There didn't seem to be an authentic space for coming together as mutually knowledgeable, but unknowing persons, to study the sometimes overlapping, complex dilemmas of teaching and parenting.

And so the separation of domains became the organizing problem for our actions. A colleague and I formed an Educational Issues Book Club. We conceived the purpose of the club as a forum to read, hear, and express concerns and visions about local and national issues that pertain to education and schooling. Each meeting, we focus our discussion with text—book chapters, blogs, articles, and movies. To date, we've discussed a host of issues such as the use of technology in education, social learning at school, discipline and 'responsive classroom' approaches, educational politics, state testing, teacher evaluation schemes, and cafeteria atmosphere.

It is rewarding that our members are now suggesting texts as springboards for our conversations, which means they are more attuned to educational issues than they would have been previously. As I see it, we collaboratively "address the cultural and existential challenges of democratic living." By reading and hearing perspectives of others, we are more likely to examine issues in multifaceted and hermeneutic fashion. In that place where the void had been, then, I hope we cast light on the plurality that deepens our own understandings, and our collective comprehension of the democracy that is still in the making.

Boni's Holistic Snapshot: Children are Beautiful

I had asked Terri, a tall, fit African American student, to stay after class to discuss his inadequate work ethic and disruptive language. "What the f★★k do you want from me, Mrs. Woz? Why do you care?" he yelled, shaking with anger.

"I care because I see who you are … what you can become! It's beautiful!" I nearly shouted back.

He burst into tears, his nearly seven-foot frame crumpling in front of me. After a moment, I asked him why he was crying. He said, "No one has ever said that to me. People don't see a future for me." His words left me breathless. How is it possible that after fifteen years, a child is never told he has the prospect of a beautiful future? If teachers can inspire, where was Terri's inspiration after 10 years in schools? How do teachers, or perhaps more personally, how had I chosen to give or withhold encouragement to particular students in my practice?

These are the moments that inspire me to grow as a professional. "Teachable moments" and positive experiences certainly give a sense of clarity to my work. However, these moments of injustice that cause a visceral anger in my being are the ones that truly engender change in my practice. Winfield (2007) cautions that when we are most comfortable is when injustice and its underlying "ideology operates in its most pernicious state" (p. 151). Terri ended up, like many students of color, in juvenile detention and did not graduate from high school. While the decisions he made were his alone, I couldn't help but wonder, whose job is it to teach children that they are, indeed, beautiful?

Teaching is a journey (Pinar, 1975). On one hand, the journey engenders growth for the teacher, a recursive process of "I am not yet" (Greene, 1998) in one's ideology and pedagogy. Similarly, it is a process of being and becoming for students, a journey via curricular forms that foster particular action through education (Watkins, 2001). Therefore, the web connecting the Subject matter with democratic Self and Social (3S) understandings is always in a fluid state, changing with daily interactions in school.

As an educator, I consider myself lucky to have had a mentor who taught with consideration to the whole child, rather than her test scores. Ms. Cleary was a ninth grade earth science teacher who frequently gave up her lunch and planning period to attend to my grief over my parents' divorce and maternal grandparents' passing, all of which occurred during the year and a half prior to me taking her class. Yet, even in dealing with an emotionally fragile teenager, she managed to spark my curiosity in science and keep me on track with other subjects. From my experiences with this outstanding educator, I constantly find myself asking, "What does Ms. Cleary's teaching teach us?" Yes, she produced high test scores. Yes, she was given several honors of excellence for her work. More significantly, she encouraged learning that did not forget that scores came second to the task of guiding children.

Beth's Holistic Snapshot: Believing in Students

During winter break, I received a kind lunch invitation from two former students accompanying the claim that because I "believed in them," they are where they are today. Actually, I identified wiggle room within the system to provide meaningful learning to guide them towards their self-defined goals.

Weeks after starting my university job, Anna visited my office soon in tears—her application to our professional architecture program was rejected because of her GPA. She explained the low average resulted from grades received during a past "difficult time." She accused me of "standing in the way of her dream" (unaware I was not part of the decision to decline her application). I rebutted, "I would be the last person on this planet to stand in the way of anyone's dream—I teach to help people attain their dreams." I asked her to share her goal. She retorted, "I want to become a registered architect." Review of her college transcript clearly indicated classroom success before and after the "difficult time." I vowed to help her, but explained that her journey might require taking an alternative path.

Tony's application to our professional architecture program was also rejected despite his decent GPA and class rank. He recalled, "My SAT score got me snubbed." Accepted into Architectural Studies (ARCS), a non-professional liberal arts-based undergraduate program that I coordinated, Anna and Tony soon became critical friends. They flourished academically and as role models. They motivated groups of underclassmen through leading design-related service projects in the community. They thoughtfully negotiated problem solving across the diverse cultures within which they found themselves. After reflecting on their collaborative learning at an ARCS Forum attended by stakeholders, Tony focused on his goal: teaching and urban design.

While investigating graduate schools, Tony and Anna requested to volunteer as studio teaching assistants continuing the forum's credo—learning to serve | serving to learn. How could I refuse? Empowered, they taught by listening to ideas, engaging in creative problem solving, and researching alongside students. Finally, they organized the annual ARCS Meet + Greet, showcasing coursework across the curriculum. They were growing in their own 3S pedagogical way.

After each received their Bachelor of Arts degrees, I championed their graduate school pursuits. Tony began teaching part-time while earning a Masters in Urban Planning, Design and Development coupled with a Masters of Urban Design. Anna's advanced studies have included a graduate assistantship charged with graphics and partial coordination of her department's lecture series as well as a peer-voted Chair position on the Student Activities Committee serving as liaison between faculty members and students. At lunch, we celebrated Tony's employment offer as City Planner/Transportation and Streetscape Specialist for the City of Cleveland's Planning Commission and Anna's upcoming spring graduation with a Masters of Architecture. Anna's architectural registration will undoubtedly follow.

These are two students—and there are many others—who were misrepresented by numbers and test scores. I believe these are the kind of graduates our professions need: leaders with a liberal arts breadth of knowledge fostering democratic humanism within societies and assuming interdependent responsibilities to earth and the cosmos.

Rationale

As described in the preface, curriculum development is one of the education profession's most important and far-reaching topics. In fact, it can be argued that curriculum development in all of its diverse aspects—including program designing, lesson planning, and student evaluating—touches on the heart and soul of educational artistry. What is the basis for such a bold claim? And why begin this text in this way? The response to these two questions highlights the philosophical underpinnings of all curriculum activities. Since the term 'curriculum' denotes the educational course to be run, curriculum decisions are justified on the basis of a *critical thinking* that is directed toward a *way of being* that is pragmatically realized through a *becoming* generally described as *educational growth*.

Schubert (1986) argues that the three "bottom line" curriculum questions are: "What knowledge is most worthwhile? Why is it worthwhile? How is it acquired or created?" (p. 1). He explains:

> Without direct consideration of *what* is worthwhile to know and its correlates of *why* and *how*, [all curriculum] activities are devoid of defensible meaning, purpose, and direction. When fundamental curriculum questions are not addressed by educators, economic or political caprice leads the way and educational practice is governed by default. (p. 1)

Though Schubert is arguing for the importance of critical thinking in curriculum work—for responsibly thinking about the 'whys' of educational courses of action—he is also recognizing the vital significance of carefully considering the 'whats' and the 'hows' implicated in the 'whys.' This introductory chapter is organized around this responsible, comprehensive approach to curriculum justification. We begin with the 'why' of this book's new curriculum development before turning to the 'what' and the 'how' that flows from this 'why.' Each of these three sections will be organized around a specific question: *Why* engage in this curriculum development? *What* is the focus of this curriculum development? *How* is this curriculum development practiced?

Why Engage in This Curriculum Development?

This book's conception of curriculum development is grounded in a progressive and emancipatory pedagogy. This interpretation of teaching is this text's inspiration, its vocational calling, its compelling voice-from-within, and its educational imagination. Pinar (2012) writes that his "work as a [curriculum] scholar and theoretician is structured pedagogically" (p. 1). In a similar vein, this book is structured pedagogically; it revolves around a particular teaching artistry. In this book, teaching is treated as not just a fundamental of curriculum, it is this text's *raison d'être*. Curriculum and teaching are not treated as separate entities. In more formal poststructural language, the curriculum and instruction binary is deconstructed in this book; and there is a critical point underlying this deconstruction.

Curriculum development theorists who separate curriculum and teaching may invite the top-down management of teachers, so why theorize in this way? What's the agenda? Are teachers not trusted to be responsible, autonomous professionals? Do teachers' activities need to be carefully structured, scripted, and supervised? Is there a worry that if teachers are not properly controlled, educational mediocrity and/or chaos will result? The consideration of these critical questions points to the chapter's opening vision of educators as lead professionals in societies with progressive and emancipatory aspirations.

The Challenges of Continuing Cultural Progress

Teachers who practice the progressive, emancipatory pedagogy that inspires and grounds this curriculum development text address the deep cultural and existential challenges of democratic living. These educators serve the key hermeneutic role of translating the spirit of their society's democratic declarations and documents into daily educational activities.[2]

In the quote that opens the preface, Dewey (1897/2013) acknowledges educators' hermeneutic role by describing teaching as a society's "supreme" art.

The way educational courses of action are theorized and then enacted is a key progressive concern due to the interdependent relationship between studying and living. In fact, much can be learned about the WAY of living in a particular society by noting that society's curriculum conversations. Pinar, Reynolds,

Slattery, and Taubman (1995) write, "curriculum … is what the older generation chooses to tell the younger generation" (p. 847). If the elder members of a particular society do not embrace dynamic and creative educational practices, their culture will, over time, become stagnant and rigid. It will eventually fade into history. Curriculum work requires the practice of "educational imagination" as advanced by Eisner (1994):

> All of us, through the process of acculturation and professional socialization, acquire a language and a set of images that define our views of education and schooling. … When we talk about learners rather than children, competencies rather than understanding, behavior rather than experience, entry skills rather than development, instruction rather than teaching, responses rather than action, we make salient certain images: our language promotes a view, a way of looking at things, as well as a content to be observed. (pp. 359–360)

Progressive education is a complex topic with a rich, multilayered history in North American education (Cremin, 1961; Kliebard, 1987). While a detailed discussion of this heritage is beyond the scope of this book, it is hoped that readers of this text already have, or can find, progressive heroes and heroines who inspire, or can inspire, their curriculum development work. After briefly acknowledging the complicated history of North American progressive education, Hansen, Anderson, Frank, and Nieuwejaar (2008) provide an overview of its guiding tenets. They note that "progressive theorists strove to create curriculum that would draw together students, subject matter, and social improvement … [focusing on] the betterment of the individual and society" (pp. 441–442). They then provide a synopsis of the work of four major American progressive educators: Ralph Waldo Emerson, W. E. B. DuBois, Jane Addams, and John Dewey. They summarize the contributions of these inspiring individuals in this way: "They [all] envision education as both a transforming social institution and as a dynamic individual experience that can liberate persons to realize their various gifts and callings" (p. 449). Hansen et al. conclude their essay by noting that Emerson, DuBois, Addams, and Dewey recognized the importance of a "critical continuity" in progressive educational thought requiring "a call to reenvision progressive curriculum in our time" (p. 456). They are inviting present-day educators to continue the progressive educational legacy through their own inspired, visionary work. They are encouraging educators to cultivate their own progressive spark. This book is designed with this present-day invitation in mind.

The Challenges of Existential Freedom

The existential challenges of *being* a human is the other key source of inspiration for this curriculum development book. Because we humans are a learning species, we have some latitude on *how* we will live our lives. Hamlet's famous soliloquy, "To Be or Not to Be," in William Shakespeare's *Hamlet* is, as Bloom

(1998) discusses, an illustration of the "internalization of the self [which] is one of Shakespeare's greatest inventions, particularly because it came before anyone else was ready for it" (p. 409).

Shakespeare's original, humanist construction of a sense of self is based on the recognition that we humans can make choices in our *way* of living. Some humans may be so culturally bound—so caught up in the habits and traditions in which they are embedded—that the question, "How will I *be* in this world?" has no meaning. Existential choices make no sense to them. However, the great American philosopher, Maxine Greene, celebrates the fact that humans have the potential to be existentially engaged through embracing a "dialectic of freedom," referring to the interplay between freedom 'from' and freedom 'to.' They can critique that which they experience as repressive, inhibiting, limiting, oppressive, dehumanizing, and destructive; and they can cultivate that which they experience as constructive, affirming, broadening, inspiring, inspiriting, and ennobling. Greene (1988) concludes, "Freedom cannot be conceived apart from a matrix of social, economic, cultural, and psychological conditions" (p. 80).

Greene also understands that teaching for existential awareness, responsiveness, and responsibility demands a sophisticated practical wisdom—a flexible, reflective practice informed by a multidimensional critical awareness, and this important insight will be a central theme in the next section of this chapter. Noting that engaging in our best practical intelligence is "the price we must pay" for our existential freedom, Greene (1988) quotes from Schaar's (1979) commentary on Herman Melville's novel, *Benito Cereno*: "Human beings, unlike cattle, must choose what they will do and be. We are not governed by our instincts or totally dominated by our keepers. Rather, we are free; and our freedom puts us under an imperative of decision and action" (p. 46). Writing in a spirit of continuing hermeneutic engagement, Greene (1988) notes that perspectives on human freedom can never "be finished or complete. There is always more. There is always possibility. And this is where the space opens for the pursuit of freedom" (p. 128).

Locating her inquiry project in the context of the best of American progressive and pragmatic thought, she notes that such individuals as Oliver Wendell Holmes, Thorstein Veblen, Vernon Louis Parrington, William James, John Dewey, Lincoln Steffens, Charles Beard, and Jane Addams all "shared a profound faith in hypothetical and empirical inquiries; and they shared an understanding of the transactional relationships between living human beings and their environments" (p. 42); and Greene argues that the "consequences of free action … are to a large degree unpredictable" (p. 46). Greene's (1988) dialectical understanding of human freedom is a careful balancing of social critique and personal affirmation. Her critique focuses on "oppression or exploitation or segregation or neglect" (p. 9). Through disciplined critical work, people can establish distance from their psychological and/or social shackles; they can responsibly express "the right not to be interfered with or coerced or compelled to do what [one] did not choose to do" (p. 16). This is the *freedom from* side of the dialectic.

On the *freedom to* side of her dialectic, Greene celebrates embodiments of responsible, authentic self-direction: "freedom shows itself or comes into being when individuals come together in a particular way, when they are authentically present to one another (without masks, pretenses, badges of office), when they have a project they can mutually pursue" (p. 16). Authentic, responsible self-direction is directed toward a "carnival" of creative human expression (Sidorkin, 1999), culminating in a robust cultural renaissance that replaces unimaginative standardization.

Greene's (1988) analysis of her dialectic of freedom is quite comprehensive and diversified. She describes a variety of forms of oppression, exploitation, segregation, and neglect in American society. These include not only those associated with racial, gender, and class relations, but more subtle forms such as "constraining family rituals," "bureaucratic supervisory systems," and, ironically, even static images of 'freedom' in the media that serve the interests of the wealthy and powerful (p. 17). She recognizes that struggles against freedom's constraints must be broad-based and multileveled. Greene's (1988) presentation of authentic expressions of democratic freedom is equally sophisticated. Tapping into American history, she draws on the writings of Thomas Jefferson, Walt Whitman, Mark Twain, Horace Mann, Ralph Waldo Emerson, and many others. She summarizes her understanding of human freedom by acknowledging the intimate relationship between personal and social emancipation.

Janet Miller, who was Maxine Greene's close friend and colleague, documents and celebrates emancipatory "spaces" that encourage and foster teachers' "voices." Miller (1990) concludes her book with this existential affirmation of teachers:

> Within these daily spaces, clearings forged in the midst of permission slips and mandated curriculum and computer print-outs of test scores, educators do recognize that the fissures of teaching and research, theory and practice, public and private, are artificial distinctions that separate us from ourselves and from the relationship in which knowledge about self and about our worlds is generated. (p. 172)

In a celebrated collection of autobiographical essays, Miller (2005) discusses her ongoing work to write the biography of Maxine Greene. Miller describes this project as a highly personal and collaborative scholarly effort, and she poses a set of questions that touch on the themes of existential transactions, reciprocity, and respect:

> What happens when the writing of Maxine's "biography" becomes an interactive, intertextual, collaborative event? That is, in what ways do my autobiographical "answers" … to [my authentic, respectful] questions interact with and influence my understandings and representations of her answers? In what ways are my constructions of Maxine's "educational biography" as much about me as they are about Maxine? (p. 258)

Miller's insightful analysis and affirmation of teachers' critically aware, authentic, interactive collaborations is a key referent for this book's focus on inspiring educational action. The notion of existential coengagement—defined as 'holonomy' in the preface—will be a recurring theme in this text, as will the passion for progressive educational engagements. Pinar (2012) captures this existential-progressive coupling in his definition of curriculum theorizing:

> I thread my subjective experience through academic knowledge, thereby reconstructing both and inviting you to do the same. Through academic and self-study we reconstruct ourselves and the world we inhabit. ... Through self-reflexive academic study, subjectivity becomes reconstructed as social democracy. Private passion becomes public service. (p. 2)

This book provides counsel for a theory of curriculum development, and it will proceed in Pinar's critical, personal, and public way.

Autio (2009) provides an insightful European perspective of this curriculum orientation. He begins by describing the interplay of personal and cultural growth that is the hallmark of the German *Bildung/Didaktik* tradition, which has been highly influential discourse in European education over the past two hundred years (Null, 2011; Westbury, Hopmann, & Riquarts, 2000). Autio (2009) notes that "Bildung can be understood as a kind of self-formation along the lines of a wider [societal] belonging and ... Didaktik refers generally to the pedagogical techniques for intertwining if not spiraling subjectivity and society together" (p. 71). With reference to these two German concepts, this curriculum development text can be described as advancing a Didaktik artistry that facilitates Bildung curricular aims. The book provides a study-based approach to pedagogical artistry that fosters the disciplined self-formation that is an essential dynamic of progressive, emancipatory culture-building.

Teachers' and Students' Journeys of Understanding

As mentioned at the beginning of this chapter, the decision to 'run' a particular educational course is justified on the basis of a *critical thinking* directed toward a *way of being* that is realized through *becoming* processes. The human growth advanced in this text can be briefly summarized as a generous and generative journey of understanding embedded in a dialectic of freedom. In an edited book entitled *The Passionate Mind of Maxine Greene: 'I am ... not yet,'* Greene composes a brief Afterword entitled "Towards Beginnings." She writes:

> I ponder my own memories as I think about past and present—and (even now) what I am not yet. Have I simply been a good student? Have I been lucky enough to be visited by inspiration—at least now and then? ... Teaching,

writing, speaking, looking at paintings, watching plays and dance performances, listening to music, reading (always reading), I know the challenges are always new. The questions still gather, and I relish my sense of incompleteness. I can only live, it seems to me, with a consciousness of possibility, of what might be, of what *ought* to be. (Greene, 1998, p. 256)

Greene is articulating and expressing her sense of becoming—her journey of understanding.

This notion of a personal journey of understanding has particular resonance in this book. This text's curriculum development invites educators to engage in autobiographical self-examination. In an important groundbreaking text in the curriculum study field, Pinar and Grumet (1976) reframe the Latin noun 'curriculum' as the Latin gerund, *currere*. They address the personal past, present, and future dimensions of 'running' an educational course of action. Pinar (1994) summarizes *currere* self-examination with a question: "How is the future present in the past, the past in the future, and the present in both?" (p. 26). With reference to educators 'becoming' lead professionals in their society, this book could be characterized as a *currere development* text.

The problem underlying this curriculum development book is the challenge of studying and practicing a particular pedagogical artistry. It is the problem of teachers undertaking journeys of understanding so that they can encourage and support their students' journeys of understanding. Because this emancipatory work is guided by the comprehensive, holistic heritage of progressive educational thought, this problem can be reframed as *teachers engaging in 3S journeys of understanding so as to teach for 3S understandings*. The 3S designation refers to Subject learning, Self learning, and Social learning. The sources for the subject learning are disciplinary topics tied to academic, vocational, and other pursuits. The sources for the self learning are a wide range of personal emancipatory concerns including the cultivation of authentic voice and responsible agency (Deleuze, 1994; Sirotnik, 2002). The sources of the social learning are a wide range of progressive concerns, including the cultivation of tolerance and empathy for diverse others and the recognition and affirmation of the deep interdependence between humans, and between humans and other species.

In their text, *Understanding by Design*, Wiggins and McTighe (2005) codify students' 3S understanding as demonstrations of one or more of six "facets." Students demonstrate their understandings when they "can explain … can interpret … can apply … have perspective … can empathize … [and] have self-knowledge" (p. 84). We will return to a deeper exploration of Wiggins and McTighe's six facets of understanding in the next chapter; however, we will do so from Deleuze's (1994) argument that human emancipation is highly diversified and idiosyncratic. We will treat Wiggins and McTighe's six facets as simply six possible "lines of flight" (Deleuze & Guattari, 1987). Teachers and their students might demonstrate their journeys of understanding in many other ways.

We are now ready to turn to the 'what' and 'how' sections of this introductory chapter. However, a brief review of the 'why' explanations in this section may assist your understanding of the key curriculum concepts that have been discussed so far. This is important since these concepts will continuously reappear throughout this book. We began with a discussion of the progressive, emancipatory pedagogy that grounds and inspires this curriculum development text. We then turned to an examination of the cultural and existential challenges embedded in this pedagogy, which are addressed through hermeneutic engagements linking the personal and the public. Becoming such a teacher constitutes a very high professional standard requiring disciplined journeys of understanding, and the referent for these journeys is a progressive, holistic 3S orientation addressing the integration of subject, self, and social understandings.

What Is the Focus of This Curriculum Development?

This section begins with a brief historical explanation of the gerund, 'reconceptualizing,' in the book's title. In a 1975 edited book, William Pinar declared a legitimate academic space for an "avant-garde" group of curriculum study scholars who critically challenged traditional and empirical curriculum work as exemplified by Tyler's (1949) curriculum development "rationale" and by educational applications of positivistic, reductionist social science. Pinar (1975) called this avant-garde group "the reconceptualists," and argued that, though they were small in numbers, they were beginning to establish a new "stage" for curriculum studies, which he summarized as follows:

> This stage has meant introducing existentialism and phenomenology to the field, in order to provide conceptual tools by which we can understand human experience of education. It has also entailed a sensitivity to contemporary historical and cultural developments: the political events of the sixties and the rise of the counterculture. The intellectual foundations of continental philosophy and the experience of life in the United States (specifically in the schools) in this last third of the twentieth century are two primary "ingredients" of the curriculum field reconceived. At its most ambitious, the field will attempt to become a synthesis of contemporary [critical] social science and the humanities. (pp. xi–xii)

Twenty-five years after the publication of this edited book, Pinar issued a reprint with a slightly changed title. While the 1975 text was entitled *Curriculum Theorizing: The Reconceptualists*, the 2000 reprint was entitled, *Curriculum Studies: The Reconceptualization*. Pinar (2000) explained the title change in the preface of the reprinted edition. He noted that, in the 1975 edition, he had settled on the 'reconceptualist' noun to signal a "paradigm shift" in the curriculum field and that the use of this term was a mistake. He explained that the 'reconceptualist' noun "allowed some to misconstrue the movement as an ideologically unified set of individuals in personal and professional allegiance with each other with a definite and agreed-upon destination in mind. Nothing could be further from the truth, as I well knew." (p. xi)

The Dominant Heritage of North American Curriculum Development

Rethinking curriculum development in this 'reconceptualizing' spirit challenges the dominant heritage of North American curriculum development, beginning with the 1918 publication of Franklin Bobbitt's *The Curriculum*.[3]

Null (2008) provides a concise, thorough overview of this heritage in his historical analysis of curriculum development. He notes that "Bobbitt was an authority on educational administration whose specialty was making systems more efficient. Curriculum, to Bobbitt, was just another process like textbook ordering and plant management" (p. 479). Tyler's (1949) *Basic Principles of Curriculum and Instruction* was a pragmatic refinement and extension of Bobbitt's text (Kliebard, 2013). Tyler advanced a "rationale" that was, in essence, a pragmatic problem-solving process organized around four questions: What educational purposes should the school seek to attain? What educational experiences can be provided that are likely to attain these purposes? How can these experiences be effectively organized? How can we determine whether these purposes are being attained?

Null (2008) points out that Tyler "believed … that he was providing educators with a scientific process that claimed to be value neutral" (p. 480). Supporters of Tyler's rationale, such as Peter Hlebowitsh in his 1993 response to critics of Tyler's rationale, entitled *Radical Curriculum Theory Reconsidered: A Historical Approach*, and Daniel and Laurel Tanner (2007) in their thoroughly researched synoptic text, entitled *Curriculum Development: Theory into Practice*, celebrate Tyler's applied 'scientific' method. In fact, Tanner and Tanner (2007) argue that Tyler's generic problem-solving orientation is still the dominant paradigm for curriculum work: "Tyler's handbook has been widely used in curriculum courses and widely discussed in the curriculum literature from mid-century to the present day. Although various modifications have been proposed, Tyler's explication of the curriculum paradigm has not been fundamentally changed" (p. 134). Arguably the most astute critic of Tyler's rationale, Herbert Kliebard (1992), provides guarded admiration of his curriculum development approach as follows:

> One reason for the success of the Tyler rationale is its very rationality. It is an eminently reasonable framework for developing a curriculum; it duly compromises between warring extremes and skirts the pitfalls to which the doctrinaire are subject. In one sense the Tyler rationale is imperishable. (p. 164)

An Alternative to Tyler's Rationale

Hlebowitsh (1993) argues for the imperishability of the Tyler rationale by making reference to Dewey's lifetime work on the logic of inquiry:

> The Tyler rationale is in the tradition of Dewey because it frames curriculum planning as an inquiry process that considers ends as open points for deliberation while simultaneously advocating sensitivity to the nature of the learner, the values and aims of the society, and the reflective reformulation of the subject matter. One may criticize Tyler for failing to discuss philosophical considerations in a more comprehensive framework ..., but the rationale encourages the main determiners of the curriculum to take charge of the curriculum; it supplies guiding questions and sources not to suffocate artful initiative but to lend a fundamental vision of growth and movement toward an ideal. ... [His rationale] represents the curriculum field's historical commitment to curriculum development as a problem-solving process. (pp. 65–66)

The conception of curriculum development that is advanced in this book resonates with, and differs from, Hlebowitsh's argument. To begin, it's important to note that current educational practitioners may never have heard of Tyler's 1949 rationale. This is not surprising since his rationale was published over 65 years ago. So what's the point of arguing with, and against, a particular curriculum development approach that is not current? Hlebowitsh's final sentence in the above quote is the response to this question. Tyler's rationale represents the curriculum field's historical commitment to curriculum development; it serves as an organizing symbol and normative referent for the way that "curriculum development"—everything from lesson planning, to program designing, to student evaluation—should be conceived and practiced. Null (2008) writes:

> Tanner and Tanner (2007) see no problem with extending Tyler's (1949) paradigm, and they see no need for it to be reformulated or rejected. Many scholars from outside the ranks of professors of curriculum and instruction agree with Tanner and Tanner. ... Curriculum development will be around as long as modern science is around. Critical discussions about modern science take place each day, but we continue to benefit from modern science in many ways. Curriculum development is part of this larger appreciation for science. (p. 488)

The 'what' of this book's conception of curriculum development stands in vivid contrast to the 'Tylerian' paradigm in all of its past, present, and possible future manifestations. Though this text draws on the Western scientific heritage in one important way, which will shortly be explained, it also draws on the heritage of emancipatory philosophy, critical social science, the arts, and the humanities. As a child of the reconceptualization of curriculum studies, this book advances a fundamental rethinking of all of the educational actions that fall within the parameters of 'curriculum development.' In short, this text is a constructive alternative to the Tyler rationale, understood symbolically.[4]

Curriculum Development's Philosophical Compass

Hlebowitsh (1993) acknowledges that the Tyler rationale is weak on "philosophical considerations;" and for this book, this is a very telling admission. As pointed out at the beginning of the 'why' section of this chapter, this text's conception of curriculum development is grounded in a progressive, emancipatory pedagogy; and this interpretation of teaching serves as the compelling inspiration for the practical details of curriculum development that will shortly be introduced. Note the design of this reconception. Curriculum development is not conceived as a stand-alone topic or as the prime driver of educational work. Rather, an inspired and informed pedagogical artistry leads the way, and specific curriculum development activities are in a supportive role. Phrases such as "curriculum and instruction" and "curriculum and teaching" are quite common in North American education and around the world. In this book, such phrases are deconstructed to capture the spirit of curriculum work that supports and nurtures the critical hermeneutics of a pedagogical artistry that advances a deepening democracy. Green (1999) provides an insightful perspective on what constitutes such a deepening:

> Deep democracy would equip people to expect, to understand, and to value diversity and change while preserving and projecting both democratically humane cultural values and interactively sustainable environmental values in a dynamic, responsive way. Existentially, deep democracy would reconnect people in satisfying ways. (p. xiv)

In short, this book advances a pedagogically based, democratically inspired, and democratically informed curriculum development.

Hlebowitsh (1993) refers to the "tradition of Dewey," but where is his discussion of educators' pedagogical *being* and *becoming*? Where in his book is his discussion of pedagogical artistry as the basis of curriculum development? Where does he describe and affirm teachers' and students' journeys of understanding? Dewey (1939/1989) writes, "We have advanced far enough to say that democracy is a way of life. We have yet to realize that it is a way of personal life and one which provides a moral standard for personal conduct" (p. 101). Where is Hlebowitsh's critical and ethical recognition that, if democratic living is to be enacted in education, curriculum must necessarily be interpreted as a particular *currere*? In fact, neither "pedagogy" nor "*currere*" appear in the index of Hlebowitsh's text.

The point of these critical questions is not to challenge the book of a dedicated, influential curriculum scholar. The point is to question conceptions of curriculum development that lack a deep philosophical and pedagogical compass. Concerning these amoral conceptions and with reference to his critique of the Tyler rationale, Autio (2009) writes that

> In Tyler there is no sight of the belief … that a sense of morality will develop through the acquisition of knowledge. The faith in method and procedure … is a kind of closed circle where the vistas for moral progress have apparently disappeared and the managerial stress on things becomes elevated, seemingly for their own sake. (pp. 89–90)

If the mission statements of educational organizations mean anything at all, if they are not just exercises in empty managerial rhetoric, and if educators' "ethical fidelity" (Badiou, 2001) has any deep moral basis, conceptions of curriculum development that are 'value neutral' simply won't do. Such an amoral curriculum development posture contributes to a moral 'illness' that is globally prevalent at this point in history. This illness, which Badiou (2001) characterizes as "*le mal*"—translated from the French as an "evil" sickness—can be described as a cancer that is exponentially growing throughout the world. It is the moral illness of separating fact and value, which Ryan (2011) calls our current "crisis of modernity."

In a recent encyclopedia essay, Hlebowitsh (2010) fairly acknowledges the critiques of 'Tylerian' curriculum development that have been advanced under the curriculum 'reconceptualization' banner. Though he doesn't offer a constructive alternative to Tyler's (1949) "rationale" based on these critiques, which is precisely the strategy taken by this book, his brief discussion of this curriculum study criticism is written in an open-minded way. As we now turn to an introduction to this text's practical wisdom orientation, it is important to recognize that many of the educators who are still tied to 'Tylerian' curriculum development may be open to pragmatically considering the merits of this book's new curriculum development. Advocates of this text's approach may find common ground with such fair-minded educators as Peter Hlebowitsh, and this will be the study topic of chapter 5 in this book.

Building Practical Wisdom Capacities

One final concept must be introduced before turning to the details of how this conception of curriculum development is practiced. It is the notion of "practical wisdom." Practical wisdom as a general normative referent for all human actions has an ancient pedigree, tracing back to Aristotle's *Nicomachean Ethics*, which was published around 340 BC. Arguing that the exercise of practical wisdom is critical for staying centered on the balanced, 'golden mean' of the virtuous life and for the happiness and flourishing that results from this way of being, Aristotle (2011) writes: "He who is a good deliberator simply is skilled in aiming, in accord with calculation, at what is best for a human being in things attainable through action" (p. 124). Aristotle's teaching mentor was Plato, and Plato's teaching mentor was Socrates. In his philosophical writings, Plato reports that his teacher, Socrates, argued that the practice of moral wisdom is the "greatest" of the human virtues. Kekes (1995) summarizes Socrates's argument,

> A just and honorable life is lived according to virtue, and Socrates recognizes five virtues required by such a life: temperance, courage, piety, justice, and … moral wisdom. He held that these virtues are related to each other more intimately than parts are related to a whole, … although "wisdom is the greatest of the parts" … because no action can be virtuous unless it is based on the knowledge moral wisdom gives. (pp. 32, 37)[5]

Schwartz and Sharpe (2010) provide a thoughtful contemporary analysis and illustration of practical wisdom, which they describe as constituted by six key characteristics: "A wise person knows the proper aims …, knows how to improvise …, is perceptive …, knows how to take on the perspective of another …, knows how to make emotion an ally of reason …, [and] is an experienced person" (pp. 25–26). Their book is mostly a troubling, critical accounting of the many ways in which current "institutions are discouraging the wisdom of practitioners" (p. 9). However, they end their book with a celebration of the "canny outlaws," who find wiggle room to engage in practical wisdom, and the "system changers," who are making more comprehensive inroads into organizational cultures.

The notion of practical wisdom is of key importance in this book due to the fact that the pedagogical artistry that serves as the inspirational and moral referent for this text's curriculum development calls for the building of practical wisdom capacities. Simply put, progressive, emancipatory pedagogy requires the disciplined exercise of practical wisdom. Educators who undertake personal journeys of 3S understanding so that they can teach for 3S understanding must engage in sophisticated, informed judgments. Pinar (2012) agrees:

> Because the academic curriculum is a complicated conversation and not a business meeting or military drill, its enactment requires intellectually independent teachers whose professional acumen is informed first and foremost by their erudition, secondarily by their savvy, always by their ethical commitment to children. This academically informed acumen becomes personified in the subjectivity and specifically the speech of the individual teacher who is then professionally obligated to exercise her or his intellectual judgment. (p. 223)

Building capacities for practical wisdom falls within the parameters of a new policy paradigm known as the "capabilities approach" that is being advanced by

Martha Nussbaum and her "human development" associates. Nussbaum (2011) describes this approach as a "social justice" orientation that,

> takes *each person as an end*, asking not just about the total or average well-being but about the opportunities available to each person. It is *focused on choice or freedom*, holding that the crucial good societies should be promoting for their people is a set of opportunities, or substantial freedoms, which people then may or may not exercise in action: the choice is theirs. (p. 18)

This book's curriculum development focus is not on following a procedure or protocol but on building capacities for 3S pedagogy. In short, this text has a *development-from-within* orientation based on the recognition that 3S pedagogy requires opportunities to study and practice sophisticated, informed judgments. This is this text's 'what.'

Explaining the Book's Title

The title of this book can now be explained. The title, *Reconceptualizing Curriculum Development*, refers to the fact that this text is a dynamic artifact of the reconceptualization heritage in curriculum studies as informed by John Dewey, Maxine Greene, and many other scholars who address complicated questions on the relationship between cultural progress and human emancipation. The subtitle, *Inspiring and Informing Action*, refers to the recognition that the overall purpose of this reconceptualizing approach is to support and nurture progressive, emancipatory inspirations and informed judgments. While the notion of *inspiring action* touches on questions of educators' vocational callings, the notion of *informing judgment* raises questions concerning educators' opportunities to cultivate responsible professional autonomy.

How Is This Curriculum Development Practiced?

This book's curriculum development is practiced through an inspired lead learning that initiates and sustains the formal and/or informal collegial study and practice of 3S pedagogy. This section's methodological discussion of this lead-learning practice is organized around Pinar's (2007) proposal for a curriculum development that possesses substantive and syntactical breadth and depth:

> Before the Reconceptualization, curriculum development was primarily procedural, epitomized in Tyler's (1949) four questions. ... [These many] years after the Reconceptualization, I am proposing curriculum development that is simultaneously substantive and syntactical. The subject matter of such curriculum development is now, in principle, open. ... As a curriculum developer, I compose synoptic texts to enable public school teachers to

reoccupy a vacated public domain, not as "consumers" of knowledge, but as active participants in complicated conversations that they themselves will lead in their own classrooms. In drawing widely but critically from various academic disciplines, from interdisciplinary areas, from popular culture, the form of curriculum development I propose and demonstrate herein creates textbooks for teachers who can appreciate that our professional calling is the intellectual reconstruction of the public and private spheres. (p. x)

This text is an application of Pinar's proposal. In substantive terms, it is organized around an *open, fluid*, and *synoptic* set of *seven key problem-solving topics* related to 3S pedagogy. In syntactical terms, it advances a *lead-professional way* of studying and practicing these topics that is *forgiving, persevering*, and *contemplative*. In short, this book provides guidance on how educators can work as lead professionals for a holistic pedagogy. This book can be described as a study-methods text. We begin with the substantive dimension of this study and then turn to its syntactical dimension.

The Substantive Dimension

The Seven Key Problem-Solving Topics

The selection of the book's seven study topics—three reflective inquiries informed by four deliberative conversations—is based on two key curriculum study principles. *First of all, complex problem solving requires a versatile and diversified reflective inquiry*. As Burke (1994) notes in his discussion of Dewey's (1938a) logic of inquiry, complicated problems often have a "multifaceted structure" (p. 160). This is because such problems are actually problematic situations containing a complex gestalt of embedded elements. As noted in the preface, the problem that organizes this text can be stated as an overarching question containing three subquestions. To repeat, the overarching question is: How can the collegial study and practice of 3S pedagogy be introduced and sustained? Its three subquestions are: How to teach for 3S understanding? How to embody 3S understanding in classroom, school, and community contexts? How to build trust for 3S pedagogy through collegial study and practice? These three subquestions constitute the substantive focus of chapters 2 through 4.

Burke (1994) continues his analysis of Dewey's logic of inquiry by noting how diversified reflective inquiries are necessarily informed by recursive deliberations:

> The process of securing a judgment … has a progressive but essentially circular or cyclical component. … In a nutshell, this circular aspect of inquiry looks something like the following: The agent observes the results of his/her/its actions, entertains possible courses of action and expected results based on those observations, experiments with the more feasible alternatives to test their viability, observes the results of such experimentation, and

around it goes—a process of exploring facts of the matter and narrowing the range of possible actions one can take, until, hopefully, a solution to the initial problem is settled on. (p. 160)

The recursive circularity of sophisticated reflective inquiries points to the second curriculum study principle: *complex problem solving is informed by open and fluid deliberative conversations.* Doll (2013) provides insight into this principle:

> In recursion, it is a necessity to have others—peers, teachers—look at, critique, respond to what one has done. Dialogue becomes the *sine qua non* of recursion. Without reflection—engendered by dialogue—recursion becomes shallow not transformative; it is not reflective recursion; it is only repetition. (p. 218)

This book's synthesis of Dewey's concept of reflective inquiry, Schwab's concept of curriculum as deliberative artistry, and Pinar's concept of curriculum as complicated conversation is guided by Doll's notion of problem solving recursion; and another brief foray into the history of North American curriculum studies provides further insight into this theoretical integration.

Schwab's interpretation of curriculum as deliberative artistry was formally articulated in 1969 with the publication of his first 'practical' essay entitled, *The Practical: A Language for Curriculum*. Pinar et al. (1995) note this date in a dramatic way:

> The main [curriculum] concepts today are quite different from those which grew out of an era in which school buildings and populations were growing exponentially, and when keeping the curriculum ordered and organized were the main motives of professional activity. That was a time of curriculum development. Curriculum development: Born: 1918. Died: 1969. (p. 6)

The 1918 date refers to the publication of Franklin Bobbitt's *The Curriculum*, which has already been introduced as the first curriculum development text in North American education. There were American scholars in Bobbitt's generation who challenged the management interpretations of curriculum that were beginning to emerge. However, these more critically oriented scholars, including the "social reconstructionists" Harold Rugg, George Counts, and Theodore Brameld (Stanley, 1992), worked within the confines of specific theoretical orientations.

Schwab, who was a colleague of Ralph Tyler's at the University of Chicago, was bothered by the limitations of both management and critical theorizing in curriculum work. He felt that both orientations missed the mark. He felt that neither the management proceduralists nor the critical theorists were working the way curriculum scholars should work. Schwab felt that neither group properly understood the discipline of curriculum studies, so he composed an essay that he first presented at an annual meeting of the American Educational Research Association and for which he received an unusual standing ovation. First, he argued that curriculum cannot be studied through any particular theoretical perspective—no matter how critically insightful. Curriculum scholars must be theoretically sophisticated; they must approach their discipline eclectically. Schwab (1969/2004) writes:

> All the social and behavioral sciences are marked by "schools," each distinguished by a different choice of principle of enquiry, each of which selects from the intimidating complexities of the subject matter the small fraction of the whole with which it can deal. The theories which arise from enquiries so directed are, then, radically incomplete. … It follows, then, that such theories are not, and will not be, adequate by themselves to tell us what to do with human beings or how to do it. What they variously suggest and the contrary guidances they afford to choice and action must be mediated and combined by eclectic arts. (p. 98)

Schwab then noted that this eclectic artistry culminates in "arts of the practical," which are deliberative in nature and cannot be reduced to precise protocols. In short, Schwab argued that curriculum is constituted by eclectic and practical arts. In this book, these arts will be combined under the term of *deliberative artistry*. Though Schwab extends his 1969 argument into three additional 'practical' essays that are published between 1971 and 1983 (Schwab, 1971, 1973, 1983), his first essay is the groundbreaking one.

As noted in the preface, Pinar et al. (1995) argue that curriculum is an "extraordinarily complicated conversation" (p. 848). Their lengthy text carefully and comprehensively documents the emergence of the multiple, diversified, and overlapping subtexts of this curricular understanding. However, in their book's concluding chapter, they worry that the critical move away from the "paradigmatic unity" of the Tyler rationale has resulted in a "particularistic … and even balkanized" field (p. 849). They call for a new holistic eclecticism:

> At this point in the field's development we risk balkanization, building nearly identical fiefdoms which do not contribute to a "common faith" or to a movement in the field as a whole. Perhaps we need a "United Nations" of scholarship sectors to formalize dialogue across discourse borders. (p. 856)

The substantive features of this book's study methodology—which, again, is based on the integration of Dewey's logic of inquiry, Schwab's deliberative artistry, and Pinar's complicated conversation—is a specific, definitive response to this 1995 call for a new holistic eclecticism.

This book's four deliberative conversations, which constitute chapters 5 through 8, inform the three reflective inquiries in important ways. With reference to the chapter 5 deliberative conversations, *cross-paradigm critique and negotiation* addresses the challenges of establishing critical distance from the hegemonic rigidity of standardized management, while cross-paradigm negotiation addresses the challenges of seeking out and working with the "wiggle room" for 3S pedagogy in the spirit of Cuban's (2003) critical insight:

> Attention to raising test scores is not the same as restricting the school's agenda to those tests. And that is the wiggle room between selective attention to tests and a sole focus on scoring better that … [schools] have maneuvered in order to retain their "goodness." (pp. 35–36).

The 'why' and 'what' sections of this chapter have already discussed this cross-paradigm issue in some detail, so a further introduction to this chapter 5 topic is not necessary.

With reference to the chapter 6 deliberative conversations on *equity in education*, this is a challenging, multilayered topic due to the many theoretical interpretations of such related terms as "social equity," "social justice," and "justice as a virtue." For example, Brighouse (2004) provides the following overview of social justice:

> Justice is one of the central virtues of any social order. It matters enormously how we distribute the burdens required to maintain social organization and the benefits that accrue from it, because none of us should suffer worse lives from being treated wrongly by others, and none of us should benefit from the wrong treatment of others. (p. vi)

He then notes that the various interpretations of social justice possess three common features: (a) not treating "the political status quo as having intrinsic authority"; (b) treating individuals as "the primary objects of moral concern, and corporate arrangements … [as justified] by reference only to their likely effects on the quality of the lives of individuals"; and (c) advancing poststructural critiques: "the government should not require people to structure their lives according to a set of values that the government believes is true and worthy, even if the government is right to believe them true and worthy" (Brighouse, 2004, pp. 160–162). Since the question of progressive, emancipatory education—as discussed in this chapter's 'why' section—touches on equity-in-education issues, a further introduction of this chapter 6 topic is not necessary.

With reference to the chapter seven deliberative conversations, the study-and-practice topic of *consciousness-raising for democratic interdependence* is informed by critiques of the Western heritage of elitist, class-based, and arrogant humanism. This heritage is so hegemonic—so deeply embedded in social and discursive structures—that establishing critical distance from elitist humanism for purposes of practicing a democratic, ecological humanism is generally characterized as a 'post-humanism' topic. In her post-humanist analysis of Iain Chambers' *Culture after Humanism*, Baker (2009) challenges "the logocentrism of the modernist humanist subject" with its dogmatic, dominating, privileged, Eurocentric, power-over, and colonializing subtexts (p. xii).[6]

Nussbaum (2010) aptly summarizes the challenges of practicing democratic humanism in education:

> The word "soul" [refers to] faculties of thought and imagination that make us human and make our relationships rich human relationships, rather than relationships of mere use and manipulation. When we meet in society, if we have not learned to see both self and other in that way, imagining in one another inner faculties of thought and emotion, democracy is bound to fail, because democracy is built upon respect and concern, and these in turn are built upon the ability to see other people as human beings, not simply as objects. (p. 6)

In the final chapter of his argument for a "post-liberal" education, Bowers (1987) discusses the work of closely affiliated and critically informed ecological groups, which he describes as

> bioregionalists … [who] are able to ask the most probing questions about the belief systems that underlie our social practices. To accord them the serious attention they deserve, readers must be able to free themselves from the control of the mental habits reinforced by the language of the liberal [humanist] paradigm. (p. 159)

With reference to the chapter 8 deliberative conversations on *inspiriting teaching through mythopoetic inspiration*, deliberative conversations on this topic touch on a wide range of arts and humanities themes, including educational aesthetics, pedagogical eros, instructional artistry, and storied spirituality. Writing with a poetic feel for education, Jardine (1998) invites,

> a different way of understanding ourselves and our place in the world, one which problematizes our aspirations to clarity, progress, mastery, and dominance as images of our relation to Earth and to each other. It brings inquiry out from under the desire for the final Word; it opens us up for the rebirth and re-enlivening of the Word in the soul, with the full richness and ambiguity that such re-enlivening requires. (p. 19)

Garrison (1997) writes that "Teaching involves *bestowing* value on others. The teachable moment occurs when teachers and students engage in meaningful inquiry regarding some problematic situation involving themselves and the subject matter being taught" (pp. xiv–xv).

Such teaching is infused with a love of wisdom, which stands in vivid contrast to all forms of human arrogance. Socrates was passionate about wise judgments—decisions that would stand the test of time. However, he understood the humility of this aspiration. He understood that humans could not be wise; they could only be transactional lovers of wisdom through disciplined inquiry and soul-searching dialogue. Henderson and Kesson (2004) write that "some wisdom traditions focus less on providing rules and regulations and more on cultivating a state of mind that is receptive to inner wisdom, or the truth of the spirit" (p. 5). They then note that the "Taoist tradition, with its emphasis on discovering the internal 'Way' of truth, reflects this non-doctrinaire approach to wisdom ..." (p. 5).

Arguably, Ted Aoki is the most historically important curricular voice on a Taoist understanding of curriculum—on embracing curriculum as silent, open-hearted Being. In a groundbreaking essay first published in 1980 and reprinted in his collected papers (Aoki, 2005), he invites curriculum researchers to "take a cue from the first line of the *Tao*: The way that can be described is not the way" (p. 110). Speaking in the collegial context of co-researchers interpreting curriculum as a way of being, Aoki (2005) explains:

> We believe education to be a moral enterprise concerned about what it means to be educated. ... The inherent logic of "application" often found in education talk—the notion of "applying thought to practice"—should be made problematic, at least when reference is made to the world of people. (p. 110)

An Open, Fluid, and Synoptic Set

A methodological concern in this text is to avoid the dogmatism that undermines democratic being and living through the recognition that the seven problem-solving topics are part of an "open set" (Badiou, 2005a) of relevant ways to study and practice 3S pedagogy. This openness, which was introduced in the preface, acknowledges that additional relevant topics could be added to the study and practice of 3S pedagogy at any point in time. May (2005) conveys this spirit of openness through his interpretation of problem solving: "Instead of seeing ... problems that seek a particular solution, we might sense them as opening up fields of discussion, in which there are many possible solutions, each of which captures something, but not everything, put before us by the problem" (p. 83). In short, May captures the recursive openness of reflective inquiries informed by deliberative conversations.

Pinar (2006) infuses this spirit of openness into his notion of 'study.' Citing Robert McClintock's 1971 essay on the topic of disciplined study, Pinar (2006) writes:

> Study is the site of education. Not instruction, not learning, but study constitutes the process of education, a view, McClintock [1971] tells us, [that is] grounded in "individuality," "autonomy," and "creativity."

> McClintock ... emphasizes the significance of our "particularity," that we become more that we have been influenced to be, that we ... refashion ourselves by engaging "freely" and "creatively" with our circumstances. (p. 112)

This book advances the open study and practice of 3S pedagogy that allows for individuality, autonomy, and creativity. In short, this book's study-and-practice counsel is organized around the paradoxical notion of *disciplined openness*.

The disciplined way of studying that will be advanced in this book has 'vertical' and 'horizontal' dimensions in accordance with Pinar's (2007) argument on the question of disciplined curriculum inquiry. Pinar defines "verticality" as the disciplined effort to acquire a historical understanding of curriculum studies with reference to the field's leading ideas. This form of disciplined study "becomes concrete and embodied through biographical studies of individuals and their contributions to the field" (p. xiv). Note how Pinar's sense of vertical study pervades this introductory chapter. Pinar defines "horizontality" as the disciplined effort to understand curriculum work in the present moment: "Horizontality refers not only to the field's present set of intellectual circumstances ... but as well to the social and political milieus which influence and, all too often, structure this set" (p. xiv). Again, note how Pinar's sense of horizontal study informs this introductory chapter.

This disciplined study is also highly fluid in its orientation. There is, necessarily, a continuous movement between diverse discourses and perspectives. Patrick Slattery is one of the coauthors of *Understanding Curriculum* who declared the 'death' of the Tylerian approach to curriculum development. In the same year as the publication of that book, Slattery (1995) published a curriculum development text reflecting "postmodern eclecticism, inclusiveness, and irony" (p. 16) through a kaleidoscopic format:

> The kaleidoscope creates constantly changing images and yet is always symmetrical within its own context. ... Postmodernism is like the kaleidoscope; this book has been an attempt to create kaleidoscopic sensibilities. The designs were constantly changing and becoming something new, and yet all of them remain interrelated. ... Postmodernism celebrates the diverse and complex understandings within each unique context. (p. 243)

This feel for postmodern fluidity is the basis of an edited book, entitled *Curriculum Studies Handbook: The Next Moment*, which is based on the argument that the reconceptualization of curriculum studies has now entered a "post-reconceptualization" moment of "proliferation," characterized by Deleuze's (1994) sense of the "multiplicity" of human meaning-making. In his editor's introduction to this book, Malewski (2010) explains:

> Multiplicity might characterize the emerging [curriculum] field in terms of the need for epistemological spaces where knowledge has more to account for in regards to the increasing complexities of everyday realities and the

world. Proliferation does not require that we see the field develop in a mode of debate and synthesis where one cluster of theories overtakes another on the way toward "one right way" approaches. (p. 23)

There is a postmodern fluidity embedded in democratic living. Democracy is not about locating and enforcing consensus; it is about creating a constructive, multiperspective "dissensus" (Rancière, 2010) that allows for and sustains robust inquiries, reflections, deliberations, and conversations.

The book's study-and-practice fluidity is also informed by Kincheloe's (2001, 2005) arguments for the practice of "bricolage" in educational research. Kincheloe (2001) writes that bricolage is an eclectic inquiry orientation that is both interdisciplinary and multivocal:

> As an interdisciplinary approach, bricolage avoids both the superficiality of methodological breadth and the parochialism of unidisciplinary approaches. The notion of the bricolage advocated here recognizes the dialectical nature of the disciplinary and interdisciplinary relationship and promotes a synergistic interaction between the two concepts. In this context, the bricolage is concerned not only with divergent methods of inquiry but with diverse theoretical and philosophical understandings of the various elements encountered in the act of research. (p. 679)

In a later publication, Kincheloe (2005) notes that bricolage applications are exercises in individual meaning-making in the context of an openness to emerging "methods to uncover new insights, expand and modify old principles, and reexamine accepted interpretations" (p. 687).

The synoptic nature of this book's study-and-practice agenda has a rich historical heritage. As Pinar (2006) notes, "Synoptic textbooks have played an influential role in the advancement of U.S. curriculum studies … [in] part because the genre … has served to summarize curriculum scholarship and suggest its significance …" (p. 7). He explains further with reference to a holistic curriculum orientation that addresses subject, self and social learning in a balanced way:

> What I am proposing is that curriculum studies scholars research "throughlines" along which subjectivity, society, and intellectual content in and across the academic disciplines run. Such "content" (itself an old-fashioned and synoptic curriculum term) becomes not simply derivative from—a "bad copy" of—the academic disciplines, but, rather, a conceptual montage enabling teachers to complicate the conversations they themselves will lead in their own classrooms. (p. 2)

Bobbitt's (1918) curriculum development text is synoptic in this 3S (subject/self/ social) sense, and many other curriculum scholars followed in Bobbitt's footsteps, most notably Ralph Tyler with the publication of the 1949 *Basic Principles of Curriculum and Instruction*; and as mentioned earlier in this chapter, Tyler's "rationale" can be read as a refinement of Bobbitt's text. There have been countless curriculum scholars who have worked with this synoptic 3S orientation; in general, their scholarship has been informed by Dewey's (1938/1998) argument that a comprehensive approach to educational experience must be based on "democratic social arrangements [to] promote a better quality of human experience, one which is more widely accessible and enjoyed ..." (p. 25).

Tanner and Tanner (2007) provide a thorough overview of the synoptic heritage in curriculum studies. They begin their book by noting that the democratic, holistic approach in American education can be traced back to Thomas Jefferson's views on the importance of education in a freedom-loving society. They quote Jefferson, "If a nation expects to be ignorant and free in a state of civilization [without the appropriate education], it expects what never was and never will be" (Lee, 1961, pp. 18–19). They then cite Lawrence Cremin's insight that "the entire course of American educational history is based on the gradual realization of the Jeffersonian ideal" (Cremin, 1965, p. 40). In the context of a thorough historical analysis of the views of hundreds of American educational leaders in the nineteenth and twentieth centuries on the importance of a democratic, holistic approach to curriculum work, Tanner and Tanner (2007) write:

> No document of the twentieth century was more influential in shaping the structure and function of the American educational system than the report of the NEA [National Education Association] Commission on the Reorganization of Secondary Education, *Cardinal Principles of Secondary Education* (1918). ... Embracing Dewey's [1916] concept of social efficiency in a democracy ..., in sharp contrast to social efficiency in undemocratic societies, the *Cardinal Principles* report called for the fullest release of human potential through the widest extension of educational opportunity. (pp. 280–281)

The Syntactical Dimension

The Lead-Professional Way

Substance and syntax are two sides of the same methodological coin. The diverse, many-sided facets of the disciplined study of 3S pedagogy constitute this book's substantive dimension, while its syntactical dimension refers to the affective, motivational subtleties of working as a collegial and societal lead learner. It is the dispositional side of this curriculum leadership text, informed by the determined and passionate courage of the world's great moral and ethical leaders. Mahatma Gandhi and Martin Luther King come to mind. Gandhi saw himself as an active and generous citizen of India, not a passive and fearful subject of the British

Empire; and he conducted himself accordingly. Martin Luther King saw himself as an active and generous citizen of the United States, not a man subjected to debilitating and dehumanizing American racism; and he also conducted himself accordingly. Both men had a strong sense of their identity, which they embodied and enacted with a deep sense of ethical fidelity.

The lead-professional way of this book is inspired by such individuals. Educators who are collegial and societal lead learners are not deterred by "deforming" (Pinar, 2012) educational policies and structures. They are active and generous professionals who understand their cultural role and responsibilities (Henderson & Kesson, 2001). Though they may be treated as bureaucratic functionaries, this is not how they see themselves. This is not their professional identity. They are deeply committed to understanding and practicing their rightful professional purpose insightfully summarized by Pinar (2012):

> The point of public education is not self-abandonment nor that suspension, until adulthood, of satisfaction too many—including "successful"—schools stipulate as scores on standardized tests. ... The point of public education is not to become "accountable," forced into positions of "gracious submission" to self-promoting politicians and profit-seeking businessmen plundering public budgets. The point of public education is to become an individual, a citizen, a human subject engaged with intelligence and passion in the problems and pleasures of his or her life, problems and pleasures bound up with the problems and pleasures of everyone else in the nation, everyone on this planet. (p. 229)

Hendry (2011) documents the powerful, but silent and silenced, history of women educators who have fought this generous and generative professional battle with courageous determination. Ella Flagg Young was one such educator. She was appointed the United States' first woman superintendent in 1909 by the Chicago School Board, and she had a deep commitment to collegial, democratic educational leadership. Hendry (2011) describes how she was publicly berated and reviled for her lead-learning actions and activism: "Young's persecution and public vilification as a 'witch' and 'feminist' attest to the threat she posed to dominant notions of educational leadership embedded in social [management] efficiency" (p. 171).

Ella Flagg Young's collegial and societal educational leadership will be vividly exemplified by the three teacher leaders in chapter 9. They embody the motivational themes that were introduced in the preface. They are educators who are deeply committed to the purposes of this book's inspired lead learning, to the mastery of the caring pedagogical artistry and the nuanced curriculum understanding that the enactment of these purposes requires, and to the responsible professional autonomy that sustains this enactment and provides a constructive alternative to distrustful accountability systems.

Though their lead-learning work might be disrupted by management structures and societal attitudes, these three teacher leaders are not deterred. They persist because, deep down, they have no choice. They have been called to democratic education. It is who they are. It is their personal and professional identity. They resonate with Palmer's (2007) call for a "'new professional' ... who not only is competent in his or her discipline but also has the skill and the will to resist and help transform the institutional pathologies that threaten the profession's highest standards" (p. 202).

Forgiveness and Perseverance

As described in this chapter's 'why' section, teaching for a holistic 3S under-standing requires teachers and their students to engage in personal journeys of understanding. Such journeys are individual and idiosyncratic ways of becoming, requiring Maxine Greene's 'I-am-not-yet' humility cited earlier in this chapter. This feeling of humility invites a lead-learning forgiveness. Lead learning does not require expertise; it requires a willingness to formally and/or informally begin and persevere. The authors of the seven lead-learning invitations are not experts; they are motivated, disciplined students of their selected topic. Their chapters are written as humble, general invitations for a continuous, persistent collegial study and practice.

Lieberman and Friedrich (2010) note that there are, increasingly, openings in the education profession for such collegial leadership; however, their optimism is tempered by a caveat:

> Roles for teacher-leaders, as well as openings for formal leadership posi-tions, are rapidly expanding. Fresh thinking about "distributed leadership" (Spillane, 2006; Spillane & Diamond, 2007), newly defined roles for princi-pals and teachers (Sergiovanni, 2004), and calls for nurturing and develop-ing teacher-leaders (Lieberman & Miller, 2004) open up possibilities for constructing these leadership positions in different ways. Many teachers, however, continue to be reluctant to claim the title and identity of leader. Teachers' reluctance stems in part from persistent, widely held ideas that define leadership as working hierarchically, having all the answers, and hold-ing power over others. (p. 7)

With respect to Lieberman and Friedrich's caveat, teachers need not be reluctant about this book's understanding of educational leadership because it is framed in forgiving and persevering "power within" (Henderson, 2010a) and "power with" (Kreisberg, 1992) terms. This text's lead-learning approach is decidedly demo-cratic and non-hierarchical. It is highly collaborative, allowing for diversified and idiosyncratic personal understandings. Barth (2008) writes that, "In our [educa-tion] profession, especially, one is a learner and THEREBY a leader. The moral authority of the educational leader comes first and foremost from being a learner" (p. x). This is, in part, the moral authority underlying this curriculum development text. The book's syntactical focus is on teachers working as disciplined lead learners who initiate and foster a study-based collegiality, not as experts but as humble "servant leaders" (Nichols, 2011). This forgiving and persevering way of working together—of practicing holonomy—is the study topic for chapter 4 and will be exemplified in chapter 9.

Contemplation

There's a contemplative side to curriculum studies that inspires and informs this book's new curriculum development. Writing in a meditative and visionary spirit, Macdonald (1995) writes that "the next step [in curriculum work] is an inward journey that will manifest itself by discovery, through perception and imagery, of human potential only slightly realized until now, and an outer journey for new communal life stages that are pluralistic ...." (p. 76). Macdonald (1995) describes this personal/communal back-and-forth movement of curriculum contemplation as engagement in a hermeneutic circle:

> In the hermeneutic circle, the quest for understanding and meaning, and as such the dialectic of theory-practice, must itself be viewed in terms of what it reveals that creates new meaning for us through our interpretation. ... The hermeneutical process is universal and basic for all interhuman experience, both of history and the present [moment], precisely because of the fact that meaning can be experienced, even where it is not actually intended. (p. 183)

As support for his explanation, Macdonald (1995) quotes another curriculum theorist, the Canadian Max van Manen, who is well known for his insightful work on caring pedagogical artistry: "Theorizing contributes to one's resourcefulness by directing the orienting questions toward the source itself; the source which gives life or spirit to (inspire) our pedagogic life" (van Manen, 1980). Writing with this spirit of pedagogical inspiration, Barone (2001) tells powerful stories of the "enduring outcomes of teaching," which he describes as "touching eternity." He explains:

> "A teacher affects eternity," said Henry Adams. "He can never tell where his influence stops." That comment by Adams expresses a hope felt by many of us who are, have been, or aspire to be school teachers. We want to believe that we can make a significant difference in the world through our work. But that remark also raises questions about the real power of teachers. What important things can be taught and learned in school that will indeed endure? (p. 1)

Block (2004) insightfully analyzes the contemplative subtext of Schwab's deliberative artistry. He introduces his analysis by asserting that, "Study, I aver, is a prayerful act. Study, like prayer, is a stance we assume in the world. Study, like prayer, is a way of being—it is an ethics" (p. 2). He then writes that, "to fully appreciate the cogency and breadth of Schwab's ideas demands an understanding not of any one particular essay, but the intertextual character of all of Schwab's essays, the 'complex back-and-forth between the particular and the more general'" (pp. 3–4). Block (2004) links Schwab's intertextuality to the Talmudic tradition and notes that, "For the Rabbis, study must be related to the practical—to the continued striving for a holiness that can only be realized in our daily lives in this world" (p. 83). 3S pedagogy—teaching for a holistic 3S understanding—is inspired and informed by this sense of practical holiness.

Badiou's (2001) ethics touches on this sense of the holiness/wholeness of democratic education in an important way. He builds his ethics around powerful, personal "events" that invite universal, "for all" inspirations (Badiou, 2005b). Badiou (2001) describes these events in contextual, existential terms: "A [loving] truth proceeds *in* the situation, and nowhere else—there is no heaven of truths. ... I call 'subject' the bearer ... of a fidelity, the one who bears a process of truth" (pp. 42–43, author's emphasis). Badiou's 'subjects' are not passive, powerless individuals but persistent, respectful bearers of inclusive, universal truths. Teachers and their students who cultivate self and social understandings of democratic living are such subjects. They voice their democratic truths, and they invite others to voice their democratic truths. This is this book's way of democratic lead learning. Kesson and Henderson (2010) write: "Without educators who can sustain their 'for all' ethics over a long period of time, there doesn't seem to be much hope for the future of democracy in education" (p. 72).

Organization of the Book

The organization of this book follows directly from this introductory why, what, and how rationale. Chapters 2 through 8 are lead-learning invitations to study and practice the three reflective inquiries and the four deliberative conversations that inform this multilayered problem solving. These seven chapters constitute part I of the text, and this section begins with an introductory essay.

Part II also begins with a brief introductory essay. Chapter 9 follows with the presentation of a narrative montage organized around the stories of three teacher leaders who have engaged in the collegial study and practice of the seven part I topics over an approximately two-year period. Eisner's (1994) concept of "expressive outcomes" informed the creation of this montage. He writes:

> Outcomes are essentially what one ends up with, intended or not, after some form of engagement. Expressive outcomes are the consequences of curriculum activities that are intentionally planned to provide a fertile field

for personal purposing and experience. … Expressive activities precede rather than follow expressive outcomes. The tack taken with respect to the generation of expressive outcomes is to create activities that are sufficiently rich to allow for a wide, productive range of educationally valuable outcomes. (pp. 118–120)

Chapter 10 is written by a highly experienced educational administrator with a strong background in leadership studies. She discusses the ways in which teachers and administrators can work together in a spirit of generative leadership to nurture and sustain this book's lead-learning vision. Chapter 11 presents a cross-cultural conversation on the possibilities and challenges of this book's new curriculum development. This dialogue is organized as a simulated panel discussion.

Endnotes

1 This opening quote is taken from a short introductory essay that John Dewey wrote in 1952 for Elsie Ripley Clapp's *The Uses of Resources in Education* (New York, NY: Harper, 1952). This essay, which is John Dewey's last publication, was written shortly before he died at the age of 93.

2 The term 'hermeneutics' is derived from the Greek god, Hermes, who served as the messenger between the gods of Olympus and humankind. Hermeneutics—in all of its religious, legal, and philosophical manifestations—is the art of interpreting the spirit of some matter for literal, quotidian purposes. For example, the Supreme Court justices in the United States have the final hermeneutic responsibility of translating the spirit of American democracy into specific laws. They are the ultimate 'go-between' the spirit and the letter of the law—between the lofty ideals and the quotidian practices of the American legal system. Positioning oneself between the spirit of a matter and the many possible interpretations of that spirit involves an open-minded and open-hearted engagement in the play of multiple perspectives. Gadamer (1975) calls this "dialogical play." Hermeneutic practices stand in contrast to all forms of literalism, fundamentalism, dogmatism, and ideological narrowness.

3 As a historically relevant aside, it's important to note that Franklin Bobbitt was a leadership studies scholar at the University of Chicago, and Ralph Tyler was one of his doctoral students.

4 Based on his understanding of current curriculum studies, Jupp (2014) provides a thoughtful and thorough critique of the Tyler Rationale. Similar to this chapter, his critical analysis is based on treating Tyler's rationale as a historically significant, symbolic framework for educational reform and curriculum development.

5 For a further discussion of Kekes's (1995) insights into practical wisdom, particularly as applied to curriculum work, see Henderson and Kesson (2004).

6 Logocentrism refers to the dogmatic strategy of dictating an 'original' meaning, perhaps attributed to 'God,' and then claiming that this original meaning is epistemologically superior to all other possible, relevant meanings. In other words, all interpretations are secondary to a metaphysical, foundational interpretation. Hegemonic, regulatory standardization relies on particular manifestations of logocentric identity. Autio (2009) writes, "The logocentric subject provides the hidden place and the source of colonialism in terms of demands for uniformity" (p. 72).

PART I

Lead-Learning Invitations

Part I is an open-ended arrangement of three interrelated reflective inquiries informed by four deliberative conversations. To quickly review, the reflective inquiries address the interrelated questions of how to teach for 3S understanding, how to embody 3S understanding, and how to build collegial and public trust for 3S pedagogy; while the four deliberative conversations are organized around the topics of management-to-wisdom critique/negotiation, social justice, democratic humanism, and mythopoetic inspiration. Over the course of six years of action research, this particular configuration of topics has emerged as a powerful way to introduce and sustain the collegial study and practice of 3S pedagogy. In short, chapters 2 through 8 are single-authored essays that function as an ensemble of lead-learning invitations that have been created in the bricolage methodological style described in chapter 1. This introduction highlights several key features of this section's eclectic, synoptic ensemble.

Educators who are introduced to part I's lead-learning agenda can quickly access a wealth of Internet resources on all seven topics. However, this initial work falls mostly within Pinar's (2007) discipline of "horizontality," as discussed in chapter 1. These Internet resources, which are a wide range of present-oriented, pop-culture material such as YouTube videos, movies, documentaries, and Wikipedia entries, generally lack curriculum history depth. For this reason, the seven part I invitations have a curriculum history emphasis. They are exercises in Pinar's (2007) discipline of "verticality."

The part I essays are also an application of Hendry's (2011) critical insight that "curriculum [history] is constituted of infinite discourses ... with no beginning or end, that is continually circulating, that enfolds, overlaps, and is pulsing with energy" (p. 6). This book is, essentially, an explanation and illustration of an innovative, experimental, and optimistic theory of curriculum development. Deutsch (2011) argues that such theoretical explanations have an open-ended, infinite reach:

> The truth is always that knowledge must be first conjectured and then tested. ... Optimism ... is the theory that all failures ... are due to insufficient knowledge. This is the key to the rational philosophy of the unknowable. ... Problems are inevitable, because our knowledge will always be infinitely far from complete. ... An optimistic civilization is open and not afraid to innovate, and is based on traditions of criticism. (pp. 89, 221–222)

Chapters 2 through 4 have a recursive design, which is characteristic of experimental problem solving (Dewey, 1938a; Doll, 2013; Ryan, 2010). There is a continuous back-and-forth movement between problem framing, pedagogical action, reflection, questioning, and problem reframing. Additional reflective inquiries, as well as additional deliberative conversations beyond the four topics constituting chapters 5 through 8, could be added at any time during this process. However, over the six years of piloting this study-and-practice agenda, educators were continually invited to take this step and never did. In effect, they felt that they were acquiring a starting kit that was sufficient for their initial lead-learning efforts. Perhaps over time, if this book's collegial leadership was to become a professional norm, additional deliberative conversations—and, perhaps, even additional reflective inquiries—would emerge as relevant considerations.

Finally, there is also an identity subtext underlying these seven lead-learning invitations. Hendry (2011) argues that selected historically based curriculum discourses can serve as "sites of identity construction" (p. 6), and this book's new curriculum development is an extension of her argument. Chapters 2 through 8 are not just an ensemble of lead-learning invitations; the seven essays are also written as openings to a personal and professional identity that Dewey (1930/1984) characterizes as a "new individualism" for American society and the world.

Over eighty years ago, Dewey (1930/1984) critiqued the pervasive influence and, at times, the domination of "a pecuniary culture" in the United States that has resulted in the perversion of the American ideal of individualism, particularly this ideal's celebration and defense of "equal opportunity and free association and intercommunication" (p. 9). Speaking as an American, he described this problem as "the deepest problem of our times" (p. 16); he called for an integrated individualism in which "equality and freedom [are] expressed not merely externally and politically but through personal participation in the development of a shared culture" (p. 17). Dewey then concluded his argument with a holistic, global vision:

> To gain an integrated individuality, each of us needs to cultivate his [and her] own garden. But there is no fence about this garden: it is no sharply marked-off enclosure. Our garden is the world, in the angle at which it touches our own manner of being. … We, who are also parts of the moving present, create ourselves as we create an unknown future. (pp. 82–83)

Reflecting the spirit of Dewey's creative challenge, Watkins (2012b) concludes his edited book's careful documentation and critique of current twenty-first century political, hegemonic pressures to privatize and corporatize American education with this affirmation of grass-roots democratic citizenship:

> Education is for the public good, not a feast for the profiteers. The notion of education as a right must be reasserted. Every human being has a right to be informed and literate. … We are going to have to do this ourselves. We choose education no matter who is in the big house [of the capitalist, wealthy oligarchs]. We citizens, educators, and students demand a WORLD CLASS school in every neighborhood. (pp. 191–192, author's emphasis)

Chapters 2 through 8 are, collectively, an invitation to advance this inclusive democratic identity. All seven authors have approached their work as lead professionals for an emerging new individualism that can be described as an autonomy-within-interdependence or, for short, a holonomy. This holonomy is ethically grounded in a deep respect for the infinite possibilities of other humans, as well as other species. Noddings (2013) describes this respect as an "ecological cosmopolitanism … that emphasizes connections, connections among the subjects taught and connections between school subject and real life" (pp. 84, 91). Blumenfeld-Jones (2012) describes this respect as an "aesthetic consciousness … that honors experiencing connection with others over systems" (pp. 106–107), and he asserts that this ethical awareness goes to the heart of democratic education:

> For us [educators] to foster democracy …, we must provide opportunities to honor the vulnerable infinity of the Other that calls out to us. In so doing, the development of a moral imagination begins; and in this, I would argue, lays the heart of democratic life. (p. 108)

2

TEACHING FOR HOLISTIC UNDERSTANDING: INSPIRATIONAL EVENTS IN STUDY AND PRACTICE

[T]hey had something to do with it, but their own selves were outside of it, detached, removed. They were involved in it but not in such a way as to care. (Pirsig, 1974, p. 26)

A New Lead Learning Paradigm

This chapter is an invitation to learn about *teaching for holistic understanding*. On behalf of the contributors of this book, I have been afforded the opportunity to serve as a *lead learner* on the topic. First, I begin by introducing myself as a public school kindergarten teacher and doctoral candidate who is intellectually passionate about the study and practice of progressive, emancipatory pedagogy. Then, I hope to express my current understanding of what it means to be a *lead learner* of *teaching for holistic understanding*. In the process of doing so, my intention is to initiate a discussion rather than provide an explanation of this topic, by taking a careful look at historical underpinnings shaping our contemporary situation. I hope opening in this manner will set an invitational tone that permeates through the chapter, welcoming readers to engage with the ideas in ways that appeal to their own study and practice of curriculum.

Since the beginnings of my teaching career in 2000, I have maintained a commitment to consider myself *in the service of* the public. As such, I am charged with the responsibility of providing beneficial educational experiences to the children entrusted in my care using my best discernment. Conversely, the professional landscape for educators in the United States is characterized by a well-established metanarrative and corresponding hierarchical structures, together presuming teachers to be *in servitude to* authority figures and mandates. Over the years, I have repeatedly encountered discord when "passionate public service"

(Pinar, 2009), comprised of academic study and experiential learning, conflicts with "standardized instructional management" (Henderson & Gornik, 2007). For me, the ongoing challenge of deciphering how to persevere in carrying out progressive, emancipatory pedagogy while immersed in the dominant structures that contextualize my practice has been an experience of recursive alienation and reconciliation.

Being troubled by common educational practices but hardly ever able to articulate my concerns made me feel alienated during the workweek and became an impetus for engaging in graduate studies. In the first course that I took as a doctoral student, *Fundamentals of Curriculum*, Dr. Henderson clarified several basic tenets for curriculum inquiry, which have remained of great consequence in my study and practice. Central were the Socratic heritage of our democratic tradition and the work of John Dewey as a foundational resource for progressive pedagogy and democratic education. Accordingly, teaching for holistic understanding calls for the practice of an egalitarian "for all" spirit. This bold aspiration strives to enact Dewey's vision of democratic education in a society wrought with habits and structures that reproduce social inequalities. This sort of pedagogical experience is an inherently ethical enterprise (Hansen, 2001) carried out by autonomous professionals deeply committed to reflective inquiry and maintaining a seamless relationship between theory and practice. Hence, I apprehend teaching for holistic understanding as constituting an ambitious calling and a determination to "walk the talk."

Additionally, Dr. Henderson presented curriculum as an "extraordinarily complicated conversation" (Pinar et al., 1995) in which I was invited to participate in the process of posing and solving the multifaceted educational problems I found compelling. Along these lines, clear distinctions were made among instructional management, instructional leadership, and curriculum leadership (Henderson & Gornik, 2007). Participating in complicated curriculum conversations as a lead learner is a dual commitment to contest the dogmatic images of thought reified through metanarratives and clandestine structural habits, while at the same time, avoiding the temptation to invoke a counter ideology. For educators who are content to restrict their focus to the technical-mechanical aspects of teaching, instructional management or leadership might be sufficiently satisfying, as asking "why" is perceived to be a tangential inconvenience. However, as an exercise in lead learning, this chapter engages in the challenge of "critical pragmatism" scrutinizing our ideas, practices, and contextualizing conditions (Cherryholmes, 1988).

Based upon this background, I write about the practice of curriculum and pedagogy from a particular "platform" of beliefs and images (Walker & Soltis, 2009). Important to note is that I experience—or, as Pirsig (1974) might say, have grown accustomed to "caring about"—curriculum in both theoretical and concretized terms. Curriculum leadership acknowledges the *what* and *how* questions, which I had grown accustomed to addressing as an early childhood educator, as important technical issues related to instructional leadership. However, considering fundamental curriculum questions such as Schubert's (1986) "what knowledge is of most worth," "how it might be attained," and "who decides," curriculum leaders also bring the underlying *why* questions to the fore. Being introduced to the concept of curriculum leadership provokes contemplation among teachers as to *why* curriculum discourses and practices are commonly carried out as they are, and to imagine possible alternatives.

Though structural challenges often constrain teachers' work, Nussbaum (2011) advances a "capabilities approach" to human development to assess the qualities of life that impact individuals' capacity to freely choose what they do and be. Spending five days a week at an elementary school, I believe, has fostered a pragmatic sensibility in my study and practice of curriculum. The proverbial chasm between theory/research and practice is troubling. I am discouraged when my teaching colleagues convey a perception of policies and programs as being fixed entities designed by remote experts. Moreover, I have been frustrated by erudite theorists who, despite having interesting ideas, seem content to retreat to a "safe place for theorizing"—a place where it is too easy to forget that labors of reconsidering dominant structures do not make hegemony cease to exist. Accordingly, this chapter is an invitation for teachers to think, speak, and act critically in two ways: 1) disruptively deconstructing taken-for-granted assumptions that set limitations upon freedom and flourishing, and 2) creatively reconstructing how we choose to imagine and enact a pedagogical artistry.

Present Conditions and Historical Groundings

The ultimate aim of "teaching for holistic understanding" is to enable educational experiences to take place that foster freedom and flourishing. Cultivating practical wisdom capacity is the pragmatic means that must be utilized "to translate the very general aims of practice into concrete action" (Schwartz & Sharpe, 2010, p. 7). But, contextualized by the contemporary milieu of curriculum in the United States, the very general pedagogical aims mentioned above often get reduced by predominant normative assumptions. Taking up a love of wisdom through his poststructural pragmatism, Cherryholmes (1988) suggests, "everyone rethink what they say and do. Rethinking may rejuvenate commitment to conventional discourse-practices or it may lead to something quite different" (p. 153). I have come to see openness to "rethinking" as a central and very reasonable professional responsibility. After all, it only stimulates diversified inquiry and obliges curriculum workers to be *open to the possibility for new possibilities*.

When teaching is perceived through the restrictive lens of technical rationality, the educational course to be run is apprehended uncritically and simply assumed to be good for all children. Deemed unproblematic, what is routinely said and done within a given "culture of curriculum" (Joseph, 2011) becomes habituated in "non-reflective experiences" (Ryan, 2011) of daily practice. Without reflection and inquiry, teaching can easily fall into default modes, which conform to dominant efficiency management culture. Accordingly, when informed by structures of instructional management or leadership, one proceeds with fidelity to intervention protocols, systematic programs, or ideas. Perhaps unwittingly, even the best intended efforts often result in maintaining of the status quo.

The dominant paradigm of thought puts forth a fragmented image of curriculum and teaching. On one hand, policy mandates that appraise qualities of teachers' work through accountability systems rely upon observable behaviors. Teachers' affect can be evaluated based upon their "fidelity in implementing evidence based practices," as they are prescribed (Rathvon, 2008); and their effect is measured by students' scores on standardized tests (March & Peters, 2008). On the other hand, proponents of "best-practice" (Danielson, 2007; Wiggins & McTighe, 2005; Zemelman, Daniels, & Hyde, 2005) rely upon specifying the key principles of rationalized ideals to set standards for assessing the qualities of teachers' work. Here, the qualities of a good teacher can be judged in terms of coherence to principles of constructivism, inquiry-based instruction, or, in my case as a teacher of young children, developmental appropriateness (Copple & Bredekamp, 2009).

The empiricism of "evidence based practices" and the rationalism inherent to ideals of "best-practices" are not the conflicting polemics they appear, at first glance, to be. On the contrary, one can see empiricism and rationalism together as the two philosophical traditions that constitute "contemporary realism" (Ryan, 2011). Contemporary realism consistently eschews metaphysical and ontological considerations. Ryan (2011) explains that in pursuit to apprehend a mind-independent reality, empiricists search through what can be perceived through the senses, while rationalists focus upon what can be conceived by the mind. Either way, human limitations of sense perception and mental capacity leave any quest for certainty a futile endeavor of endlessly making efforts for closer approximations of reality. Indeed, these conventions of modern thought assemble what Cherryholmes (1988) describes as the predominant structures of discourse and practice that ascribe meaning to curriculum development and teaching. Although Cherryholmes (1988) provides an extensive list of defining attributes of discourse-practice informed by structuralism, here I highlight three. For curriculum workers, apprehending these structural attributes helpfully raises our awareness to the subtle scaffolding that upholds the professional knowledge, most regularly taken for granted.

Three attributes of structuralism are notably present in the mainstream curriculum and teaching discourse-practices in the United States. First, binaries distinguish the content of discourse-practices (Cherryholmes, 1988). For example, a specified behavior is either observed or not noticed. Practices are evidence-based or capricious efforts. A classroom experience can be regarded as developmentally appropriate or in contrast to children's developmental needs (Copple & Bredekamp, 2009). Teaching can be deemed to exemplify constructivist, inquiry-based instructional techniques or didactic forms of direct instruction.

Secondly, "word concepts" do not exist outside the system (Cherryholmes, 1988). Using examples above, "evidence-based practices" do not exist beyond instructional protocols endorsed by experimental and quasi-experimental methodological design (Rathvon, 2009). For early childhood educators, developmental appropriateness is not only overreliant upon developmental psychology, but systematically fails to acknowledge the existence of perspectives from other disciplines (Kesseler & Swadener, 1992). Construction of knowledge is contrasted with direct instruction as an opposite negating the possibility that each can be utilized in fitting situations to ensure the most authentic, meaningful, and valuable educational experience.

Third, especially since I have now alluded to "valuable educational experiences," structures of discourse-practice claim ideological neutrality (Cherryholmes, 1988). Alleged value-neutral ways of understanding curriculum and teaching restricts dialogue to narrowly focus upon describing and mapping processes rather than clarifying and envisioning the purposes of professional practices. Ralph Tyler (1949) provided the most enduring systematic rationale for mapping the process of planning educational courses of action, also known as curriculum development. The four-step procedure of the Tyler rationale, which was discussed in chapter 1, aptly names the four most habituated moments of planning curriculum and instructional courses of action. If one is to formally engage in curriculum and pedagogy clarifying educative purposes, then planning experiences, organizing those experiences, and evaluating the degree to which the stated purposes are being achieved seem to be necessary. Hence, recognizing both the "imperishability" (Kliebard, 1992) and the intellectual lifelessness of traditional customs of curriculum development are central to teaching for holistic understanding.

The Tyler (1949) rationale is, indeed, an enduring structure of curriculum development. The first chapter highlighted how some influential curriculum theorists such as Hlebowitsh (1993), Tanner and Tanner (2007), and Wraga (1999) have maintained a steadfast commitment to the customary role of systematically advising practice. Also underscored was the shift of the contemporary field from the "scientific management" of curriculum to focus upon understanding curriculum most poignantly asserted by Pinar et al. (1995), who proclaim curriculum development to be dead via Joseph Schwab's (2004) indictment that the field was moribund. However, the waning influence of curriculum scholarship on daily practice, announced by Schwab in 1969, did not curb the proliferation of various versions of the Tyler rationale.

One popular and current example mentioned in the previous chapter is Wiggins and McTighe's (2005) *Understanding by Design*. The authors provide a framework which reorders the four Tylerian components of curriculum development to promote six facets of understanding by "beginning with the end in mind." Pre-arranged in rubrics, facets of subject-matter understanding such as explanation, interpretation, and application are deepened by the personal and social aspects of perspective-taking, empathy, and self-knowledge (Wiggins & McTighe, 2005).

In Deleuze and Guattari's (1987) terms, the six facets of understanding serve as potential "lines of flight," with possibilities undoubtedly hindered by Wiggins and McTighe's (2005) proclivities toward structuralism. Subjective becoming is central to the mode of curriculum development put forth in this book. Hence, the lines of flight that define one's process of becoming are addressed as an essential aspect of teaching for holistic understanding, rather than a predetermined "end in mind" or a compartmentalized "facet of understanding."

Defending the usefulness of recapitulating the Tyler rationale, Wraga (1999) protested the reconceptualization of curriculum and the prognosis that curriculum development had reached its demise. If scholars make use of esoteric theories for erudition of complexity rather than customary structures for practical advising, Wraga (1999) argued, curriculum scholars will exhibit little utility. Pinar (1999a) provided a prompt rejoinder, warning of the inherent shortcomings of two means by which people cling to traditional structures. Using the Southern Baptist Christian tradition as an analogy, Pinar (1999a) described criticisms, such as Wraga's (1999), as versions of Old Testament preaching and New Testament witnessing that must be avoided. I will elucidate Pinar's important analysis, juxtaposing it with an analogy from Alain Badiou (2012) and drawing upon my reflections of teaching.

Through the analogy of "Old Testament preaching," Pinar (1999a) explains that some scholars are eager to restore the historically gendered power imbalances associated with the field of education. A reestablishing of hierarchal order is implicitly carried out when professors advise and guide the work of practitioners. Formal expertise and institutional authority allow privileged individuals to image themselves as heroic figures saving their subordinates from their own ignorance. Proponents of evidence-based practices come to mind, as do accountability management reformers. Borrowing from Badiou's (2012) historical analogy of epic poetry, one must wonder if these authority figures envision themselves to be epic warriors, restoring order by heroically demanding "what works." Carrying out the traditionally masculine roles, researchers set protocols for practice and improvement processes, while administrators manage and oversee the process. Of course, as Pinar (1999a) reminds, this scheme presumes the traditionally feminine role of classroom teaching in a position of gracious submission.

Pinar (1999a) concomitantly shuns another dogmatic method with the analogy of New Testament witnessing. A presumptuous stance of experts informing school practice remains. This time, experts are those who have "traveled among the multitudes (i.e., schoolteachers) with timeless curriculum ideas, thereby raising them up from the dead" (Pinar, 1999a, p. xiv). Here, from positions of privilege, experts and authority figures enlighten the common curriculum workers by sharing the "good news" of ideal practices. Proponents of totalizing discourses and generalized "best practices" come to mind. Borrowing from Badiou's (2012) historical analogy of postromantic lyrical poems, one must wonder if these New Testament witnesses envision themselves to be soldiers fighting for the principles of ideological causes. To be clear, this is an example of a rationalist variation of contemporary realism, guided by idealistic visions of alleged "best practices." Hastily generalizing, such visions are based more upon unwarranted optimism than an actualized universal benefit.

Pinar (1999a) contends that while Old Testament preaching and New Testament witnessing may appear to be dramatically different ventures, they end up leading individuals down very similar paths. In sociopolitical terms, Apple (2005) might concur that under the umbrella of "conservative modernization," neoliberal profit motives and neoconservative value traditions affably coexist through the process of managerial auditing. In philosophical terms, Frank Ryan (2011) might describe contemporary realism as taking an analogous path that incorporates rationalism and empiricism unproblematically. Ryan (2011) further cautions about what John Dewey deemed to be the "crisis of modernity," that our technological advancements were far outpacing our moral evolution. For our purposes, the epic warriors demanding evidence-based practice and the romanticized soldiers championing ideals of best-practice are two forms of structuralism that perpetuate the status quo. Badiou (2012) elucidates,

> The great problem is to create a paradigm of heroism beyond war, a figure that would be neither that of the warrior nor that of the soldier, without for this reason returning to Christian pacifism, which is only the passive form of sacrifice. (p. 46)

To realize a new paradigm for curriculum development, which does not return to Christian pacifism, classroom teachers must refuse to assume the "positions of gracious submission," which Pinar (2004) illustrates using an analogy of a gendered Southern Baptist tradition. As mentioned in the first chapter, the disciplined study of holistic pedagogy provides the substantive basis for informing reconceptualized curriculum development. Curriculum development is an essential aspect of teachers' daily practice, which Pinar (1975) has long recognized as no longer being the purview of education professors. Consequently, situated within the intellectual history of curriculum scholarship, curriculum development is often described as a canonical era of study which has come to pass: died in 1969 (Pinar et al., 1995).

Sixteen years after proclaiming curriculum development to be dead, Pinar (2012) conceptualized "allegories-of-the-present." He quotes author Hilary Mantel: "The dead … are never quite as dead as we think; they are part of us, not just genetically but psychologically" (as cited in Pinar, 2012, pp. 113–114). Pinar connects allegory and reconstruction as concepts that undertake remembering the past to rebuild the present and envision future possibilities. "The past is recalled …" according to Dewey (1920), "… not because of itself but because of what it adds to the present" (p. 2). In this chapter, recalling the basic precepts of traditional curriculum development via Tyler (1949) sheds light on the nonreflective moments of curriculum development that routinely transpire in contemporary classrooms.

Revisiting the structural demands, which have become obscured in the shadowy habits of classroom teachers' daily grind, enables two important forms of critique. First, through deconstruction, one can disrupt the established routines of traditional curriculum development. Then, disruptive problem posing must be followed by constructive problem solving. If one is not troubled by their contextualizing state of affairs, then the established customs put forth by the culture of curriculum require only technical reflection. However, articulating critical problems is a vital first step for those of us who are troubled by the situation in which curriculum is currently practiced. A first step in a recursive and fluid cycle, critical distance opens up opportunities for curriculum workers to envision alternative ways of talking and acting for new pedagogical possibilities (Cherryholmes, 1988; Pinar, 2012). This cycle of deconstruction and reconstruction constitutes the syntactical dimension of educators working in troubling times. The next section will underscore the challenging process of deconstruction and reconstruction.

The Syntactical Dimension: An Ethical Challenge

Alas, the notion that schools do not provide equal opportunities *for all* in the United States is nothing short of obvious (Pinar, 2013b). The democratic rhetoric routinely touted by educational institutions such as the leveling of playing fields and providing of equal opportunities *for all* has outreached the coinciding logic that has been applied in policy and practice (Cherryholmes, 1988). The reconceptualization has enlivened curriculum study with epistemological diversity, bringing to bear matters of power, identity, and discourse (Pinar, 2012; Pinar, 2013b). However, Pinar (2013b) points to international studies and professional ethics to possibly supplant politics as the unifying concepts for understanding curriculum, authoritatively asserting that the key concepts of the reconceptualization, reproduction and resistance have become intellectually exhausted.

In response to the exhaustion of key concepts, Pinar (2012) guides us to look back for allegories-of-the-present. In the opening lines of *Reconstruction in Philosophy*, Dewey (1920) similarly appreciates the value of historical memory, contending that humanity "differs from the lower animals because he preserves his past experiences" (p. 1). As we begin to think of teaching for holistic understanding and the corresponding reconceptualized approach to curriculum development, it is vitally important that we recognize that this challenge is situated in the beginnings of what some consider to be a post-reconceptualization era (Malewski, 2010). Therefore, the search for new concepts must be mindful of the ways in which the scientific management of Bobbitt (1918) and Tyler (1949) may have become dated and deconstructed but remain genetically and psychologically part of us, as curriculum workers. Attuned to reconstruction, I humbly suggest that Pinar et al.'s (1995) death narrative, mentioned in chapter 1, could be revised in the following way:

> The main concepts for tomorrow will be birthed from an intellectually vibrant era of epistemological diversity, when circumventing the order and

structures of schooling was necessary for persevering in being. *That was a time of the reconceptualization.*

Curriculum Development: Born: 1918. Conceptually exhausted: 1969

Deconstruction through Reconceptualization: Born: 1969. Conceptually exhausted: 2013

Reconceptualized Curriculum Development: Conceptually reconstructed: 2014.

This exercise in lead learning embraces Pinar's (2007) humble assertion "that no totalistic grasp of the field's structures is possible. We are participating in a conversation larger, more complex, and finally elusive than any single individual or school of thought can grasp" (p. xiv). Accordingly, the substantive grounding in progressive pedagogy and the syntactical tenor of pragmatic cycles of deconstruction/reconstruction are provisional expressions proposed to invite study and provoke dialogue. With the intention of being mindful to both the challenges of our contemporary sociocultural milieu and the intellectual history that informs our practice, my unmistakably Deweyan influence is worth noting. Indeed, the substance and syntax that structure this chapter are informed by various interpretations of Dewey.

Professional ethics, which Pinar (2013b) suggests lies at the heart of reconstructing the study and practice of American curriculum, takes form here as the perseverance of an emancipatory, progressive pedagogical artistry. Though Dewey thoroughly articulated this vision long ago, instantiating pedagogy with a "for all" quality within the past and present sociocultural milieu has remained an unrealized dream. Continental philosopher Alain Badiou (2001) broadly explains the "intellectual tendencies of our time were at best variations on ancient religious and moral preaching" (p. 90), as Pinar (1999a) illustrated metaphorically with Old Testament preaching and New Testament witnessing. Then, Badiou (2001) continues that contemporary thought is "at worst a threatening mix of conservatism and the death drive" (p. 90), as captured by contemporary realists' recapitulations of the traditional structures of curriculum development and postmodern deconstructions absent of reconstructed alternatives.

Curriculum practice is contextualized by the realities of our sociopolitical situation as well as the intellectual tendencies of our time and their corresponding histories. Teaching for holistic understanding involves a deeply personal journey of becoming (see chapter 3) and a collaborative process of enduring (see chapter 4). From this perspective, teachers are quite literally *lead learners* engaged in the ongoing study of the 3S (self, subject, and social) implications of their own practice. The common challenge among each of these three interrelated reflective inquiry artistries is that they go against the grain of predominant ways of being, practicing, and collaborating in schools. Images of mastery are preserved by formalized rules and taken-for-granted knowledge promulgated by disciplinary structures and intellectual tendencies. In other words, established discourses and practices of curriculum development stifle the possibility of new possibilities. Thus, the disruption and reconstructing cycles of lead learning definitively break from customary practices.

The formalized rules and taken-for-granted knowledge used to define the qualities of an alleged "master teacher" are according to Badiou (2001) simulacra— mere representations or semblances of reality. Reality is experienced not through illustrative demonstrations, but in the moments of lived events. For Badiou (2001), events are situated at the edge of the void, that which is not enunciated or apparent amidst the abundant customs and recognized knowledge. Moreover, each individual possesses the equal capacity to become subject to the truth of an event, which is void from the abundant situation. Becoming subject to a truth process is initiated with the declaration of the truth of an event, not evidence from simulacra.

For example, I work within a culture of curriculum that is attentive to both sides of the contemporary realist coin. In many ways, my colleagues and I are required to adhere to the demands of "evidence-based" practices, particularly regarding standardized assessments. Additionally, we are also encouraged to inquire into what is known about "best practices," including the design of constructivist learning experiences. But, in our collaborative efforts, something else can occur, which cannot be apprehended by evidence-based protocol or visions of best practice. The declaration that an event has occurred supplements the prevalent knowledge readily available in my culture of curriculum. Events afford us the possibility to speak about and act in accordance to ideas outside of the structural confines of mainstream discourse-practice.

From the lenses of ethical consistency and commitment, Badiou (2001) delineates two additional signposts marking the challenges inherent to the enterprise of teaching for holistic understanding. On one hand, a becoming subject might abandon the truth of an event by succumbing to a dominant paradigm of thought or simply giving into the pressures to conform to cultural customs. Badiou (2001) regards this as the betrayal of a truth event. On the other hand, fidelity to a truth process can become misguided should one lose their 'for all' quality, or impede others' capacity to become subject to their own truth processes. Badiou (2001) deems the former 'disaster' and the latter 'terror.' The take-home point here is that taking on the challenge of being a lead learner for 3S pedagogy is a decision to venture down uncharted paths requiring great amounts of perseverance and a deep sense of commitment. Interested readers may find Jenkins (2004) and den Heyer (2010) helpful for a more detailed exploration of the signposts alluded to above.

In the next section, I will review a selection of resources, which I have experienced as study events. I selected these particular resources based upon the following criteria. First, each study resource disrupts an aspect of traditional curriculum development, as it is commonly understood. Secondly, following critical analyses, each also reconstructs an alternative possibility for enacting an emancipatory, progressive pedagogical artistry. Third, these study resources make a compelling case for a quality of pedagogical artistry that is absent from conventional discourse and practices. And, finally, each resource invites further reflection and inquiry rather than providing clear-cut protocol. In other words, esteemed education professors Nel Noddings and Elliot Eisner, as well as Frank Ryan (a Deweyan scholar) serve as illustrative examples of lead learning. Their intellectual labors model cycles of deconstruction and reconstruction along with the ethical fidelity of innovating new possibilities.

Moments of Disruption and Reconstruction

Moments of disruption become possible when problems arise within the practice of nonreflective curriculum development. Such moments are characterized by the reflective process of experimentation and problem solving a curriculum worker engages in to resolve inconsistencies and contradictions noticed within the quotidian of curriculum development. Teachers critically deconstruct dominant discourses and practices and reconstruct alternatives with a hermeneutic commitment that disrupts the customary "standardized management" (Henderson & Gornik, 2007) procedures for curriculum development. These moments of disruption/reconstruction initiate circuits of inquiry and valuation (Ryan, 2011) where the curriculum worker qualitatively deepens or reinvents Tyler's four principal demands.

From Purpose to Holistic Aims Talking

Nel Noddings informs a reconstruction of conventions of clarifying educational purposes into aims talking. According to Noddings (2003), continuously discussing educational aims is a necessary component of both democracy and education. More recently, she advanced aims, goals, and objectives to be a hierarchy of ends (Noddings, 2013). Noddings (2013) laments, "[m]ost *why* questions, if they are asked at all, arise … at a lower more specific level" (p. 40). Today, teachers typically take on a subordinate role, receiving state sanctioned measurable learning outcomes. Eisner (1994) explains how the language of traditional approaches to curriculum development has changed over time, transitioning from educational to instructional, to behavioral, to performance objectives. Moving from general to specific, the degree to which planned learning outcomes are necessarily "educational" becomes less obvious. Noddings (2013) encourages critique and imagination, calling on curriculum workers to begin with and maintain focus upon broad general aims that "connect objectives to life;" an ambition that is indeed difficult to pinpoint and nail down. Aims talking is an evolving process that avoids the tendency of thoughtless pigeonholing.

Indeed, Noddings's (2013) vision is a version of progressive education that extends Dewey's insights into a contemporary context. She calls for interdisciplinary synthesis that leads to a less fragmented curriculum and an emphasis on problem-based learning. Like Dewey, Noddings is committed to developing an understanding of educational ends through sustained inquiry and dialogue. Reconstructing the aspirations of Dewey's (1916) *Democracy and Education* in the twenty-first century, Noddings envisions curriculum aims evolving attentiveness towards ecological cosmopolitanism. Conventions of curriculum development would thus demand answers to the question: What learning experiences foster ecological cosmopolitanism?

From Learning Experiences to Pedagogical Transacting

Ryan's (2011) analysis of Dewey's final work, *Knowing and the Known* (1949), which was written in collaboration with Arthur Bentley, refines and deepens notions of educative experience through the concept of transaction. As mentioned prior, contemporary realism has informed two mainstream methods by which one can know about curriculum and teaching. Ryan's (2011) analysis of Dewey's final work, Knowing and the Known (1949), which was written in collaboration with Arthur Bentley, refines and deepens notions of educative experience through the concept of transaction. Of course, many classrooms incorporate a combination of the two, justifying, for example, certain practices because they are evidence-based and others because they are developmentally appropriate. However, inter- and self-action constitute taken-for-granted structures of professional knowledge, which are often nonreflectively experienced by curriculum workers.

In his final words on educational experience, Dewey articulated the concept of transaction (Ryan, 2011). With transactional knowing, Dewey and Bentley (1949) put forth an axiom of ontological pluralism. The interactive and self-active ways that our world is pervasively known provides us with basic assumptions to proceed in our daily affairs—in our case, pedagogy—with some degree of efficiency. After all, every aspect of one's life and every decision one makes cannot be afforded time for in-depth deliberation. We go about our pedagogical business, tentatively trusting the utility of evidence-based research and recognized best practices. Then a problem arises that is specific to a particular individual, group, or context.

Experiences with pedagogical transacting can be provoked by moments of disruption where one must deal with the reality that what one knows though interaction and self-action are "not *the* answer to how things work, but *an* answer" (Ryan, 2011, p. 35). Ryan continues, "self-action and interaction look at a whole as the sum of its parts, transaction sees the parts as determined by the whole" (p. 35). Using Cherryholmes's (1988) terminology for further illustration, self-active and interactive knowing are two different forms of structuralism that define a mind-independent reality. Under these circumstances, Cherryholmes (1988) decries meaning as derived from the structural system, not the individual. Transactional knowers are able to circumvent structuralism through critique because they "see together mind and object as joint contributors to problem-solving activity" (Ryan, 2011, p. 36). The former succumbs to "vulgar or naïve pragmatism;" whereas, transactional knowing is an enactment of "critical pragmatism" (Cherryholmes, 1988). Next, conventions of curriculum development demand answers to how pedagogical transactions ought to be organized.

From Organization to Creative Designing

Elliot Eisner's (1994) seminal book, *The Educational Imagination*, offers a useful provocation for deepening our understanding of how curriculum is designed and organized. Eisner supplements the conventions of "scientific management," which were initiated by Bobbitt (1918) and refined by Tyler (1949), with a profound perspective of artistry. The traditional approach of organizing predetermined and predictable learning objectives is qualitatively deepened with a concomitant consideration of "expressive outcomes." Describing the dominant scientific management approach as an algorithm, Eisner (1994) advances a heuristic for minding meaningful educational outcomes that cannot, or even ought not, be anticipated with any degree of precision.

Expressive outcomes are derived from expressive activities, which contrast the conventional means-end approach to curriculum planning. With clearly defined and standardized ends, organization becomes a means by which fragmented components become coherently, logically, and systematically sequenced. Depending upon one's conceptual schema, a systematic organizational structure can be state sanctioned, imposed by a privileged culture, or implied through predominant ideologies. However, expressive activities can foster multiple worthwhile outcomes, allowing educational programs to nurture diversity and individualism. Eisner (1994) differentiates between processes of educational planning that either set out to conform individuals to a common structure, or set out to promote diverse individuals becoming more distinct by engaging in meaningful and interesting experiences.

There are many variations of contemporary realism reified through mainstream organizational structures. March and Peters (2008) draw upon the predominance of state sanctioned educational standards to give advice regarding how curriculum is best organized for "standards-based instruction." E. D. Hirsch (1988) provides a comprehensive list of essential knowledge he deems to constitute a "culturally literate" person's education. With the current induction of Common Core Learning Standards, such an organizational structure is sure to find prominence, as will constructivist-minded models provided by Lynn Erikson (2007) who writes about structures of knowledge, or Grant Wiggins and Jay McTighe (2005) who suggest a backwards design for beginning with an end in mind.

In contrast to the organizational approaches above, Eisner and Noddings challenge us towards creative designing. Eisner (1994) suggests visualizing a staircase to apprehend the preplanned progression of well-organized systems of educational objectives. Noddings (2013) protests that common knowledge, learning standards, and cultural values shared among educated people are an educational achievement and not a fixed point of departure from which to initiate educational experience. Further, drawing on Dewey (1916), she argues that such achievements are attained through conversation among diverse people and not a prerequisite for dialogue or civic participation. The desire for such inclusiveness that characterizes participatory democracy in a diverse society calls for the incorporation of expressive activities "that are engaged in to court surprise, to cultivate discovery, to find new forms of experience" (Eisner, 1994, p. 122). Eisner stimulates such a vision for creatively designed curriculum by disrupting the linearity of "staircase" habits with an image of a spider web, inviting engagement rather than enforcing control. Next, conventions of curriculum development demands answers to how the expressive and diverse outcomes of creatively designed curriculum are to be evaluated.

From Evaluation to Critical Appraising

Teaching for holistic understanding requires a reconstruction of the mechanical rationality pervasive to traditional approaches of curriculum evaluation. Curriculum evaluation may very well be the principle that anchors the persistent influence of Ralph Tyler's approach to curriculum planning. Foundational curriculum questions of *what knowledge is of most worth* and *how is it attained* are accompanied by queries of *how will it be measured*. The reductionist aphorism "if it isn't measured, it doesn't matter" is undoubtedly engrained in the "audit culture" (Apple, 2005) that has become the most pervasive mindset toward curriculum in the United States. Moreover, penchants for evaluative measurement implicitly assume that greater importance ought to be attached to qualities of educational experience, which can be measured and hence easily observed.

For decades, reconceptualizers of curriculum have burgeoned expansive ways of knowing, understanding, and critiquing curriculum. A multitude of critical poststructural epistemologies have shed light on the predominant discourses and hegemonies that underlie common practices. According to Pinar (2013b), reproduction and resistance emerged as the key concepts of the reconceptualist era of curriculum studies. Poststructural critique and historical archaeologies of power have effectively explicated how dominant discourse-practices have reproduced inequalities in ways that must be resisted. However, to commence reconstruction, critically deconstructing the past and present situation must be augmented with visionary projections of enhanced discourse and practice yet to come.

Formulation of educational connoisseurship and criticism serves as an excellent starting point for considering how one might appraise pedagogical artistry without disavowing perspectives from the social sciences (Eisner, 1994). Educational connoisseurship is "a private act; it consists of recognizing and appreciating the qualities of a particular" from a perspective of broad experience and knowledge (p. 219). Connoisseurs can distinguish the subtle and important qualities that typically go unnoticed both by unrefined eyes and by the methods of "clean experimentation" that constitute procedures for standardized evaluations. Eisner explains that the close look of a connoisseur provides the substance for educational criticism.

Educational criticism takes on descriptive, interpretive, and evaluative dimensions (Eisner, 1994). Here, I only briefly elaborate on the implications of each dimension for our purposes of advancing teaching for holistic understanding. The descriptive dimension requires one to be present. A synergistic relationship between theory and practice is essential. A description of the daily discourse-practices of a given culture of curriculum is bound to be superficial at best if one is not intimately engaged in that culture. The interpretive dimension reminds us of the importance of collaboration and eclecticism. As meaning is attributed to various events and situations, understanding can be derived using a myriad of possible theoretical frameworks. Eisner (1994) reminds us, "looking is essentially a task one undertakes; it is seeing that is an accomplishment" (p. 220). Schwab's (2004/1969) eclectic artistry inspires us to remember the benefits of seeing from multiple vantage points and having an inclusive curriculum dialogue. The evaluative dimension calls on us to establish normative assumptions. The democratic standard and hermeneutic commitment of our Socratic heritage provides us with norms evolving egalitarianism. Hence, this version of reconceptualized evaluation is exemplified by the evaluator's presence and the eclectic collaboration of the community held against an egalitarian, evolving norm.

Prompting Further Reflection

I wish you well in your ongoing explorations and future study and practice. I conclude with questions to propel your personal reflections forward.

- What perceptions and conceptions of curriculum structure the discourse-practices in your culture of curriculum?
- What experiential encounters and/or study resources have instigated moments of disruption, enhancing and/or troubling your understanding of curriculum work? Can you foresee your curriculum work embodying a greater sense of ecological cosmopolitanism (Noddings, 2013); becoming more transactional (Ryan, 2011); more creatively designed with greater emphasis on expressive activities and outcomes (Eisner, 1994); appraised from a standpoint of educational connoisseurship and criticism (Eisner, 1994)?
- What qualities of your curriculum platform are abundantly represented in your local settings' discourse-practice; and what inspirations have you experienced or studied that are void from your present situation?
- Can you remain true to carrying out discourse and practices that exemplify equal interest *for all* stakeholders, without succumbing to self-interest or sociopolitical pressures?
- Can you envision yourself persevering with your ethical commitments to *teach for freedom through understanding* and not give in to dominant and dogmatic images of thought?

3

EMBODYING HOLISTIC UNDERSTANDING: DEMOCRATIC BEING IN TRYING TIMES

Yesterday I was clever, so I wanted to change the world. Today I am wise, so I am changing myself.—*Rumi* (Shener, 2012, p. 33)

My skin felt heavy as I sank into a random seat after sharing expressions of love and embracing bodies I had not seen for years. I sat in silence staring at old, pristine floral wallpaper and a white Victorian staircase. I watched in awe as an endless stream of people squeezed through the door. They represented all stages of life: infants, elders, and every age in-between. On display were collages of family photographs alongside flowers and letters sent by those who could not attend that evening's outpouring of love. As the event unfolded, I felt as though I was committing a social faux pas as I pulled a pen and a small notebook from my purse. Although I knew words could never capture everything, I had to document what was transpiring before me. My hand feverishly jotted down words and phrases spoken by attendees, which served as inspiration in shaping the poetic expression below.

Wonderful Happenstance

The universe
brought together
a school,
students,
and a teacher.

To encourage,
challenge,
inspire,
and transform each other.

Their trips weren't about
Riding buses,
Taking tours,
Snapping photos, or
Seeing monuments.

Sitting atop battlefields,
Contemplating lives lost,
Wandering through history,
Feeling it together,
Restoring it for others.
These were special.

Giving so much to your
craft…
students…
community…
We will remain forever touched.

The memorial service was a stunning display of remembrance for a man who I felt I knew well but realized I knew so little about. I had known Denny for many years, and my friendship with his daughter, Kara, allowed me to see him as a joyful, supportive father figure. Never once were our imaginations belittled when we did things such as construct floor-to-ceiling paper sculptures late at night, battle with light sabers around the neighborhood, or take vows of silence, communicating solely by writing in spiral bound notebooks. Having gone to a different school district, I was only aware that Denny taught middle school social studies. He loved history, particularly anything surrounding the Battle of Gettysburg, and he took students there annually. Beyond that, my understanding of *who* he was as a teacher and *what* he believed about teaching and learning were limited at best.

Denny dedicated over thirty years of his life-energy to teaching, and people's gestures of gratitude deepened my awareness of the educator he was. While there were many, two recollections remain vivid inside me. One of Denny's fellow teachers shared reflections from his first Gettysburg trip with students and Denny. "While standing in a circle next to our bus waiting for parents to arrive, I saw the pure genius in your teaching," he remarked. This teacher, who I shall call Steve, went on to describe the space Denny created as everyone shared smiles, laughs, and final thoughts about their trip. Steve was deeply touched as he watched seventh and eighth graders shed tears reflecting on their experiences of coming into proximity with the lives of individuals during the war. The other moment came in the form of a letter sent from a former student. The student opened with sympathies and continued by beautifully expressing how her class's Gettysburg trip impacted her. At the time, it was fun and exciting to leave school, and she learned a lot about the war. However, in the years that followed, her experience of the trip inspired her degree choice in university, and later her career working at a nonprofit fighting for veterans' rights and benefits.

Even though Denny's physical body is gone, I felt his presence that evening pouring from the hearts of colleagues and generations of students. Sharing in their emotions and in honoring Denny's life, I feel as though I connected to Dewey's (1897/2013) idea of teaching as a "supreme" art and Eisner's (1994) vision for "teaching artistry." In describing artful teaching, Eisner (1994) stated:

> Teaching can be done as badly as anything else. It can be wooden, mechanical, mindless, and wholly unimaginative. But when it is sensitive, intelligent and creative—those qualities that confer upon it the status of an art—it should ... not be regarded, as it so often is by some, as an expression of unfathomable talent or luck but as an example of humans exercising the highest levels of their intelligence. (pp. 154–156)

The attendees reflections on Denny's "teacher being" (Fowler, 2006) illustrated, for me, how an educator can indeed embody the holistic pedagogy at the heart of this book's argument for curriculum development. The knowledge Denny had about teaching and how he transmuted that into his pedagogy demonstrates to me that teaching can be all at once caring, fluid, creative, and emancipatory. The memories of the Gettysburg trips exemplified a teacher with his students and his colleagues engaging in 3S journeys of understanding together for "the betterment of the individual and society" (Hansen et al., 2008, p. 442). Denny's life is also a reminder to us that as educators, who we are, what we believe, and how we act affects the lives of the people we encounter in often unknowable, withstanding ways; we are indeed "touching eternity," as curriculum studies scholar Tom Barone (2001) advised us.

While Dan's chapter before mine is a lead-learning invitation for you to engage in the study topic of *teaching for holistic understanding*, this chapter builds upon the idea of holistic understanding with a particular focus on the study topic of *embodiment*, which beckons serious consideration of the complexities between curriculum, teaching, learning, experience, and bodies (Bresler, 2004; Christodoulou, 2010; Springgay & Freedman, 2007). At the heart of this chapter is the question: How might educators embody 3S understanding in the contexts of classrooms, schools, and communities? A question, which I confess, is impossible to answer within the words of this chapter alone because understanding how one might embody holistic pedagogy is interdependent with all of this book's chapters. The question is also challenging to answer because the inspired pedagogical artistry being argued for by this book is not commonplace in much of mainstream education—a feeling I am certain you are sensing and will come to understand more deeply through studying this whole book. Consequently, I am merely a lead learner alongside you studying how we, as educators, might become full-bodied examples of holistic understanding.

I take up the above question by first presenting an overview of the concept of embodiment, weaving together various historical and contemporary perspectives from the field of curriculum studies. I then transition by investigating the relationship between embodiment, holistic understanding, and "recursive, experimental reflective inquiry" (Dewey, 1938a; Ryan, 2011). Like Dan's chapter before and Chris's after, reflective inquiry is a central element to holistic understanding; through reflective inquiry processes, we educators can cultivate new habits necessary to practice 3S pedagogy. Please know the references I use throughout this chapter are just the tip of an iceberg that extends well beyond the scope of what can possibly be covered. What I present in this chapter is my tentative understanding of how I am making sense of embodying holistic understanding at a particular moment in time. Nothing written here should be taken as absolute or complete. Nor should the ideas be treated as doctrine because doing such would be contrary to the hermeneutic, existentialist process of becoming at the heart of this book. It is my hope that this chapter will ignite your reflexive capacities within as I invite you to explore the relationships between yourself, current educational trends, and embodying this book's vision for emancipatory, caring, holistic pedagogy within your teaching.

Creating Disembodied Education

Existing curriculum studies literature on embodiment draws from a wide range of academic disciplines including philosophy, sociology, psychology, art, history, communication, and so on. Many supporters of embodied teaching and learning do, however, make reference to the significant influence rationalism has had, and still has, on humans' understandings of the world and the institutions we create—in our case, institutions of education (Blumenfeld-Jones, 2012; Hendry, 2011; Miller, 2005; Springgay & Freedman 2007, 2010). Ushered in by the philosophy of René Descartes, rationalism creates a dichotomy in which the mind is positioned as superior to our bodies and senses; the "objects [that make up our material world] conform to [our] mind[s]" (Ryan, 2011, p. 8). Through our mind's capacities for reasoning and logic, knowledge becomes certain and objective since it is "independent of human concerns or values" (Tuana, 1992, p. 36). With rationality, the mind is "detached from the needs, desires, and particularities of the body" and "true knowledge" resides in subjects like science and mathematics (p. 37). Our senses, emotions, memories, and imaginations are seen as inferior and not 'valid' sources of knowledge, and our bodies become something that we must overcome if we have to find truth (Tuana, 1992). To be fair, rationalism, reasoning, and logic as ways of knowing the world have brought important advances into our lives, (for example, medicines and technologies), but the dominance of rationalism has come with a cost, which many a scholar such as Grumet (1988), Hendry (2011), Miller (2005), and Orr, McAlister, Kahl, and Earle (2006) have vigorously challenged from various feminists viewpoints.

Cutting up our human experiences of the world into dichotomies of either/ or thinking fostered by rationalism, according to Ryan (2011), has resulted in a "crisis of modernity," which you may recall being mentioned in chapters 1 and 2.

The crisis of modernity refers to the idea that objective scientific institutions (e.g., pharmaceuticals companies) avoid engaging deeply with moral concerns, while moral institutions (e.g., churches) avoid scientific considerations. When our scientific institutions and moral institutions opt to ignore, even discredit, each other, this is problematic because a vision for reflective and transactional understanding is not fully recognized (Ryan, 2011). The crisis of modernity may at first seem like some battle-of-wits-and-words between philosophers isolated from everyday curriculum and teaching. The crisis is, however, thriving in our daily lives; it has disembodying consequences when considered in relationship to the educational visions we choose and how those visions reverberate through our governments, our curricula, our schools, our students, our pedagogies, and our senses of selfhood.

A certain understanding of objective rationality results from the crisis of modernity and infiltrates educational actions, which results in a narrowed understanding of the world and our human capabilities. According to Eisner (2001), such rationality carries with it a certain type of ethos. The qualities inherited with such thinking about humans and the world carry desires to: (a) control and predict, (b) compare and contrast, (c) use extrinsic motivations, (d) demand clear, specific outcomes, and (e) use measurements to evaluate performance. Take a moment to ask yourself, can you sense any of these qualities within your present teaching situation? If so, where is this particular ethos, and how does it make you feel as an educator? How might your students, colleagues, and administrators be embodying such ethos as well? In studying the topic of embodying holistic understanding, I along with other individuals in the field of curriculum studies see the byproducts of such beliefs thriving in mainstream education thanks to the encroaching dominance of standardization and management mentalities (Eisner, 2001; Henderson & Gornik, 2007; Noddings, 2007; Pinar, 2012). Much of education today takes shape as disembodied curriculum "connected to some external-to-the-self sources" (Christodoulou, 2010, p. 331).

A pattern of disembodied curriculum can be seen through educational reforms including, but not limited to, *No Child Left Behind*, *Race to the Top*, and most recently, the push for and acceptance of *The Common Core State Standards*. Reforms are part of the never-ending, intensifying quest for "what works" and will fix the seemingly broken system of education in America (Pinar, 2012, p. 213). Although possibly well intentioned, reforms are an attempt to oversee and control educational experiences and curriculum making (Henderson & Gornik, 2007). Even more troubling, the bureaucratically led agendas and reforms strive to not foster communities and schools, rather to: 1) push public resources "to private management," 2) take down the opposing "independent, collective voice of teachers," and 3) limit teaching and learning, thus education, to "a single narrow metric that claims to recognize an educated person through a test score" that has little to no merit or evidence (Ayers, 2012, para. 4). Instead of engaging in nuanced curriculum deliberations and "educational connoisseurship" (Eisner, 1976) like this book promotes, reformers and politicians create and push "one-size-fits-all" approaches with the assumption that all students, teachers, administrators, and schools are identical and interchangeable (Ayers, 2010; Cuban, 2003). The message is clear: our lives, our experiences, and our differences do not matter. The disembodiment created by reforms is monumental with formidable pedagogical ramifications.

Disembodiment thrives with standardized testing. One-size-fits-all reforms always result in some form of standardized content and standardized tests in the name of accountability (Henderson & Gornik, 2007). Tests are not in and of themselves a problem, and I am sure all teachers, myself included, have used them at one point or another. Tests have merit in certain times and situations. However, "problems arise when tests are rushed through just for the sake of a score and then are linked to high stakes—the promotion of students, the pay [and job security] of teachers, and even the jobs of administrators" (Noddings, 2007, p. 211). Moreover, the high-stakes tests and those who create them have a "significant amount of control over the context, knowledge forms, and pedagogies at the classroom level," and such tests fragment understanding into "bits and pieces … for the sake of the tests themselves" (Wayne, 2009, p. 298). Such testing creates "cram schools" (Pinar, 2012) and a "banking concept" of learning (Freire, 2003) in which students are seen as minds memorizing pieces of information for the sole purpose of depositing what they received on a test. Such testing focuses on a very narrow scope of subject learning (e.g., English, math, and science), and there is little regard—or use—for democratic self and social learning, which as you read in chapters 1 and 2 are essential to holistic pedagogy.

Policies and standardized tests have a "dehumanizing effect" (Nussbaum, 2010) on local teaching practices (Noddings, 2007). Because of the demands and pressure for higher and higher scores, the teaching artistry gets reduced to drilling skills and implementing curriculum dictated from "higher-ups," and teachers become "de-skilled … [by] technical control procedures" (Apple, 2009, p. 199). There is a false assumption that if teachers follow the curriculum assigned (e.g., textbooks, curriculum maps, standards, rubrics), then students will learn (Null, 2011). The concept of curriculum gets reduced to a set of documents rather than how it is framed within this book as developing human capacities for freedom with self and social understandings of democratization (Ayers, 2010; Henderson & Gornik, 2007).

Chapter 2 beautifully illustrated the disembodying effects of standardized management in teaching through the daily routines that revolve around habitual moments rooted in Tyler's (1949) four principles: purpose, experience, organization, and evaluation. When educational institutions function with such ingrained habits, being trusted as a professional, transformative leader and studying of one's teaching as a site of knowledge is not valued, if even recognized at all (Henderson, 2010b). The embodied consequences teachers glean include a feeling of isolation from teaching (Eisner, 2001), a sense of alienation from colleagues and administrators (Macdonald & Shirley, 2009), and a loss of vocational calling (Palmer, 2007), voice, and empowerment (Miller, 2005).

Instead of individuals' perspectives and differences being valued as irreplaceable, as Dan highlights in chapter 2, testing, collecting, and analyzing data for the purpose of pleasing reforms runs the risk of becoming all consuming, shaping everything from instruction to the sense of value and worth in teachers and students mind. We continue to see what Jackson (1986) points out decades ago about the daily happenings in classrooms and schools; that is, they are many times sites of conformity on social and psychological levels. Students' bodies are not only engaged with a mind-centered "doing," but their bodies are inscribed with certain cultural morals and values (O'Loughlin, 2006). When this occurs, education is not about a process of "freedom from" and "freedom to" (Greene, 1988) described in chapter 1; rather, it becomes a process to "silence, conceal, and limit [students' and teachers'] bodies" (Springgay & Freedman, 2007, p. xix). Learning is also not framed as inquiry or a "journey of understanding" (Henderson & Gornik, 2007), but is instead the reduction, absorption, and memorization of predetermined skills and facts for the purpose of passing tests, which is equated to success (Eisner, 2001; Wayne, 2009). Students' holistic well-being is outright ignored (Noddings, 2007), and little or no room is left for students' voice or input on the curriculum matters or for cultivating deep, holistic understandings of themselves, society, and democracy (Henderson & Gornik, 2007). If not already, you will come to recognize more on why this is problematic, especially with Boni's deliberations in chapter 6 about issues of equity in everyday schooling, and how schools position students' ways of being and knowing as problematic, particularly for marginalized individuals (Watkins, 2001).

Affirming Our Holistic Being

Through the prior section, I hope you glimpsed what is in part feeding our trying times in mainstream education—the disembodiment of teaching and learning through an incessant focus on reforming, standardizing, and testing. The disembodiment of teachers and students is quite disturbing when we stop to seriously consider Blumenfeld-Jones's (2012) reflections on the intertwined nature of education, experience, what we come to know, and how we become in the world: "Through educational experience we learn ways to be and these ways, perhaps more than cognitive learning, stay with us throughout our lives" (p. 29). Our educational experiences are undeniably "lived" (Pinar & Irwin, 2004), and our ways of "knowing and being are intimately entwined" (Kane, 1994, p. 2). Although not solely responsible for students' well-being, we need to acknowledge that experiences in and around schools influence and reinforce how we exist in the world, our ways of knowing, our ways of being, and the value we see in ourselves, in human beings, and more than humans. Studying your embodiment of holistic pedagogy is in part about contemplating the lasting effects of educational experiences—an idea exemplified within many of the authors' personal, pedagogical anecdotes shared throughout this book.

When we study embodiment, it brings a richness and depth to our reflections, conversations, and actions around educational policies, theories, and practices. Embodiment invites us to reconnect with our bodies because they are, after all, the vessels through which we live. Our bodies are not "lump[s] of matter mechanically cranking" along; rather, through our bodies, we interface with the world around us feeling, communicating, and perceiving our existence (Johnson, 2002, p. 344). Embodiment in curriculum and pedagogy embraces and acknowledges that our minds, bodies, and spirits (Hendry, 2011) are central to "the [everyday] experiences of people" (Christodoulou, 2010, p. 331). Knowledge, reality, and the world are not stagnant or separate from us, but they are fluid, idiosyncratic, and constructed through our minds and bodies. An embodied interpretation of holistic understanding embraces and affirms many dimensions of experience as affective, intuitive, relational, spiritual, and more.

The vision for holistic understanding in this book is anchored in the existentialist notion of a "journey" that is at the same time personal and social (Henderson & Gornik, 2007). Such holism strives to "cultivate fully developed human beings by attending to their physical, emotional, psychological, moral, and spiritual growth" through pedagogy, fostering "personal meaning and fulfillment, love for lifelong learning, and connection to others and the natural world" (Joseph, 2010, p. 445). When we are embodying holistic understanding, we are attuning ourselves to the notion of journey as an ongoing process of becoming different, where we "enter the multiple provinces of meaning that create perspectives" (Greene, 2001, p. 5). Reflective inquiry is part of this process; it asks us to be part of a never-ending practice of disrupting, questioning, reconstructing, engaging, and deciding (Ryan, 2011). Akin to Dan's chapter 2 and Chris's chapter 4 to follow, this chapter's aim is to nurture your sensitivity and courage to engage in reflective inquiry not only about your practice of embodying holistic understanding but your relationships with others.

Reflecting on Embodiment

The philosophy of John Dewey (1938a) grounds this book's conception of reflective inquiry. Discussed at length in chapter 2, Dewey's stance on human experience is transactional. Dewey's interpretation of experience has been acknowledged as supporting embodied teaching and learning (Christodoulou, 2010; O'Loughlin, 2006) because he conceived of human experiences through a relational lens—a sense of "togetherness" or "with-ness" (Ryan, 2011). What are often seen as dichotomies (e.g., self/other, mind/body) merge and are part of a "qualitative whole" of experience (Ralston, 2013). Therefore, embodying holistic understanding is concerned with not only your "inner landscape" (Palmer, 2007) but also your *interembodiment*. None of us exist alone, and interembodiment refers to how your embodiment "is never a private affair, but is always already mediated by our continual interaction with other human beings and non-human bodies"

(Weiss, 1999, p. 5). Holistic understanding asks us, as educators, to blend and see the relationships between mind-body, self-other, senses-intellect, teacher-student, theory-practice, personal-social, known-unknown, and so on.

While chapter 2 articulated *moments of practice* to guide your reflections around teaching, I describe four *moments of becoming*, which are intended to deepen your understanding of what it means to embody holistic pedagogy. Building upon chapter 2, the reflective problem solving in this book can only emerge when we begin noticing the problems and limitations of educational policies and practices. When we acknowledge and engage with problems, we are poking holes in them and in habitual ways of being in and thinking about schools. We are challenging ourselves—alongside others—to think critically, disrupt, and seek alternatives. The moments in this chapter can help you pose your own problems and, through disrupting, allow for new possibilities to emerge. New possibilities are part of the process of reconstructing what we know and how we exist. Reconstructing can be tricky because we all have to work in/with organizations that do not always permit nor support robust reconstruction. Reconstructing teaching and learning happens in small ways and in relationship to the constraints of a given situation.

The four becoming moments I will highlight (inspired awakening, mindful enacting, heartfelt self-examining, and persistent envisioning) are intended to be a starter-kit to begin and sustain your investigations into embodying holistic understanding in the contexts of your classroom(s), school(s), and beyond. The moments are written as gerunds (*-ing*) to attempt to capture a sense of problem-solving fluidity and the disrupting-reconstructing spirit described above. Verbs, also, by their nature, imply the acting and becoming inherited in "curriculum as *currere*" (Pinar, 1994) discussed in chapter 1. In keeping with the spirit of togetherness and fluidity, the four moments actually overlap and do not follow a certain sequence or hierarchy, even though in writing they appear separate and in an order. You may experience one moment at a time or maybe a couple together. You may experience all of them at once. You may even decide to eliminate some, merge others, or let new ones bloom based on your study and practice. In this lead-learning invitation, I am working with adjectives and gerunds that work for me. However, other adjectives and gerunds may be a better fit for your journey of understanding; therefore, you may have your own unique language for these moments of becoming. Finally, I want to point out that my recursive moments intermingle with Dan's moments of *practice* and Chris's moments of *enduring*. All our moments are interdependent and will help you to engage with the professional ethic of this book. When working on your teaching, you are shaping how you exist in the world, which affects your interactions with others (e.g., colleagues, administrators, parents) and how you create community.

Inspired Awakening

Throughout this chapter, I hinted that teaching artistry through studying and practicing is unfortunately not a norm in education. Therefore, part of the challenge for those of us intrigued by this lead-professional way is the need to continuously nurture our "aesthetic attentiveness" (Blumenfeld-Jones, 2012) in sensing the "qualitative whole" (Ralston, 2013) or "is-ness" (Stuhr, 1997) of emancipatory, holistic pedagogy. *Inspired awakening* involves exploring how we might awaken our embodiment through tapping into the bodies, minds, emotions, and hearts of others and ourselves. Moments of inspired awakening are about provoking and imbuing our "teacher being[s]" (Fowler, 2006) with the spirit of holistic pedagogy and pushing ourselves towards recognizing that this work can be and is possible with curriculum and pedagogy.

Think back to Dan's chapter 2, where he critiqued teaching's daily habits as not supporting emancipatory holistic pedagogy. He suggested that at any time, "events" (Badiou, 2005) can occur in which we, teachers, can separate ourselves from the dominant cultures of curriculum. The notion of inspired awakening extends his notion of event. Identifying and reflecting upon events (e.g., teachers, films, artworks, conflicts, public figures, and so on) are ways in which we can foster deeper understandings of, and commitment to, this book's ideas. I opened this chapter recounting my memory of Denny's funeral because it lives on inside me as an event awakening me to how teachers can embody this book's mission, even on an intuitive level. Can you begin identifying events in your life where you have experienced embodiments of this book's vision? How have those influenced you? In addition to exploring personal event(s), I strongly believe chapter 8, written by my wonderful colleague Petra, will further your inspired awakening through her deliberations on mythopoetics and the wonders of stories and feelings in teaching.

Mindful Enacting

Take a moment to revisit the quotation I used from the thirteenth-century Sufi poet, Rumi, to open this chapter. For me, his words touch at the heart of mindful enacting. Even though much of what is happening in education might seem to be out of teachers' control, on a small scale, you do have control. You have control over your critical thinking and actions. Change is possible, and it starts from within by you choosing to find ways of enacting a "new professionalism" (Palmer, 2007). Embodying holistic pedagogy urges us to not only experience inspired awakening but to also embed our understandings in lived experiences. "Knowing is not a result of transcending the body, but staying embodied, trusting our lived experience" (Hendry, 2011, p. 97). Moments of *mindful enacting* call us to merge thought and action by plugging the ideas throughout this book into our daily lives mindfully. The idea of being mindful can be understood as the opposite of "mindlessness" in which rules, habits, regulations, and customs direct what we do (Dewey, 1938a; Langer, 1997). Being *mindful* entails us being open and willing to explore new information (Langer, 1997), as well as trying to the best of our abilities to be "fully present" and "wide-awake" to holistic understanding within our educational contexts (Greene, 2001).

You may be wondering how you can begin bringing the spirit of this book alive through your interactions and relationships with others, especially if you feel your context may not be overly supportive. Seek out and act upon moments in your daily life where "wiggle room" exists (Cuban, 2005). In both Chris's chapter 4 on building community and Wendy's chapter 5 on negotiating barriers around enacting holistic pedagogy, you will delve into this concept even more. Wiggle room is about finding ways to "negotiate the official discursive terrains of schooling that bound the 'design and development' of curriculum as well as 'identities'" and to "glimpse spaces through which to maneuver, spaces through which to resist, spaces for change" (Miller, 2005, p. 223). Acting upon wiggle room is a way for you to develop courage and move forward with intention and thoughtful actions, making your teaching a mindful practice of holistic understanding.

Heartfelt Self-Examining

We all cloak ourselves in beliefs, which is okay. Holding steadfast to who we think we are and our beliefs, however, can work against the spirit of curriculum development within this book. In order to develop our capacities within, we need a willingness to not only affirm efforts but also an open-mindedness to contemplate challenges and critique ourselves as lead learners. This idea is at the center of heartfelt self-examining. The *heartfelt* quality is a reminder to us about the caring and compassionate nature of this work. While you are journeying forward with your study and practice, you need to be sincere as well as forgiving in your reflections on how you are enacting holistic pedagogy. *Self-examining* at its core asks you to reflect upon your self. Through examination, you pause, go inward, and cultivate an awareness of your actions; you are in a sense asking yourself to be vulnerable. The facet of *examining* is one of "immanent critique" (Henderson, 2010a) in which you ask yourself to consider the issue of your fidelity to embodying holistic pedagogy through questions such as "To what degree am I walking the talk of holistic pedagogy, and how am I responding to resistances?"

The process of self-examining requires us to engage in deep introspections by probing our "inner landscape[s]" (Palmer, 2007). Doing this, we delve into our pasts, presents, and possible futures in order to strengthen our critical self-reflective capacities as teachers around holistic pedagogy. Embodying holistic pedagogy asks us to contemplate complex questions such as:

> *Who* in the world am I by now? *Where* am I and how did I get here? How do I go on from here? What interpretations can I make of my professional being and practice? How can I move into a mature, meaningful, aware, compassionate, knowledgeable, effective teaching being? How do I remain present amid difficulty? (Fowler, 2006, p. 17)

Through such examination of our sense of *self*, we are also pushed to reflect upon how we exist in relationship with others in our everyday teaching lives. Curriculum studies scholars Springgay and Freedman (2010) offer an essential reminder about embodiment when they encourage us to consider:

> How we come to know ourselves and the world around us, our subjectivity, is performed, constructed, and mediated in relation with other beings. It is this relationality that is crucial. Rather than knowledge formed through the rational autonomous I, knowledge is the body's immersion, its intertwining and interaction in the world and between others. (p. 230)

From their words, we can glean that self-examining is not only about ourselves but also about how we are being in relationships. Therefore, embodying holistic understanding must take into consideration how we are entangled in relationships with other people as well as other "organic and inorganic bodies, natural and cultural objects ... [because these] all are affective" (Bennett, 2011, p. xii).

The insights gathered from self-examining should not just remain locked away in our minds, which circles us back into the notion of action. Reflection is about manifesting action through the "taking of initiatives; it signifies moving into a future seen from ... [one's own] vantage point as an actor or agent" (Greene, 1995, p. 15). Consequently, the inner reflecting we do should in turn help us as we continue moving forward with mindful enactments and educational visions. The persistence, action, and fidelity around being a lead learner are picked up in Chris's chapter 4. With great sensitivity, she turns your attention to lead learning with those outside of your classroom, including teacher colleagues, administrators, and students' guardians.

Persistent Envisioning

The concept of uncovering and holding educational visions is central to this book. As you are familiar with by now, the book's vision is one in which teachers are autonomous professionals and visionary artists of their craft teaching for holistic understanding in a society striving for democratic ideals. Chapter 1 opened with a quotation by Macdonald and Purpel (1987), in which these two curriculum scholars spoke to the origins and powers of the curriculum visions we hold. As a refresher, the visions we hold arise from "who and what we are, where we come from, and where we are going" (p. 192). In choosing particular educational visions, holding them in our mind's eye, and acting upon them, our visions find ways to manifest outwardly into our classrooms and schools.

Throughout this book, and during your continued study and practice, you will be cultivating "beliefs and images" (Walker & Soltis, 2009) surrounding what for you embodies emancipatory holistic pedagogy and a new lead-professional way of being. The notion of *persistence* refers to you continuing to reflect upon and hold visions despite the difficulties or oppositions that might transpire while lead learning. The idea of *envisioning* is about tapping into and excising creative, imaginative capacities for living democratically. Envisioning asks us to give careful, serious attention to the power of our "educational imagination[s]" (Eisner, 1994) and "social imaginations" (Greene, 2001, 2010) as part of our process of wide-awakeness, which holds the potential to break from the habits and taken-for-granted ways of knowing and being. Our wide-awakeness can be done individually on an internal level (i.e., through heartfelt self-appraising) but also socially through coming together through reflectivity, inclusiveness, agency, and plurality (Baldacchino, 2009; Greene, 2010). Persistent envisioning, therefore, continuously directs our attention to the importance of "aims-talking" (Noddings, 2009a) and our relationships with our educational visions as well as with visions of humanity and the cosmos. In chapter 7's deliberations written by my colleague, Beth does a fine job building upon the importance of considering "how might one live" (May, 2005), while envisioning teaching and learning that fosters consciousness-raising for democratic interdependence.

Feeling Your Way Forward

As you continue forward, my hope for this chapter is that you begin to not only find embodiment as connected with other chapters but that you also actively question and sense your own embodiment of holistic understanding. Know that there are others out there with a deep desire to, as Parker Palmer (2007) states, "deepen, renew, and sustain" our sense of "vocation in trying times" (p. xiv). I even glimpse hints of a growing public awareness among educational stakeholders (Abeles & Congdon, 2009; Guggenheim, 2010; Robinson, 2011) that the current trends in mainstream education have disembodying consequences. We need to keep our eyes open for comrades who find the current climate troubling. We need to connect with them and share how we, too, are looking for new possibilities in teaching and learning. We need to forge relationships of support for our bodies, minds, and spirits. As the philosopher Deleuze (1990) reminds us, "we do not even know what a body is capable of ..." and "we do not even know of what affections we are capable, nor the extent of our power" (p. 226). Studying and practicing this book professional vision asks us to sense our way forwarding; we are exploring the yet to be known possibilities within ourselves.

Together, may we explore more holistic possibilities of our educational bodies and those of future generations. I hope this chapter continues to challenge and support your exploration of self and your beliefs about what it means to be a teacher. May the resources I use help you begin studying the topic of embodiment. As you embark on lead learning, may you also make sense of the study scaffolding in a way that is your own. In closing, I leave the following questions to further your thinking on embodiment and possibly begin conversations with colleagues in all kinds of lead-learning contexts—colleagues who are concerned and, perhaps, preoccupied and disenchanted by the 'modernist' pressures for a narrow rationalism, standardization, and testing:

- Becoming a teacher is a social process, and we must consider how we have undergone "many changes and nevertheless retained impressions or traces" from our journeys (Spinoza, 1959, p. 2). To what degree were living expressions of holistic pedagogy's qualities present for you? How have you been affected by and are you affecting others?
- How are your school and your teaching materials shaping the bodies-minds-spirits of students? How might you work to create educational experiences and environments that take into consideration the holism of your students?
- How are your daily thoughts and actions living embodiments of holistic understanding? How might you either alone, or with colleagues, begin enacting tenets of holistic pedagogy in your educational context?
- How might you, perhaps with fellow educators who are also feeling drained or disconnected from their careers, find ways to reignite and revive your vocational calling? What imaginative and creative ways might you use to better understand the dimensions of holistic understanding?

4
SOWING HOLISTIC UNDERSTANDING: BUILDING A DISCIPLINARY COMMUNITY

It is now the task of education in the broadest sense to identify, to radically resist, and to begin to alter these continuing conditions that block community and intimacy and foster domination and opposition. (Stuhr, 1997, p. 245)

Reader, by now you have realized the *way of being* supported within this book is not the thing to make lesson planning and assessment easier. It cannot answer the demand for ever-increasing test scores, or mend debates about school funding. Why even entertain the notion of cultivating wisdom-oriented inquiry in concert with others as described in chapter 1? Who has time to trouble themselves with community, intimacy, and endowing the world with new meaning?

The endeavor described within this book has everything to do with the deeper meaning of teachers' work, not just the more narrow efficiency of our techniques. I invite you to come along on this journey—a departure—in spite of and because of the time-stressed conditions in which we teach. For me, the work satisfies a deep yearning that has to do with calling and wholeness, with the desire to affect posterity, with the opportunity to be a part of something bigger than myself—to "be the change I wish to see," as Gandhi so profoundly dared us all. In this way, I enliven my fondest hopes for my vocation, the very things that drew me to it in the first place. I give voice and space for what matters most, not only the things that are easily measured. For, as Eisner (2005a) said, "we need to be concerned about more than the measurable. Not everything that matters is measurable, and not everything that is measurable matters" (para. 20).

Essentially, this journey involves us, teachers, remaking our roles—teachers as reflective inquirers, seekers embodying the worth and promise of education in a deep democracy *that has yet to be realized*. How can we fit ourselves for this work of *enduring* in the face of thwarting social conditions? Stuhr (1997) holds, "…we almost have given up concern for the eclipse of a community or public and effective publicity. Still we must realize that this state of affairs is incompatible with a democratic way of life" (p. 251). He contends that we need knowledge producers (and, in my view, teachers qualify) to work at the *cultural* frontiers that mark the limits of our collective advancement. Stuhr names the gap between "actually existing American *society*, on the one hand, and the realization of a genuinely American (and global) *community*, on the other" (p. 238) as the site for this work. The "effective publicity" to which Stuhr refers is the agency borne of actual full participation by all members of a society, so as to transform it into a community.

The effort demands a reckoning of the distinctly moral nature of teachers' work. Behm, Rankins-Robertson, and Roen (2014) aptly note:

> Democracy is more than an election cycle, campaign rally, or party platform; it is a way of being in and acting on the world. It is a disposition that emphasizes bridging differences, coalescing relationships, reflecting critically on values and beliefs, and developing knowledge to address a community's core challenges. (para. 8)

If one recognizes vibrant democracy is dependent upon the widest array of persons, all suited for the aim of "addressing a community's core challenges," rather than posturing in a political parade, then teachers have much to offer in cultivating this disposition in the citizenry. Educators are obliged to engage in critical reflection so their students may do so. Teachers cannot impart in their students awareness of relationships unless they themselves become attuned to merging relations. It behooves us to attend to such matters, since they pertain to our highest responsibilities to our students and our communities.

If there were ever a time for attending to building community and trust for deeper democracy, it is now. The following excerpt from Melton's (2014) blog provides a heartening backdrop for 3S pedagogy. She is speaking as a parent who visited her son's fifth grade teacher:

> We talked about teaching children and what a sacred trust and responsibility it is. We agreed that subjects like math and reading are the least important things that are learned in a classroom. We talked about shaping little hearts to become contributors to a larger community—and we discussed our mutual dream that those communities might be made up of individuals who are Kind and Brave above all. (para. 4)

I bring these words to your attention early in this chapter, lest you think the academy is the only site for disrupting and reconstructing. Although the standardized management paradigm with its technical-rational conceptions of teaching appear all around, do not overlook the potency of a small, committed group of individuals. Parents have a great stake in their children's education; many are beginning to recognize the ways that standardized testing has perverted schooling experience. Keep your eyes peeled, and you will witness individuals from widely assorted backgrounds engaged similarly in reconsidering aims for education and schooling, some of which connect quite closely with 3S pedagogy.

An essential feature of this undertaking is building public and professional intellectual capacity. Think 'learning organization' and widen the circle to include parents, teachers, administrators, students, and community members. The *quality* of that collective, intellectual, moral, and social development is key. Within the myriad of interactions between humans, we share an overarching concern for the way we stand in relation to each other, and in relation to ourselves.

Arendt (1958) wrote that "plurality is the condition of human action because we are all the same, that is, human, in such a way that nobody is ever the same as anyone else who ever lived, lives, or will live" (p. 8). I believe the plurality of human experience paves the way for *autonomy-within-interdependence*, which draws forth contributions that would be impossible otherwise. It is an element of practice in corporate and religious settings, but largely absent as schooling exists today. Autonomy-within-interdependence, or holonomy, is cut off when we fail to recognize relations other than codependency (as agents of the state, passive recipients of policy mandates) or sole independence (shut the door and teach).

Rather, for the sake of our students and ourselves, it is imperative to tune our ways of being toward agency in working "within, without being of, this situation," as Dan has invited us in chapter 2. At first, it may seem foolish to take on commitments when the teaching 'plate' is already overfilled. But, unless we reprioritize how we spend our time, the integration of practices and beliefs is not likely to occur. Building a disciplinary community for 3S pedagogy takes the "carnival" of creative human expression mentioned in chapter 1 as its default mode. Let me emphasize that unlike other paths, the road involves the *doing of* it (inquiring, searching, developing) from within, as generators of knowledge and change, not only recipients of them (i.e., *having it done to* us).

I want to provide metacognitive guidance for building a disciplinary community around the aims of curriculum development through wisdom-loving, democratically laden 3S pedagogy. Specifically, and as introduced in the preface, I want to offer some advice on building trust for 3S pedagogy through collegial study and practice. I find myself asking: What would be helpful for those along a continuum of development for a holonomic way of becoming and being? How can I counsel lead learners so that an invitational stance is rooted in their ways of being and becoming, and so that others would feel compelled to join them in study? Or, as Jen has previously written in chapter 3, to "remain present amid difficulty"? How can I keep company with those who are on the road? How can I make what was my private journey more collegial?

Chances are that you have surveyed the landscape 'in the trenches' and the knowledge you have acquired is invaluable in the road ahead. In this book, you are in good company and at the front end of a pioneering effort. This book's invitation maps a difficult terrain, but the beautiful vistas and hopeful new possibilities can be convincing. Your own progress on this journey is idiographic; still, there may be some gain to be had from my path so far.

You have been invited in the two previous chapters to engage in the study topics of teaching for holistic understanding and of embodying holistic understanding. I now summon your engagement in the study topic of building a 3S disciplinary community through moments of disrupting and reconstructing. Within the moments threading through these early chapters, and in the spirit of holistic understanding, consider the multilayered, iterative nature of your study.

Dan's invitation pertains largely to *practicing*, Jen's to *embodying*, and mine to *sustaining and enduring*. However, because the quality of this work is dynamic and recursive, rather than sequential or hierarchical, you will find yourself noticing overlapping dimensions, and you may also recognize new moments emerging in your own disrupting-and-reconstructing ways of being a teacher. These are valid and important for you to pursue as you practice, embody, and endure for holistic understanding. I am grateful for the insights of many authors cited here, who provide me with continuing enlightenment for my journey, but they are not meant to be an exhaustive listing of the only places to find inspiration, expertise, or satisfaction while you tread this path. I urge you to put on the mantle of researcher and inquirer while you study. It will sustain you in ways that none of us can anticipate.

In the next pages, I offer an overview of a disciplinary community, its aims, and how else it may be different from current conceptions of professional learning communities. I explain altered relations and changed priorities of the disciplinary community, and describe some of the significant distinctions between dominant ways of being a 'teacher leader' and those advanced in a wisdom-loving and democratically tuned pedagogy. The remainder of the chapter describes moments threading through much of my own experience with that pedagogy, in my elementary classroom, with adult learners as a graduate school instructor, and with parents in an educational issues book club. For the sake of organizing the chapter, I describe these moments with adjectives and gerunds meaningful to me: *graceful inviting, radical resisting, conscious cultivating*, and *peer and public reviewing*. I hope my scaffolding approach assists your study, practice, and reflective inquiry.

Disciplinary Communities

There are many types of communities— e.g., residential, professional, athletic, cult. Here, the word 'disciplinary' does not refer to obedience and punishment or regulation of behavior. Instead, we are speaking of the development of specific knowledge-based capacities. In this case, the specific branch of knowledge is a 3S pedagogy that advances a deepening democracy.

Reconfiguration and More: Transfiguration

What struck me immediately upon my initial exposure to the concept of 3S pedagogy was the novelty of it. Imagine, *teachers* actually studying their own practice for the purpose of developing the knowledge that propels them forward. The idea that I could harvest daily transactions in my work and use them to become a better teacher was a decidedly different way of viewing my responsibilities. It reminded me of the old adage "only the one who wears the shoe, knows where it pinches." For me, it represented a certain liberation. This was not a matter of 'connecting the dots' differently; instead, a whole new realm entered into view. I claimed freedom to transform what formerly existed as a standard-centric, somewhat fragmented, and largely unconscious practice into a more thoughtful pedagogy with deepened self, social, and subject matter understandings as its aim. The upshot has contributed to a hopeful vision of moral authority and collective agency—a new way of *being a teacher with others*, which opened up possibilities for my own public intellectual work.

Allow me to trace more of the history that brought me here. Much of my teaching career has reinforced a few pervasive assumptions about my role as a teacher. First, someone outside the field of teaching provided knowledge I was to study and enact. I learned by omission, more than explicitly, that any teacher would be unlikely to possess enough skill (let alone time) to fuel either her or his own professional growth, or the achievement of students and colleagues. Although I was expected to apply outsiders' wisdom in my own classroom, it was never suggested that I examine philosophical underpinnings of curriculum standards, assessments, data collection methods, or related teaching practices.

Second, teachers' study was meant to be subject-matter centered. Meaning, in order to become a better teacher, I was to store up knowledge about the content of subjects I taught and the carefully prescribed standards for my grade level. The 'study' generally involved reading technical texts and watching videos of instructional procedures for particular subjects and standards to an age range of students. More recently, there has been emphasis on professional training devoted to testing metrics, such as quantitative analysis of assessment scores, rates of improvement, and prospective learning trajectories as predicted by value-added scores. At the present time in the United States, this is what counts as 'legitimate' knowledge.

Moreover, once teacher certification was completed, it was not expected that I maintain a habit of inquiry, reading, or collaborative study related to my profession. "You passed the test, now give it a rest" seemed to be the accepted mode of operation. This longstanding paradox of anti-intellectualism in education is confronted directly via my moments of radical resisting and conscious cultivating, which I will expand upon shortly. In fact, critical distance was rarely on my radar during my early teaching career. As a public intellectual, however, whatever influence or support I hope to lend or gain is tied to my own continuing inquiry.

In retrospect, I recognize my teaching practices were based on an amoral, petrified kind of problem-solution process. I disregarded the premises underlying my instruction and glossed over aberrations that might have prompted inquiry. I believed my expertise was encompassed entirely in my technique. Although at times I felt myself bucking these notions, I was unaware of how they distanced me from my own understandings of being a good teacher, and my agency in becoming better.

Reflecting on my professional enculturation, I noticed that my teaching practices were most influenced by two things: what happened in my classroom and what happened when I came together with other teachers, questioning, discussing, reading, brainstorming, and troubleshooting. During mostly informal meetings, the conversation always got back to our students—sometimes particular ones, or sometimes the class as a whole. When we ourselves posed the problems we encountered in our daily school lives, and then attempted to find solutions within our contexts, I recognize now that we engaged in a cycle that was quite apart from officially sanctioned standardized management procedures. Further, I can identify a kind of reciprocity between what my students experience and what I experience as a teacher at school.

Why Do We Need a Disciplinary Community?

In reforms masquerading as *simplicity, neutrality*, or *efficiency*, we unwittingly proliferate fundamental images and beliefs that do not serve our students, our profession, nation, or humanity well (Apple, 2001; Berliner & Biddle, 1995; Henderson, & Gornik 2007; Jackson, 1986; Kincheloe, 2005; Noddings, 2007; Pinar, 2012). Most of all, presently, educators lack power, time, and space where they can do the important work of thinking about their students' learning and their own, carefully considering the assumptions and theories that are held in practices. Collective inquiry allows investigation into attendant contexts, historical referents, and long-term impact of current policies, of which Apple (2001) has written form "a regime of control [that] is based not on trust, but on a deep suspicion of the motives and competence of teachers" (p. 51).

Before any alternative can be generated, the current conditions of hyperscrutiny, labor intensification, deskilling, and dysintegration call for explicit acknowledgment and delegitimization. For those involved in building disciplinary communities for holistic understanding, inquiry into such conditions constitutes moments of disruption, which call for deeper understanding of the current culture. We are caught in the same conundrum that Cinderella faced when she wished to attend the ball: "Only when you finish this endless list of chores that subversively seeks to prevent your admission." Cinderella enlists the help of the subservient creatures in her midst, using them as resources to get the work done. Rather than colonizing the ones around us (or waiting around for a fairy godmother), disciplinary community envisions ways to take issue with

the posture of gracious submission that Dan has described, and to resist disembodied education Jen's chapter prior illuminated. Moreover, in the workings of
a disciplinary community, we carve out a construction site for individuals to
entertain possibilities of new identity, including altered priorities. We do this by
transfiguring power relations so that the destination *and* vehicle are changed.

A disciplinary community is necessary to fortify each other for this journey;
to keep watch and be inspired by others who keep watch over their priorities; to construct the professional norms that will allow for reciprocal learning
and trust. Our students need an infusion of democracy, agency, and joy in their
learning process, and so do we. In order to develop schooling in ways embodying principles of deep democracy—of each person's potential contribution being
irreplaceable (den Heyer, 2014)—we form disciplinary communities that incite
inquiry, reflection, reconceptualization, and action.

Building a disciplinary community requires trust. As Jim argues in chapter 1, its
success depends on a 'grass-roots' kind of movement to address the cultural and existential challenges of democratic living. An organic and collective cultivation of study
and inquiry distinguishes the disciplinary community I am describing here from
some other types of professional learning communities. The transactions in a disciplinary community revolve around concerns that surface through daily experience in
classrooms and schools, reading, dialogue, and study at the zone, which "continues to
mark the limit of our expansion, development, and civilization" (Stuhr, 1997, p. 238).

In order to explain some distinctions between organizations with standardized-
centric ways of being, and those advanced in building trust for 3S pedagogy through
collegial study, my description is necessarily simplified. In the spirit of hermeneutic
inquiry, however, please consider that any representation of holistic understanding in
3S disciplinary communities falls short of the actual complexity of the thing. Griffiths
(2005) wrote, "practices are fluid. They are also leaky and viscous. Their boundaries
are not sharp" (p. 7). The interplay of 'spirit' and 'letter' enriches inquiry; what might
have been conceptualized as 'noise' is, in this way of being, a deliberate and desirable
condition. In building trust for a 3S disciplinary community, we strive to loosen the
cultural boundaries that impose limits on democratically oriented ways of being with
each other. On purpose, we create priorities that demand alternative foci for study
and stand in contrast to the ones prevailing in current school reform efforts.

In a disciplinary community, the ways persons stand in relation to themselves
and others are deliberately shifted toward new ways of 'being with.' Broadly, it
involves deconstructing entrenched, habituated constitutions in an organization
and (at times, simultaneously) reconstructing relationships. For instance, we can
move deliberately from separate camps, a lack of attention to power relations,
hierarchy, and alienation toward collective, shared knowledge bases, support for
developing critical distance, and mutual high regard and valuation.

Similarly, when one considers the priorities of practice and pedagogy, altered
foci for study come into play. These stand in contrast to the ones prevailing in
current reform efforts. For example, in building a disciplinary community, we

study with the aim of developing capacity for reflective inquiry in each other, instead of focusing solely on following mandates. We rely on a transactional dialectic of understanding, rather than on the external 'truth' of policies. We promote associating theories, practices, and missions, and go after deepened, hermeneutic, pluralistic aims. The 'information flow' is *expectant*—in advance of judgment and decision, rather than doled out on a 'need to know' basis.

Graceful Inviting

Building trust for holistic understanding can begin with inviting. Moments of graceful inviting are issued in the inclusive spirit of 'come as you are.' After all, we can only take up building a disciplinary community from the actual starting places and persons that exist at a given moment in time. In that regard, each one of us is no better, but certainly no less, than any other one. In this instance, we are about creating freedom to

> break with the 'cotton wool' of habit, of mere routine, of automatism, [which] is (as we shall see) to seek alternative ways of being, to look for openings. To find such openings is to discover new possibilities—often new ways of achieving freedom in the world. (Greene, 1988, p. 2)

Although daily we must contend with many imposing and alienating qualities of school transactions, inviting persons to form a disciplinary community need not be one of them. The call to disrupt the usual focus of mandates, received agendas, and fragmented practice can take place informally, as we actively 'sit with' our colleagues to hear the openings they present—the ones that crack open shared concerns and mutual aspirations. Even if colleagues decline this invitation, they will be aware that the freedom to engage in collective inquiry exists.

We teach amid strident reform policies that impose ever-increasing pressure to yield ground in our relations, in our study, in our classrooms and communities. Creating the space to examine current practice in a time-stressed environment is a delicate feat that encompasses both building relationships and nurturing responsibilities. It involves a conscious effort to create new ways of *being* and new ways of *being with*. How does one offer invitations to create hospitable ground for *counter* change?

Casting a wide net is imperative; one that sifts through moments at the copy machine, hallway meetings, parent conferences, and board meetings, all with an eye toward gathering persons interested in actively and collectively constructing a viable alternative to what now exists. If one considers discouragement of teachers' work conditions as a possible opportunity for invitation, then a single day in a public school will yield many opportunities! Some teachers will respond positively at the chance to marshal their creativity and insights in divergent professional development rather than conforming to predetermined rubrics. When others consider the prospect of breaking out of the arid conditions of the teaching profession, they may harbor a belief that it cannot be done. Even those persons may be more willing to 'hitch a ride' if they see glimpses of caring pedagogical artistry in action. In such instances, the individuals often see the potential for reconnection with their early visions of being a teacher. Many colleagues will be curious about the possibilities for remedying the rift between what they know and believe and what they find themselves doing in their classrooms.

An important advantage of graceful inviting is that it gathers a wide array of persons, practices, and perspectives. Griffiths (2005) claims that:

> If there is enough diversity within a practice there is room for some communities to develop within the larger practices. Therefore diversity makes it possible for the practice itself to be more fluid, flexible and nonhierarchical. It can become a community of learners, rather than a set of novices seeking a single model of expertise. (p. 7)

Griffiths underscores the positive effect of widespread invitation. It increases the chance that we can assemble individuals and practices with enough diversity so that there can be room for communities of learners to develop. This is part of what building a disciplinary community is after.

For me, it was important my invitations be understood not as one more tier of an infinitely defined pathway to perfection. Barth's (2001) previously cited conception of 'lead learner' is useful here. Inviting a person to be a lead learner, and the charge of cultivating lead-learnership for holistic understanding, gives permission to fumble, to be humble, and to learn from all around. Both in my experience with elementary students and as a lead learner in the role of teacher for graduate students, I find there are many times when I need to let the students lead me. They know which concepts are fuzzy, what kind of work would improve their learning, and where they need support. This opens new possibilities for us *being with* each other; together, we can craft new lessons, altered assignments, and different performances of understanding. The premise of fallibility is at once a humanizing and unifying element in this posture for study.

The felt quality of inviting is interdependence, integrity, and wholeness of practice. We reach for collectiveness within difference, trusting that we can see and hear in the other. It is a recentering of practice that attunes to questions such as: *Who is being excluded? Where are there walls between us? How can those persons be invited to the table?* The only deftness in moments of inviting is grace: to preassign value to all present; to believe in and admit the irreplaceable contributions of all (den Heyer, 2014); to soundly commit to the introspection and openness required to be fully present. Therefore, moments of graceful inviting permit us to turn toward moral sources of authority, or the "felt obligation and duties derived from widely shared community values, ideas, and ideals" (Sergiovanni, 1992, p. 39).

Radical Resisting

To work within professional norms that circumscribe narrowly defined objectives and prescriptive remedies has become increasingly difficult. As it is used here, radical resisting is meant to convey a comprehensive awareness of and resistance to the root sources of the stunting boundaries we actively seek to transgress. Radical resisting involves "take[ing] up residence in marginal territories and new lands" and *being with others* within, but not of, those bounds (Stuhr, 1997, p. 233).

In a disciplinary community for 3S pedagogy, we strive for an openness that leaves room for what Eisner (2005a) has called "being flexibly purposive." Speaking of the restricting consequences of highly technical-rational conceptions of teaching, Eisner explains his use of this phrase:

> In the first place, means do not always follow goals—goals can also follow means. New goals may emerge during the process of implementing means. As we go through a process, we often discover opportunities that we could not or did not anticipate before we took action. Our aims, when we are at our best, are *flexibly purposive*. Being flexibly purposive means that we are open to new opportunities that we did not foresee. One consequence of our preoccupation with standards is that it freezes our conception of what we want to accomplish in our schools. (para. 4)

What could come of such resistance? Acts of personal and collaborative reflection have the potential to make the familiar strange; they present the occasion to disrupt the habitual, disembodied problem-solving operative at work in our thinking. For instance, with the intent to radically resist, we can investigate the anti-intellectual paradox in education: *What losses ensue when the scholar is severed from the school? To what extent do I/we reinforce the false dichotomy of identity as scholar OR practitioner?* In tandem, there arises potential to reorient our ways of being and being with: *What gains might be had in taking up collective study and inquiry (with students, colleagues, administrators, parents)?*

Radical resisting entails commitment to suspend judgment while we unearth and dwell in various perspectives and positions revealed during study. Thus, it constitutes a turn toward professional and moral sources of authority, rather than those assumed in technical-rational, bureaucratic, or psychological authority. Sergiovanni (1992) analyzed various modes of knowing and their implications in leadership. He noted that secular, science, and deductive logic are 'official' modes of knowing. Jen has explained further that the fallout of Descartes' rationality reinforced 'true knowledge' (i.e., sanctioned truth) as the domain of science and mathematics. Repercussions of this primacy abound today in dominant notions about 'researched-based practices' and the assumed validity of standardized psychometrics. That sacred and sense experience are delegitimized ways of knowing is of significant consequence for educators at the present time. Investigating the results of devaluing sense and sacred experience is an example of radical resisting.

Related to reconstructing, professional sources of authority take for granted that no one best way exists, and the breadth of experience with students and the contexts of presenting problems are valued bases in developing collective practice. A premise of professional authority is that scientific knowledge is meant to "inform, not prescribe, practice" (Sergiovanni, 1992, p. 39). Moral authority hinges on the existence of a community with shared values and commitments, and assumes that what is right and good is of as much importance as what works and is effective. In a 3S disciplinary community, we take on pedagogy based in moral authority, enacting ways of being and being with to foster collective, expanded, and sustained capacities for holistic understanding and inquiry.

Therefore, the substance of 3S collegial study stands in stark contrast toward much of the professional training that takes place today. It is *not* driven by pre-conceived agendas, mandates and policy, or standardized test data, although these topics are certainly recognized as having bearing on teachers' work. Instead, the artifact of our inquiry is more inquiry, a fundamental generating of points of entry, and practical and collective transactions to prompt further development of holistic understanding.

One helpful way to fuel development, I have found, is to introduce language that more fully captures qualities of classroom life. Terms like data-driven decision making, rate of improvement, benchmarks, expected trajectory, and value-added score pertain to a host of measures supposed to be 'objective.' In fact, these are rightly conceived as a means to gauge achievement, but have now been conflated to become both means and ends. They fall short in rendering the qualitative aspects of learning and teaching and, in the process, dispatch attendant historical, contextual, and cultural features which deny difference, and (at least in part) account for the manner and degree of the learning taking place.

I would submit that qualitative aspects of schooling have as much to do (if not more than test scores) with a mission of advancing intellect toward deeper understandings, caring, and commitment to the tenets of our democratic way of life. Eisner (1976) maintains that the kind of instruments and the corresponding language we use for observing and evaluating have a profound effect upon what we are able to see. He warned:

> Instead of talking about aims and aspirations, we must talk about dependent variables, performance objectives, or competencies. …This shift would not present much of a problem if it only represented a shift in language, but the problem exceeds the matter of language per se. The problem is that in de-emotionalizing expression and proscribing suggestive language, the opportunity to understand empathically and to communicate the quality of human experience diminishes. (p. 138)

By tuning our language, we can heighten attention to those dimensions of pedagogy that would have been invisible otherwise. We radically resist disembodied teaching.

Conscious Cultivating

Conscious cultivating begins with making consciousness visible—that is, building a *self*-consciousness. Such transacting allows us to penetrate what has been obscured, to surface paradoxical commitments, to gaze into the voids. Qualitative deepening of understanding cannot occur without establishing critical distance from present ways of being, and conscious cultivating allows us to make 'object' (taken-for-granted worldviews) what we were formerly only 'subject' to. Because conscious cultivating risks revealing our indifference in being up-standers for our students' or our community's plight, the groundwork of building trust cannot be overemphasized.

The members of the community must first have assurance that they can present themselves, in all their flawed glory, to one another. They begin to reveal their aspirations for their profession, their beliefs about their roles and their students, their dilemmas and gaps in understanding. Together, we consciously cultivate the relation of critical friend, witnessing and prompting the steps along the journey, but resisting prescription. We serve as the flesh-and-blood (human) links to a generous and generative (humane) vision of education and schooling.

At the same time, we recognize that our ways of knowing anything are pinned to our being, and cannot be comprehended inertly. Marty Grundy suggests there is "a way of knowing that is not of the intellect. We don't have very good words for this (in our present time and culture), so have to fall back on 'intuition' or 'heart knowledge' or something of the sort" (M. Grundy, personal communication, January 14, 2014).

In a disciplinary community for 3S pedagogy, we deliberately attend to development from within ourselves individually and from within a collective study group. We conceive our roles as agents and generators of knowledge rather than passive recipients of policy and information. And it is, as Hendry (2011) posits, "the spaces of contraction, paradox, and 'unknowing' that move us to spaces that are generative" (p. 208). That is not to say that we disconnect from the knowledge generated through other sources; instead, the goal is to situate that knowledge within the context of daily schooling, to accomplish the aim of qualitative deepening of understandings.

We resist conceptions of knowledge and learning as inert phenomena. Rather, we draw on Greene's (1988) characterization of consciousness, which entails "the capacity to pose questions to the world, to reflect on what is presented in experience" (p. 21). Greene explains further that perspectives are always partial, but that,

> there is always more to be discovered, each time he/she focuses attention. As important, each time he/she is with others—in dialogue, in teaching-learning situations, in mutual pursuit of a project—additional new perspectives open; language opens possibilities of seeing, hearing, understanding. (p. 21)

In moments of conscious cultivating, we actively nurture the capacity to 'see' in the full-bodied, holistic ways Greene describes. It is an interdependent aim that relies on trust to speak our own truths, *expecting* that they are plural. In some respects, the idea of conscious cultivating has some commonality with the Quaker practice of *discernment*. Grundy (2014) describes the process of discernment as involving,

> suspending judgment in terms of our assumptions of how this has to work out or move forward, [it] does not mean that we disregard reason, logic, or common sense. There is a dance, if you will, between being open to new revelation, to an unexpected "third way" of looking at and resolving an issue, and evaluating potential solutions. ... Discernment is an art, and requires practice. (M. Grundy, personal communication, January 14, 2014)

As explained in Grundy's words above, there is artistry in remaining open to new revelation, turning things over, and hearing others making meaning of issues and dilemmas we share. It potentially dislodges entrenched reference points for teaching practices. The move to examine what others perceive *and* what I perceive provokes an essential shift from unconscious acceptance of one reality and the simultaneous attribution of neutrality toward *on-purpose* investigation of interpretations of reality. Beyond that, conscious cultivating paves the way for *repositioning*, a concept described by Apple (2001):

> It in essence says that the best way to understand what any set of institutions, policies, and practices does is to see it from the standpoint of those who have the least power. While it is not preordained that those voices that will be heard most clearly are also those who have the most economic, cultural, and social capital, it is most likely that this will be the case. After all, we do not exist on a level playing field. Many economic, social, and educational policies when actually put in place tend to benefit those who already have advantages. (p. 199)

In this manner, we make approximations toward knowing what we do not know. Headway in the quest to discover how we may be complicit in domination or oppression can be illuminated through questions such as: *Where do I harbor preconceived notions or stereotypes in my practices or my omission of attention? How do these gaps affect my perceptions? Upon what premises or assumptions am I basing my practices? How do these align with my current mission/personal commitments? What wiggle room is present, or can be created?*

Peer and Public Reviewing

My experience with moments of peer and public reviewing are taken from a few different contexts. Some were informal conversations (as asides from the predetermined agendas of delayed start/in-service days, grade-level meetings, or "data" meetings). Others occurred during speaking engagements outside my district, or in a more formal setting of teaching graduate students in a teacher-leadership endorsement program. Some took place during the Educational Issues Book Club meetings I co-facilitated. I viewed these occasions as comprising the 'wiggle room' for advocating a different way of being a teacher, and being with a community. To the extent possible, I invited participants in the spirit of collective self-governance, and development-from-within, to become lead learners along with me.

Our inquiry was focused on the limits of current understandings, and *coming to know* in a qualitatively different way. Freire's (2003) words hummed in my head: "any situation in which some individuals prevent others from engaging in this process of inquiry is one of violence. The means used are not important: to alienate human beings from their own decision-making is to change them into objects" (p. 85). Likewise, Stuhr (1997) has recognized that those who "have been denied full membership in a society will not likely identify with those who exclude them" (p. 244). Knowing this then, our study was deliberately poised to investigate the situated, partial knowledge of a wide array of individuals regarding issues of practice and relations. Our inquiry included educating ourselves on the merits and limitations of test instruments and forms of evaluation, the validity of assessment results, and the consequences of prevailing views of legitimacy regarding data.

Most often, we found a way into perspective-gathering during study and conversation about how teachers themselves experience their practices and demands upon it, how students experience curriculum, or how parents receive it. We called for enduring issues of practice as the events to spark inquiry. Texts (articles, books, movies, blogs) were mined as additional information sources, ones that qualitatively deepened the inquiry and brought various perspectives into higher relief. In addition, we conceived of our own narratives, those of the students we serve, and the other texts as sources of data—data writ large. As such, our inquiry constituted an instance of self-study, an action-research initiative that relies on hermeneutic means, which Samaras and Freese (2006) describe as encompassing "shifts forward and backward through the data with no predetermined assumptions to allow for the emergency of seemingly unrelated ideas and part-whole relationships" (p. 12). Our work was flexibly purposive, one might say.

The dialogue that transpires during moments of peer and public reviewing lifts us outside current standardized-centric protocols to create a space to examine the fit between our walk and our talk. Pertaining to development from within, we are tending to an aspect of practice involving attunement and awareness. The process is highly iterative. We need to see ourselves seeing, and in the process become aware of something's implications. In moments of peer and public reviewing, we were sifting into the hollows, bringing omissions into our gaze, and regarding what heretofore was not subject to scrutiny.

To those immersed in present "school deform" (Pinar, 2012), it is immediately apparent that standardized test scores and value-added data carry no power to render the *qualities* of schooling and teaching; indeed, they often occlude it. A different language and different instruments are necessary. Since qualitative measures are not at this point easily accessible, we have to invent ways to cull the qualitative, experiential data available to us. One possibility is to ground observation and evaluation in the "connoisseurship" advanced by Eisner (2005b) more than 30 years ago. He writes:

> The features of classroom life are not likely to be explained or controlled by behavioral laws, [so] I conceive the major contribution of evaluation to be a heightened awareness of the qualities of that life, so that teachers and students can become more intelligent within it. (p. 40)

Building a disciplinary community involves fostering sensitivity to the qualities of classroom life, including the breaches. As we review our practices and transactions, our inquiry work permits us to become more intelligent within classroom life. Thus, we are with each other in ways that take up the null curriculum in questions such as: *Is all learning and knowing scrutible? What does the absence of attention teach us, and what does it teach our students? Is noticing such aspects of practice of any value in the art of teaching? How do my own practices stimulate or stunt possibilities to 'be' in ways that are generative?* And, more widely, *how do present modes of operation (including mandated policies) position us as enemies rather than allies of each other, our students, and their parents?*

By holding small moments to the light of inquiry, we gathered the perspectives and experiences of the individuals in the community, teasing out the opportunities to reorient toward caring pedagogical artistry and responsible professional autonomy. For example, teachers in Kent State University's Teacher Leadership Endorsement Program (TLEP), which you read about briefly in this book's preface and will encounter again in chapter 9, created a service-learning initiative to alter punitive consequences for students who had minor disciplinary infractions at one high school. Several teachers constructed staff-development initiatives to confront and resist the typical teacher-and-assistant model of relations in interventionist/teacher pairings. They sought to alter partnerships between intervention specialists and regular classroom teachers to benefit students. Other teachers managed to design and implement occasions for teacher networking to advance 3S holonomy, in spite of constricting ideas of professional 'training.' Another teacher developed a "Tech Tuesday" program in which elderly residents could visit the school to receive help in using digital devices from middle school students.

Within the context of the TLEP project work, students put together a developmental portfolio for self-study. Samaras (2011) suggests that the developmental portfolio self-study method can provide a scaffold for inquiry, making that inquiry "public and open to the feedback and critique of your peers" (p. 89).

(An incidental benefit of this study method was that it easily yielded 'evidence' for teachers seeking Ohio Department of Education's Master Teacher or Lead Professional designations.) Teachers collected artifacts of their learning such as project plans, research memos, students' performances of understanding, email threads, rubrics, and other pieces that illuminated progress and problems. These artifacts offered readily available, organic sources of data that gave rise to potent transactions surrounding the quality of students' expressive outcomes, teachers' collegial study commitments, and community engagement in 3S holistic understanding.

In addition, teachers began to explore each other's initiatives and projects as critical friends—"trusted colleagues who seek support and validation of their research to gain new perspectives in understanding and reframing of their interpretations" (Samaras, 2011, p. 5). They reflected on their self-study by exchanging memos, reviewing designs for student learning, and considering transactions with other colleagues or the larger community. They sought and responded to specific calls for advice. Discussions provided assistance in considering and sorting out the dilemmas the author of the self-study found in teaching; in other words, teachers began to seek review and offer genuine support of colleagues' study and practice. Frequently, teachers discovered that they shared similar concerns. In my experience, that phenomenon increased the investment in and authenticity of the feedback they gave each other—an emerging example of autonomy-within-interdependence.

In my work with community members in the Educational Issues Book Club, we discussed topics including classroom discipline, the use of technology, private schooling, standardized testing and comprehensive core standards, and homework. During one of the most thought-provoking conversations, the possibility of parents choosing to 'opt out' of their child's standardized testing came up. Members of the group were unaware that the option existed (a breach). My own highly ambivalent feelings about bearing the news became part of the content of the conversation. Looking back on it, I felt discomfort because I was unaccustomed to *being with* the parents of students in this way. It was a completely new experience to facilitate parents' critical distancing! I am still very much learning alongside Dan, who expressed the challenge of figuring out "how to persevere in carrying out progressive, emancipatory pedagogy" in chapter 2.

More recently, I have proposed that interested parties join me to create a counter to the Ohio Department of Education's "District Report Card"—a 'report card' that focuses on some of the attributes of schooling experience missing from the officially published rankings, but which parents deem just as important to their children's education. It is stimulating and satisfying work that we undertake alongside each other in a novel assembly of persons who have something significant at stake in education and democracy. I like to think that we have collectively practiced a broadened attunement to democratically laden transaction, surfacing issues and dilemmas that would otherwise go unheeded.

Stirring Disruption and Reconstruction

So, dear reader, the invitation stands. Launch even one small bit of inquiry that refuses to accede to the 'given.' Greene (1988) says of Frederick Douglass:

> He continued to find new meanings in his lived situations ... he continued to endow his world with different meanings, to question the significance it already seemed to possess. This is one way of conceiving of what freedom signifies—the freedom to alter situations by reinterpreting them and, by so doing, seeing oneself as a person in a new perspective. Once that happens, there are new beginnings, new actions to undertake in the world. (p. 90)

As you consider the world and your verse in its song, here are some questions that may entice you:

- Are there times when you stand ready to learn from others (students, colleagues)? How are you enlisting and assigning value to their contributions? In what manner do you foster trusting relationships that defy hierarchy?
- Do you consider your beliefs about learning, and whether you are living out those beliefs (walking the talk)?
- To what extent are you able to prioritize trustworthy study, reflection, and inquiry while dealing with multiple, competing demands?
- Are you posing questions regarding your own practices and supporting others to do the same?
- What is the felt quality of your own intellectual development and that of your students?

5
DELIBERATIVE CONVERSATION: CROSS-PARADIGM CRITIQUE AND NEGOTIATION

The present affects the future anyway. The persons who should have some idea of the connections between the two are those who have achieved maturity. Accordingly, upon them devolves the responsibility for instituting the conditions for the kind of present experience which has a favorable effect upon the "future." (Dewey, 1938b/1998, p. 50)

Paint-by-Number

I spent a great deal of time at my grandparents' house when I was young, and I have a distinct memory of a new picture my grandfather had recently hung in a highly noticeable position, the grand entranceway into the living room. My family gazed in awe at the work of art: a lone man on a lost boat, cruelly tossed on a rough sea, facing the life-threatening elements of an uncontrollable storm. I was amazed that I had gone my whole life without the knowledge that my grandfather was a world renowned artist, the magnitude of which even he had only recently been made aware. The owner of a forge shop by day emerged, quite out of nowhere, as an expert in watercolors, worthy of laudable attention. How had he accomplished this task in such a short time? Had he been studying the arts, secretly developing his skills, harboring the dedication that it took to create an original masterpiece? Imagine my disappointment when I was told that this apparent masterpiece was an imitation, a paint-by-number creation. Anyone who had the means to purchase the kit and the ability to read the directions satisfied all protocol to be an artist. The illusion was the creativity necessary to actually create an original piece of art.

I offer this example as a disturbing analogy to present-day, neoliberal educational reform where every child is allegedly capable of producing a Rembrandt, at the same level, in the same period of time, regardless of expertise, experience, or ability if we can only get our teachers "highly qualified" (No Child Left Behind, 2002). A similar unreasonable premise for educating children is imposed on our profession where teachers are portrayed as feeble-minded individuals in dire need of assistance from the federal government in order to secure the necessary tools to teach (Bush, 2007, as cited in Taubman, 2009), thereby saving the nation's economy. To solve the perceived problem of unqualified teachers, today anyone can "Teach For America" regardless of your pedagogical background or experience in the study of education. We find ourselves in an aggravated state with apparently no platform to speak, where silent retreat into the status quo is the path of least resistance. "There is a withdrawal, a widespread speechlessness, a silence where there might be—where there ought to be—an impassioned and significant dialogue" (Greene, 1988, p. 184).

This chapter is a general introduction to cross-paradigm exploration of standardized management and curriculum wisdom with research into the critique (how curriculum problems are framed) and negotiation (political and structural obstacles to professional fluidity) with a critical pragmatism orientation. My intent is to encourage professional educators to engage in a lead-learning, collegial, reflective inquiry approach to curriculum development. Such an approach is informed by both curriculum and collaborative inquiry by all participants involved and designed to be a constructive alternative to Tyler's (1949) rationale. It is my hope that the material shared in this chapter provides a general overview of suggested resources to assist in our continual search for meaningful curriculum development. I also strive to contribute historically based information as a general guide for those who believe in empowerment through critical pragmatism.

I invite you to embrace study as curriculum development. Move past the current systems-based management and embrace the challenge of reconstructing education and curriculum development in a thoughtful process where teachers become the curriculum theorists who lead their own "currere" (Pinar, 2004). Embark upon a "complicated conversation with oneself (as a 'private' intellectual), an ongoing project of self-understanding in which one becomes mobilized for engaged pedagogical action" (p. 37). Specifically for teachers, *currere* offers the opportunity to embark upon a journey of change, for yourself and for your colleagues with the possibility of changing society in the process. Pinar supported "students of curriculum to study the relations between academic knowledge and life history in the interest of self-understanding and social reconstruction" (p. 35). With this process as a guide, becoming a lead learner (Donaldson, 2008) supports this love of wisdom while encouraging deep learning through deliberative conversations focused on enhancing democratic practice. In order to undertake this intellectual leap, participants on this journey must question their place in the bigger picture. Finding this deep moral, ethical, and intellectual meaning is "fundamentally related to whether teachers are likely to find the considerable energy required to transform the status quo" (Fullan, 2007, p. 39).

I write as an administrator on a lead-learning path, and I invite you to come along on the journey as an active participant and a valuable soldier in the endeavor to strive for human freedom realized through deep understanding.

Cross-Paradigm Critique

Collegial reflective practice encapsulates the standardized management and curriculum wisdom paradigms. Today, standardized management is focused on the problem of standardized test scores and the continual battle to add value to the prior year. Curriculum wisdom delves into constructivist best practice with an explicit commitment to "add the value" of democracy as a moral way of living. Every day, we see the standardized management paradigm gain momentum. We tout the "excellent with distinction" banner at a cost to our technology, arts, and basic philosophy of how we know children learn. We bow to standardization at a cost to curriculum wisdom, and I witness our teachers sinking into a depressed state of apathy, feeling powerless amid the pressures of a mandated standardized curriculum. In the last few months, I have had several exemplary teachers come to me completely distraught over curriculum dilemmas.

At various times and for different reasons, they have hit their limit. One teacher said with tears running down her face, "I feel like I cannot do this job any more, and worse, I feel like I am spending so much more time trying to do it. I am no longer a good mom at home because of the time devoted to paperwork, and I'm not as good of a teacher because I cannot prove what I know I do." Another teacher said, "I am forced to reduce, once again, the writing we do in class, and it's the best part of what I do. I don't even like this job any more." One second year teacher shared, "I went into this because I love teaching and kids but I don't think I will finish my career in this field. I can't keep up with the pressures and it's not what I thought it would be." As discussed in chapter 8, what we felt we were called to do is the opposite of what we are being forced to do. In chapter 8, Petra lovingly refers to this pull to teaching as the spirituality of a vocational calling that connects us to the students with whom we are entrusted. Under the domination of the standardized management paradigm, this attractive magnetic field is experiencing profound disturbance.

Standardized Management

To fulfill a central tenet of democracy, citizens must strive to see all viewpoints in a fair-minded fashion when trying to understand different concepts and competing perspectives. Tom Kelly in chapter 11 highlights the importance of methodological believing and methodological doubting (Elbow, 1986) when seeking to fully understand different viewpoints. Methodological believing would support wholeheartedly inquiring into all the potentially virtuous details of a topic, and methodological doubting would explore potential distortions of the same topic. Applying these inquiry principles to standardized management, standards are not the enemy and, in fact, are a necessary part of education. As an administrator, I cannot do my job without having standards that are set and met; truthfully, neither can any good teacher function in a classroom without some bar to qualify and quantify achievement. We use standards successfully when we collaborate in developing assessments and policy decisions that are data driven to move schools and districts forward (Carr & Harris, 2001). Many books give us examples of using data for academic achievement that are based on theory and practice (Blankstein, 2004; Marzano, 2004; Reeves, 2010), and you would be hard pressed to find a teacher who does not use multiple forms of data to make informed classroom curriculum decisions. However, the exaggerated importance or overdependence on standardized test results alone has caused multiple negative effects: teaching to the test, student cheating, control of curriculum from educators to organizations, and harmful levels of stress, to name only a few (Armstrong, 2006). Even done well, evaluation and the use of the data is a messy process engaged in through probing and embracing dialogue, eventually producing knowledge and moving to action, as a part of thorough and deliberative questioning of the subject matter (Schwandt, 2002). Unfortunately, our current nationalized curriculum idolizes standardized management to an unhealthy degree.

I believe in what Jim Henderson refers to in the preface as the poetics of an authentic, responsible self-direction, which culminates in a cultural renaissance that replaces today's unimaginative standardization. I also wholeheartedly support the notion that we are professionally obligated to exercise our intellectual judgment when choosing what knowledge we feel is of most worth. Where I struggle daily is with the lack of power to do so. We have allowed ourselves to be managed by standards obsessively fueled by assessments, which are compared to other buildings, schools, districts, states, and countries. "Out of fear of dominance, uniformity and homogeneity have emerged, now couched in the problematization of nationalism" (Autio, 2009a, p. 93). We are force fed a multitude of mandates directly from the federal government with little or no input into the "what" of curriculum development. How did this happen?

My own study currently leads me to neoliberalism. Capitalism in education presently views public education as a "matter of producing workers and consumers for the economy and for global economic competition" (Saltman, 2012, p. 56). The world is changing, and we cannot predict with any certainty which way public education will go, if it will survive at all. "Disregarding public input, corporate forces now possess extensive near monopolistic powers in re-imagining, reforming and restructuring public education" (Watkins, 2012a, p. 25). Privatization of education advanced by venture philanthropic foundations such as the Bill and Melinda Gates Foundation and the Broad Foundation have taken on the public school agenda and made monumental changes. Funding charter schools, affecting teacher preparation, scholarship, and tax credits are only a few examples of supporting private agendas masked as initiatives for the public good (Saltman, 2012). Why is today so different from past threats to education? Taubman (2009) suggests,

> Its uniqueness lies in its pervasiveness, its threat to the very foundations of public education, its wide embrace by the educational establishment, its direct assault on the intellectual, aesthetic, and ethical life of teachers, and its radical misunderstanding of teaching. (p. 5)

The battle over public education consists of two distinct camps: what we believe to be the right thing to do in terms of emancipatory education versus the totalitarian grip that we are witnessing, which prevents us from growing professionally in our field and making the best educational decisions with our students and our colleagues.

As Dan's chapter 2 implies, many hold Tyler (1949) accountable for excessive standardization, given his key role in developing a particular model of curriculum development, literally "changing the behavior patterns of people" (p. 5). For many years, I placed blame on the Elementary and Secondary Act of 1965 for the initial dictation of effective school processes when, in reality, the National Defense Education Act of 1958 was the first legislative act at a federal level to give monetary aid to all levels of public and private education (Zhao, 2009). The No Child Left Behind Act (NCLB) of 2001 became the number one contributor to high-stakes testing, reducing education to "the right answers" grounded in the view that "the federal government should expect results in return for the money it spends" (Bush, 2007, as cited in Taubman, 2009, p. 57). This level of standardization, including the negative impact for failure to reach preordained quotas, does cause one to question the impact that continual high-stakes testing takes on the validity of the data being extracted. "Fundamentally, tests provide little more than data, but just as one must question the confession, extracted under torture, one has to wonder just how reliable that data is, when it is wrung out of the students by constant administration of tests" (Taubman, 2009, p. 28). Beyond the anxiety and stress that continual high-stakes testing places on children, teaching primarily to the test prohibits the needed critical dialogue, deep questions, and contributing to the democratic culture in which "citizens must learn in order to participate in reworking civil society with others" (Saltman, 2012, p. 62).

I remember several years ago being in charge of testing in K–3 and experiencing several teachers loudly verbalizing their concerns with the then called "kindergarten screeners." That year, we made the decision, based upon the recommendation of the county office, that we would give the kindergarten screener at the beginning of the year to get a baseline on what children knew so we would know what to teach (now called formative assessment). As a central office employee, I was somewhat removed from the everyday battlefield that elementary teachers face; however, I pride myself on listening when I heard repeated rumblings from the frontline. So, I visited a kindergarten class while the children took the screener. I could not stay the entire period because I was repulsed with the distress I witnessed as a result of a removed decision based on data and not the welfare of children. Teachers were given strict instruction to read the directions but not answer any questions, just encourage and redirect students back to the original instructions. It was a nightmare. Gifted children were essentially paralyzed. They sat and could not move forward for fear of being wrong. Not having the background information required to complete the question, they reread the questions, raising their hands repeatedly to ask for further information, eventually getting angry and crying. Children who were possible special education or Title I students breezed through because they did not know the answer and had no point of reference to even stop and question the answer; so they guessed. The remainder of the class was a mix between the two. It was the most unnecessary display of forced testing I have ever witnessed. With much finagling, we worked to adjust the testing schedule for our district the following year, but the fact remains I had made a decision affecting children in a negative manner. This experience changed me and my decision-making process as a central office employee. I developed a support group of exceptional teachers whom I trusted and consulted with them frequently before making blanket decisions.

Zhao (2009), a previous student in China and now a professor at Michigan State University, contends that we are moving toward authoritarianism, allowing our government to dictate our curriculum whereas at the same time, China has been adopting many of our concepts of diversity and creativity. Why are Asian countries emulating our educational system, abandoning their own standardized system, as we strive to adopt theirs? I am reminded of a Chinese student at our high school many years ago, here on an exchange scholarship. She presented to our school board about the differences between her country and ours and elaborated on the freedom of content choice in the United States. Here, she discovered her deep love for photography through extracurricular opportunities in the United States where she took art and developed a talent she never knew she had. We have since cut time from many electives (e.g., industrial arts, home economics, art, computers, band, and orchestra) to allow more time for intervention and core area subjects. A nation that once shined, preparing our students for a creative array of innovation and imagination with an entrepreneurial spirit, has, since Sputnik in 1957 and the release of *A Nation at Risk* (National Commission of Excellence in Education, 1983), gradually armed ourselves to be a nation that protects the market and private property on a global basis, arguably to the point of neglecting our own responsibility for society in our own country.

Today, the United States has a teach-to-the-test form of standardized management. We have replaced authentic discovery with regulatory controls that present the illusion of quantitative advancement. Dewey (1938b/1998) would remind us that we are in a "situation," where emphasizing one form of education over another form, relying only upon standardization, significantly restricts constructive interaction. Rather than this either/or philosophy of education, we need to adopt a transactional knowing toward our current affairs (Dewey, 1938b/1998; Dewey & Bentley, 1949), where all facets of our human potential are reviewed, not disregarding standardization or emancipatory education but drawing on a "collection of useful yet fallible human practices open to ongoing modification" (Ryan, 2011, p. 39). Embracing a more eclectic paradigm rather than the narrow standardization of present-day testing supports evaluation as "making people morally answerable rather than technically accountable for their actions" (Schwandt, 2002, p. 21). Cuban (2003) would agree and states:

> I argue that reducing the notion of a "good" school and "good" teaching to an age-graded school with a uniform curriculum, one brand of instruction, and one kind of testing—the current official ideology—undermines public education in a democracy. It does so because the present orthodoxy ignores the many different kinds of "good" schools and teaching in the past century that have responded to the competing purposes of tax-supported public schools and the diversity of students in their motivation, backgrounds, and academic talents. (p. 24)

There is more to the bigger picture of curriculum development than mere test achievement. Curriculum development, as framed in this book, is compatible with 3S pedagogy and involves a sense of the social and moral sensibilities that contribute to and go beyond our own self-worth.

Curriculum Wisdom

Henderson and Gornik's (2007) definition of the 3S design is the "integration of subject matter understanding with democratic self and social understanding" (p. 8). Curriculum wisdom presents a view that encapsulates a vision of direction, in my opinion, a pathway that helps us on our *currere* journey (Pinar), emphasizing democracy as a way of being. Nancy (2010) highlights the dynamic, identity-shaping, transactional nature of democracy "whereby what is produced is a transformed subject rather than a preformed product" (p. 31). The following informative example contrasts sharply with the ideals of democracy Nancy would applaud, but the example illuminates well the problematic nature of a standardized management moment.

Sitting in a room with about 75 administrators from various counties for the Ohio Teacher Evaluation System (OTES) training, I took an active role in participating in an example of forced conformity. After viewing a video of a teacher, we were to use the new evaluation rubric to rate her performance. One hundred percent of the room raised their hands to choose the *accelerated* label for her outstanding techniques, and one hundred percent of us were wrong. The amount of experience, education, or consensus of the participants in that room did not matter; we were just wrong. The state wanted her rating to be at *proficient* (despite the fact that we later looked online and that teacher was nationally board certified). As you would expect, we loudly voiced our concerns at this rating system and our disagreement in the label, but were encouraged to move to the next video to get more experience. By the end of the three-day training, our cohort was aligned with the state's rubric. There was an undertone of defeat, dismay, and disgust, but ultimately, we conformed.

Maxine Greene (1988) believes that conditions must be intentionally created for freedom to take place. "Crucial is the recognition that conditions must be deliberately created to enable the mass of people to act on their power to choose" (p. 18). If the stage is not set, people do not take the initiative to dialogue and silence is perpetuated. Through creating conditions for freedom and dialogue, people can come together and fully advance society. Praxis, or "reflection and action upon the world in order to transform it," must be sought with democracy as the goal (Freire, 1997, p. 33). People working together to achieve praxis will move our society forward. The leader, in this case, the lead learner, cannot dictate theory or practice but instead grows with his or her colleagues. The lead learner sees this forging "not in terms of explaining to, but rather dialoguing with the people" (p. 35). With democracy, a different form of education can exist. We need to see curriculum development as transactional: not a quest for quantitative certainty or truth, but a qualitative "collection of useful yet fallible human practices open to ongoing modification" (Ryan, 2011, p. 39). Transaction involves looking at things as they are experienced, all things that comprise the whole experience (Dewey & Bentley, 1949). Dewey defined transaction as seeing together things that are generally thought of as opposites in other philosophies; it is an ongoing process that progresses with collective inquiry (Ryan, 2011). Explored in their book, *Knowing and the Known*, Dewey and Bentley (1949) state that science tends to explain phenomena in terms of a single theory or cause. Transaction is flexible—willing to configure evidence in a variety of ways depending upon needs and contexts. This inquiry suggests looking at the full picture when making an observation. This is an ongoing process that progresses with collective inquiry, thus demanding the full participation and enfranchisement of everyone involved (Ryan, 2011). Freire (1997) so eloquently put this social emancipation as "faith in mankind, faith in their power to make and remake, to create and recreate, faith in their vocation to be more fully human (which is not the privilege of the elite, but the birthright of all)" (p. 71).

I believe in democracy for each and every person, not the thrust of power over people, but the common struggle for reflective inquiry. I believe in the existence of justice and the rights of each person to pursue knowledge, contribute their opinion, and grow in their own journey of understanding. So we must ask ourselves, how do we achieve professional fluidity amidst the political and structural obstacles? How do we seek the "implications for emancipatory education conducted by and for those willing to take responsibility for themselves and for each other" (Greene, 1988, p. 56)? Through curriculum development rooted in critical pragmatism we can pursue the analysis of designing curriculum that positively affects our schools and society as a whole (Cherryholmes, 1988).

Cross-Paradigm Negotiation

It is imperative that we, as administrators and teachers, create a collegial platform that supports the design of curriculum wisdom; a platform with an eclectic design that "recognizes the usefulness of theory to curriculum decision, takes account of certain weaknesses of theory as grounds for decision, and provides some degree of repair of these weaknesses" (Schwab, 1978, p. 295). When we combine theories and explore informed judgments along the way, we can support the change in participants' beliefs—a change that we need to strive for and expect. This transactional approach involves looking at things as they are experienced, seeing things together that are generally thought of as separate, an ongoing process that progresses with collective inquiry (Dewey & Bentley, 1949; Ryan, 2011). With this type of inquiry, there is a willingness to configure evidence in a variety of ways, always looking at the full picture when making observations. Avenues for communication emerge through creating conditions for open dialogue where people can come together to support a democratic society in its fullest sense (Nancy, 2010). These openings can be accomplished through professional development and educational lead learners who are active citizens in a democratic society (Noddings, 2003, 2005, 2006, 2009a). Those who embrace democratic education "embrace human artistry" and "whenever possible, they establish critical distance from the incessant pressures to conform and standardize" (Henderson & Slattery, 2008, p. 2). We have a moral obligation in a democratic society to teach in a way that our students can participate intelligently as adults in the political processes that shape their society (Zeichner, 1995). Just as "all students deserve rich educational experiences that will enable them to become active citizens in a democratic society," adults, too, deserve and should strive for such experiences (Noddings, 2005, p. 5). But how might we overcome the constraints of the current power-hold?

Kincheloe (2005) discusses both the power that people have or perceive that they have and the outside forces that constrain human subjectivity. By taking an eclectic approach to curriculum development and educating ourselves on the dynamics of the many factors shaping inquiry, there are "context driven articulations" that shape the individual experience (Kincheloe, 2001, p. 688). Two realities exist: the world reality and each person's individual experience. Power in the social structure shapes human subjectivity, which influences individual experience. How does influence (world and individual) lead to transformative action that helps produce a change in cultural meaning (Kincheloe, 2005), ultimately producing a sustained change?

I have been reflecting on Kincheloe's idea of human subjectivity in light of something that happened a few months back after I went to training for the OTES. One of our senior teachers (also an elected member of the teacher negotiations team) asked me about the training. He got loud, defensive, and angry when I said what the training consisted of and how the evaluation tools were devised. When I mentioned using teachers as leaders, he said "Fat chance! Do you know how much resentment you would create?" He ended up walking away. An opportunity presented itself a few weeks later, and I apologized for any hard feelings from our previous conversation. He briskly said he did not at all agree with using teachers as leaders, never making eye contact with me during the conversation, and although I wanted to talk further, the bell rang and we were corralled into the conformity of the day. Later that week, he attended the same OTES training I had previously attended and came into my office to talk. We ended up having a deeper discussion about using teachers as leaders. Although he did not wholeheartedly agree with the idea, he did open his mind to the possibility of a mentoring system. We discussed the use of evaluation/observation as a mentoring tool, not an evaluation tool, and how wonderful it would be if it were based on trust and learning.

I actively seek "wiggle room" (Cuban, 2003; Donaldson, 2008) to support teachers struggling to find their voices and feel empowered as professionals who can move society forward through holistic education (Dewey, 1938b/1998; Greene, 1988; Hargreaves, 2000, 2001). Change is difficult. Change in teacher beliefs is tied into teaching and learning, which ultimately ties into classroom practice (Edwards & Hensien, 1999). Kegan (1982, 1994) fully explores the concept of adult change that endures and he defines sustained change as maintaining a different mindset than previously embraced through disciplined self-inquiry. Kegan and Laskow-Lahey (2009) state that in order to create a change that is sustained, we must change the way we think and feel; we must change our mindset. In adult learning, we must change the meaning making system, the mindset, and behavior rather than changing only behavior because "neither change in mindset or change in behavior alone leads to transformation, but that each must be employed to bring about the other" (p. 309). Therefore, sustained change requires a change in one's mindset. When this type of emancipatory change has transpired, a person knows when they have changed their belief system and they are a different person, on a different level. Walker (1971) studied the ways people work in groups, what they discuss, and how they share their points of view. People spend time talking about their beliefs, laying the groundwork for their curricular platform. Through discussion, persuasion, problem solving, and weighing all information presented, they deliberate to reach the best course of action, thus altering their original curricular platform. This type of transformative deliberation necessitates time to develop an atmosphere of trust.

Lately, I know I need to do more than wait for the opportunity for wiggle room to present itself. I believe that a platform for professional development that is pre-established in the school system is a necessary venue for critical pragmatism to develop. With this platform firmly in place in the educational setting, there exists opportunity for teachers to improve their professional knowledge as a group in an unthreatening environment. In the book, *Leading Educational Change*, Malone (2013) recognized that authorities in school reform gather their expertise to encourage providing a platform so teachers, as a unit, can pursue a common vision of curriculum development through collaboration. We must trust that our teachers, given the right venue as lead learners, have the ability and will seek the information to forge the highest standard of education for all learners. Through trial and error, I have learned the hard way to value a platform for professional development. I share my story to illustrate my continued struggle with being a lead learner.

I was in charge of professional development in my district for nine years, and I began to notice a pattern of short-term change in practice that was directly tied to and evaluated by standardized measurement. The frustration of this limited, short-term change in practice prompted me to begin a quest to find the key characteristics of what constitutes adult change through meaningful professional development that is sustained and impactful. Low scores on the standardized Ohio Achievement Tests in short answer and extended response items prompted an initiative in professional development entitled, *Writing about Math*. The focus began with math teachers in fifth and sixth grades and grew over the next year to include all math and language arts teachers in fifth through eighth grades. As I was in my doctoral program the time this unfolded, it was an easy fit for me to research theory about professional development to set the stage for this initiative. The results of the two-year initiative were staggering. In 2003–2004, students scored at or above the state average on only 33.3% of the problems ($N = 12$), whereas this number increased to 75% of the problems in 2004–2005. Furthermore, the percent of problems ($N = 12$) that students scored below the state average dropped from 66.7% in 2003–2004 to 33.3% in 2004–2005. The initiative was considered a success; practice was assumed to have changed, which in turn raised test scores.

Four years after this professional development initiative, the middle school results resorted back to below the state average. This turn of events prompted our curriculum director to distribute a short narrative survey to teachers and ascertain topics that could be addressed in future professional development initiatives. Surprisingly, the teachers responded by stating that there was a need for professional development in extended response and short answer questions on math achievement tests and that this topic had not been previously addressed. Not only was the professional development initiative to increase scores on short answer and extended response reversed, it was forgotten altogether. Why had change not been sustained? The basis for the initiative was not one that was commenced or supported in trust. There was no platform in place for teachers to discuss, elaborate, or question this initiative. It was put into place with no prior articulation and forced into practice by a placebo of glory through testing incentives. This is not how people are naturally motivated.

Daniel Pink (2009), in his book, *Drive*, delves into the topic of what motivates us. We currently follow an archaic top-down authoritarian business model of management in schools. Pink contends that we are not motivated by money (merit pay failures are a prime example), and in fact, extrinsic motivators can lead to dishonest behavior and stifle creative thinking. Nor are all goals (e.g., short-answer/extended-response math goals) necessarily a constructive motivator. Instead, they can actually cause people to fixate on short-term results, losing sight of "the potential devastating long-term goals of the organization" (p. 56). Pink explains a Type I person is intrinsically motivated, self-directed, and ultimately will strive to connect excellence to a larger purpose than themselves, whereas a Type X person usually seeks short-term gratification. The question then becomes "How do we nurture and motivate a Type I person?" Pink (2009) suggests we pay them "enough" to take external motivation off the table and provide a platform for their innate drive to work for the greater good (p. 59). Teachers are already motivated in their field; we need to hire good people and let them go (Collins, 2001).

> The most successful people, the evidence shows, often aren't directly pursuing conventional notions of success. They're working hard and persisting through difficulties because of their internal desire to control their lives, learn about their world, and accomplish something that endures. (Pink, 2009, p. 77)

We have outstanding people in our schools who are not currently motivated to succeed but instead feel threatened with a "bad score" and termination based upon students' test scores. We need to rekindle a spirit of internal motivation and provide the time to discern what is relevant in curriculum development. Schwartz and Sharpe (2010) know that our best intentions erode with an overreliance on incentives. When preaching and practice are disconnected, we lose sight of practical wisdom. We need to concentrate on "building institutions that pay attention to creating communities of learners with a commitment to do right by those they serve" (p. 273). Such a synergizing, thought-provoking community culture will nurture practical wisdom in education.

Creating conditions for the transformative leadership to take hold is based on collegiality and creating trust. Zull (2002) is clear in pointing out that our emotions directly influence our thinking. Cain and Cain's (1997) approach to change is to support teachers with the goal of reshaping their environment into one that leads to deliberate, desirable, and enduring change. Presently, the top-down model of leadership in schools does not support a learning community model (DuFour, 2004) based on authentic learning where opinions (even if opposed) are welcomed and discussed. Educational institutions shy away from this collegial type of leadership because a by-product of this management style is conflict, the unsettling discomfort that is inevitable when educated people gather to brainstorm higher level thinking goals. The best managers of top companies suggest ways to embrace conflict in order to find mutual resolution. Collins (2001) quotes phrases such as "loud debate," "heated discussions," and "healthy conflict" when referring to "*Good-to-Great*" companies. The process of conflict resolution is "like a heated scientific debate, with people engaged in a search for the best answers" (p. 77).

The top companies value opinions and do not hide from heated discussion between colleagues. Buckingham and Coffman (1999) insist that the best leaders are those who support and encourage colleagues to change through mutual resolution; they change together.

For me, conflict should be expected, embraced, and looked at as an opportunity for discussion and growth (Elbow, 1986; Feiman-Nemser, 2001). Kegan (1994) acknowledges that when conflict occurs, the focus should not be on solving the problem. Instead, focus should be on ways to let the conflict transform the participants through resolution of (or attempts to resolve) the problem. The main goal is not to solve the problem; rather, it is to transform the participants while they discover together a mutual resolution through negotiation. Fisher, Ury, and Patton (2011), in helping disputants "get to yes," offer a richly instructive outline called principled negotiation for conflict resolution. The current dominant form of positional negotiation involves clarifying your position and then defending it against attack. This is typically an antagonistic and egocentric process, which often impedes sound judgment conducted in the WIN-WIN spirit of generosity. I witnessed this positional bargaining at mediation between the school and a parent of a special education student. The parent truly believed we had not provided appropriate services for her child. We, of course, believed that we had provided adequate services, going above and beyond. Our positions were further separated by the lawyers suggesting separate rooms and the mediator going back and forth with demands between parties. By the late afternoon, angry, exhausted, and no further along than when we started, one party left and mediation ended.

Principled negotiation involves separating people from the problem, seeking to identify and satisfy the interests of the people involved in the dispute, inventing options for mutual gain, and insisting on using objective criteria. A number of helpful perspectives stand out for me. In terms of relating to disputants, if you want to influence someone, you must "understand empathetically the power of their point of view and feel the emotional force with which they believe in it" (p. 25). This will maximize the opportunity for having constructive dialogue. In the above example, had we been in the room together, understanding that both parties have the student's best interest at heart, the idea would be working side by side for various options of educating this student.

In terms of interests, negotiations must focus on the desired goals that the different parties seek rather than on their initial and often narrowly singular conception of the only way to achieve those goals. If you are trying to change someone's mind and/or work collaboratively with them, you must figure out where their minds are now and what ends or values they are hoping to achieve. On the first of these two points, Kegan (1982) would agree and further assert that the truth as one person knows it is a truth for them. The second of these two points overlaps with the vital *getting to yes* principle related to the liberating realization that multiple, promising, overlooked, or underexamined options frequently exist. That is, thrillingly, and most often, there is more than one answer! It is thus advisable to separate brainstorming ideas from deciding on one solution. This separation elicits trust in the brainstorming process that all ideas are potentially viable solutions and even wild ideas should be explicitly encouraged (Fisher, Ury, & Patton, 2011). In terms of the fourth *getting to yes* principle of insisting on using objective criteria, "The more you bring standards of fairness, efficiency or scientific merit to bear on your particular problem, the more likely you are to produce a final package that is wise and fair" (p. 84). In all, it is my belief that through a forum of cross-paradigm negotiation that seeks to emphasize empathic listening, identification of common aims and interests with a spirit of mutual exploration, constructive change can emerge.

I created a platform for negotiation in our school. We call the meetings RTI (Response to Intervention), which was a state initiative but one that had merit. The philosophy of the team (consisting of special education teachers, school psychologist, guidance counselors, and administrator) is to provide a trusting venue to discuss students who have academic and/or behavior problems, brainstorm interventions, provide alternative ideas for education, and follow the student's progress. We try to apply Elbow's (1986) concepts of real learning into our platform, applying already learned concepts as well as constructing new ones. When two people have a disagreement, we try to be open minded and "let their ideas interact" in order to "produce ideas or points of view that neither could singly have produced" (p. 42). We trust that although the format is messy, we strive for critical thinking, trust each other, and embrace conflict. Year three of this initiative is trying. We have the platform but consistently run into roadblocks because of lack of programming, nonexistent funding, and restrictive laws. However, I take valuable information from these meetings back to the chain of command and work with "wiggle room" opportunities to make gains. The progress is slow and frustrating at times, but we move forward always with the best interest of our students in mind and with a lead-learning focus as our drive.

Ending Thoughts

The challenges we face in our chosen field are many. I wholeheartedly believe it is time to stand together and with both determination and respect, call "red rover" to the outside forces instilling changes we know are not philosophically sound educational practices. We owe it to our profession, to ourselves, and to our society as a whole. Let us lock arms and join in. I conclude by posing three questions that could possibly organize lead-learning practices on this chapter's topic:

- Do you have an atmosphere of trust in your building, one that elicits freedom for ideas that may be contrary to current curriculum standardization?
- Is there time that is utilized specifically for sharing ideas in a venue of collegiality specifically for the education growth of curriculum development?
- Are there areas of wiggle room in your education setting for embodying a lead-learning platform?

6

DELIBERATIVE CONVERSATION: POSSIBILITIES OF EQUITY IN EVERYDAY SCHOOLING

Children learn more from what you are than what you teach. (DuBois, 1898, p. 18)

The collegial study and engagement in a deliberative conversation on social justice in education is difficult for several reasons. First, it tends to be extremely personal. As seen in my snapshot in chapter 1 of this book, this personal experience can be found at the intersection of educational ideologies of mentors as they affect students in a teacher's current practice. For some individuals, social justice resonates deeply with a personal experience of marginalization. For others, the study of it means a reflection and reconsideration of self, or, as DuBois notes, the importance of "what you are" rather than "what you teach." Second, thinking about social justice means attending to the philosophies that underpin the curriculum. This process questions not only what is taught but is an explicit examination of the null curriculum, what is unintentionally left out of lessons (Eisner, 1994). Third, attending to questions of equity can challenge the normalized structures and culture in schools. The hidden curriculum, what students learn through school culture (Giroux & Penna, 1983), is often so deeply embedded into the everyday of schooling that it continues unabated. The study and daily practice of social justice can therefore be seen as a call to reconsider not only a teacher's practice but also his or her ways of being.

Because social justice is a deeply personal topic, resistance to the ideas, resources, and reflections are certainly plausible. The process of rethinking what is normal in schools and in ourselves is one of action, resulting in a possible change in the way teachers see and be in the world (Watkins, 2001). Therefore, this chapter has been written to invite critical reflection. The critical examination of one's teaching, the ideas and ideals that form the foundation of those practices, and how they impact others is an important task to influencing how one is in schools. What follows is a consideration of the normalized structures of schooling through a social justice lens, one intended to provoke reflexivity towards embodied understandings.

> One morning, as I passed a colleague's classroom, I could hear several students talking loudly as she was teaching. Notably frustrated with the general chatter, she set her sights on one child and said, "That's it! I've had enough of you! You people are always so loud! Turn your desk around." I glanced into the classroom to see Alisha, the only student of color in the room, slowly turning her desk to face the back of the classroom. The other students stopped talking for a moment but then resumed their conversations. I waited, but no discipline was taken toward the other students. Alisha sat, for the rest of class, with access to the room but not to active participation or being treated with dignity and respect.[1]

Why is the pursuit of social justice significant? It is certainly not a new idea (Cooper, 1892; DuBois, 1903; Woodson, 1933) and is one that has been critically examined through many lenses (Ayers, Quinn, & Stovall, 2009). Similarly, because of its well-trodden historical roots, social justice has been enacted in important ways in schools that are, among other reasons, designed to foster a sense of "civic mindedness and responsibility" in students (Leistyna, 2009, p. 51).

While social justice is not new and its importance has been well documented, social justice is important to my daily life as an educator because, despite talk about equity and access, gay students are still committing suicide at an alarmingly high rate (Patterson, 2013), a countless number of lives lost when equity is not foregrounded in practice. Further, the ways of being and knowing of students of color are consistently viewed as a problem in schools (Dubois, 1926; Varenne & McDermott, 1998; Watkins, 2001). This contributes to their disproportionately high arrest and suspension rates compared to their Anglo peers (Henning, 2012), making it considerably difficult for these students to keep up with course content or eventually graduate. These are but two examples of how marginalized student populations in schools are affected by the (un)intentional lack of social justice in education (den Heyer, 2003). In short, social justice is significant because there are children who suffer, in very visceral ways, for the lack of equity and access they experience in their daily lives at school.

The longstanding history of institutionalized discrimination in schools (Ayers, Quinn, & Stovall, 2009; Winfield, 2007) is often burgeoned by educators. The point here is not that teachers are inherently unjust individuals who do not strive to foster a democratic, supportive environment. Rather, it is my position that social justice in schools is often seen as a curricular additive (Freire, 1997; Schoorman & Bogotch, 2010) similar to "culture days" or some character education programs. However, in seeking a more just educational experience, social justice becomes a process with the concrete, material goal of equity and access. To be socially just in education is a question of providing equity and access to all students (Gershon, 2012). Social justice is therefore a process that people do with, to, and for other people. It is similarly enacted and embodied by people. Because people interact with each other in such a wide variety of ways, defining social justice and how it might manifest itself must be open to multiple interpretations and possible forms of practice. Therefore, as schooling pushes toward standardized measures for both students and teachers under a seemingly never-ending stream of tests and teacher evaluation systems, educators must be aware of the many everyday possibilities to enact social justice and resist reducing it to merely a measurable objective.

In light of the complex nature of what social justice can mean and how it might practically function, the aim of this chapter is threefold. First, I argue for an attention to social justice as a process through which dominant social structures can be critically analyzed (Cooper, 1892; DuBois, 1903) rather than a "commodity with readily recognized features or a product for consumption" (Grant, 2009, p. 76). However, without a pre-defined structure, it is often difficult to conceptualize when an environment is considered "socially just" or that social justice has been achieved. As I outline to come, the pursuit of social justice in schools has no measurable assessment at the end of a program. Further, as most veteran educators are aware, there is no silver bullet to education or "good teaching" (Ladson-Billings, 1995). Similarly, there is no singular formula to achieving social justice in schools. Approaching equity and access with a "one-size-fits-all" form of understanding has a high potential to be harmful to children (Gershon, 2012), for if not all children and school cultures are the same, how can one approach the topic of social justice with a singular formula?

Additionally, discussions about what social justice might mean continue to be approached from diverse sets of histories and positions (see Ayers, Quinn, & Stovall, 2009; Gershon, 2012). For this reason, there is a concern in adopting one set of ideas and ideals in that it may falsely order the causes for justice an individual or group may seek (e.g., race, sexual orientation, religion, etc.). Yet, in the context of this chapter, while attending to one position can be as detrimental to the students as not attending to questions of social justice entirely, my argument does follow certain trajectories. By this, I do not intend to remarginalize traditionally marginalized groups such as ESL students or those with (dis)abilities, but rather, this chapter foregrounds social justice as it relates to sociocultural questions of race, gender, and sexual orientation.

Secondly, this chapter argues that awareness needs to be followed by action. Discrimination happens in schools. There is a longstanding history of describing and analyzing the social injustices that take place in schools toward marginalized students (Apple, 2006; Au & Jordan, 1981; Brown & Brown, 2010; Cooper, 1892; Delpit, 1995; DuBois, 1903; Pascoe, 2007; Patterson, 2013; Weiss & Fine, 1992; Willis, 1981). While scholars write that it is the perception of social, political, and economic contradictions in schools that push teachers toward action (Ayers, Quinn, & Stovall, 2009; Freire, 1997), it is not clear that awareness alone necessitates action. To be clear, this critical interrogation of awareness is not a dismissal of the significance of being conscious or the action that this cognizance can engender. This is instead an attempt to "frame critique and yet maintain the recognition of all that is valued and respected in the work" (Hooks, 1994, p. 49). If educators are aware of injustice but do not move to take action, how are students served by educators' knowledgeable inaction?

Finally, this chapter aims to position social justice at the intersection of how one knows (i.e., the epistemological) and one's way of being (i.e., the ontological). Social justice is a process (DuBois, 1903; Grant, 2009) that is not solely a journey for students. An educator's daily interactions with the sociocultural norms and values, whether it is in her or his classroom or in the often chaotic halls of the school, are crucial to attending to ideals of justice. Or, as Gershon (2012) writes, social justice is inherently about the social. Further, as how and what someone knows is in many ways tied to broader social and cultural understandings of what counts as knowledge (Fuller, 2002), the (de)construction of that pre-constructed knowledge to better view its constituent parts is inherently significant. However, one's emergent ways of being, the many ways a person interacts and moves through the world, is equally important. This is because a teacher's way of being in school—his or her "is-ness" (Gershon, 2013)—is as significant as a strong, socially just curriculum.

As stated above, social justice is not best served as a mandate from the state or a box to be checked off on a teacher evaluation, but instead, it often becomes most meaningful as a bottom-up struggle adopted and embodied by teachers (Grant, 2009). It is similarly difficult to discuss questions of equity and access in schools without the inclusion of students' narratives. How can one discuss access for students without giving their narratives space in the discussion? How can one expect students to eventually embody a sense of equity when their voice is not equally heard? Perhaps more importantly, if teachers are going to have an ethical fidelity (Henderson & Kesson, 2004) to social justice and engage in a dialogue that attends to questions of school, social norms, and students, what happens when the voice of the marginalized is left out? In an attempt to honor student voice, but recognizing that its inclusion here is not nearly sufficient, the rest of the chapter will begin each section with a relevant narrative from one of my ongoing studies in order to ground the theoretical and practical points in students' stories.

Social Justice as a Process

> I know I come to school knowin' that there's probably like an 85% chance that the office is going to call me down for something I didn't do. Just something stupid is going to go down. I could be laughing [pause] just laughing loudly in the hall with my friend and then it's going to go back that we were skipping class … so I'm usually prepared. There's just something small that happens at least once a week that makes you think. For example, one

thing, I mean it's super small but I was going to buy my Homecoming ticket. There were like eight kids walking up there … I think I was the only black kid walking up there. A *teacher* asked me what I was doing. I said I was buying my Homecoming ticket. He watched me buy my ticket and then was like, "I want to see it!" All the other kids can buy their tickets and walk past him. Why? Why did he need to see mine? I just don't get it.[2]

Schools, like all places, are socially created through very specific historical and political lines (Gupta & Ferguson, 1997; Helfenbein & Huddleston, 2013; Kincheloe & Pinar, 1994). This is not to say that other factors do not contribute to the formation of place. However, students are not marginalized solely through current contexts in schools. It is the political and historical lines from which communities are formed; identities are shaped; and identification, differences, and deficits were designed (Hendry, 2011; Winfield, 2007). For example, particular discourses have been silenced in implicit and explicit ways. Implicitly, the hidden curriculum, what is not taught in schools, has produced a kind of discourse that intentionally leaves out the accomplishments and diverse histories of particular student populations (Brown & Brown, 2010; Eisner, 1994; Winfield, 2007). Explicitly, aside from studying slavery or particular lessons coinciding with Black History Month, how often are African American ways of knowing and being celebrated in the curriculum?

Through the historical and political exclusion of marginalized people, those known and viewed as the "Other," hegemonic influences have been upheld through schooling by "defining what is legitimate knowledge and by controlling access to it" (Elmore & Skyes, 1992, p. 195). Any discourses not affirmatively legitimizing dominant paradigms have been both neglected and subordinately positioned (Brown & Brown, 2010). Eugenicists known today as the "fathers of education," such as Thorndike, Charters, and Bobbitt, explicitly formed curricular ideals and tests that supported Othering in a way that ensured control of the "inferior blood … of the worm eaten stock" (Winfield, 2007, p. 6). The histories, literature, art, and music that are attended to in school today were chosen as a design to precisely espouse and maintain a particular power structure (Watkins, 2001). As such, the constant and consistent negation of specific discourses strongly contributes to contemporary marginalization of students. Social justice serves as a counterprocess, a way of deconstructing injustices and (re)building ideals of equity and access in schools.

Deconstructing normalized structures questions universal truths that are often rooted in mainstream, Western ways of knowing. Critically analyzing universals creates *friction*, which can both serve to precipitate local change and draw further lines of exclusion (Tsing, 2005). This is because friction can "inflect motion, offering it different meanings" (p. 6). Yet despite the multiple meanings friction creates, it does not transcend universal values and structures. For example, friction can greatly affect a local context, both affirmatively and negatively, but it does not change broader universal ideals under which sociocultural norms and values are practiced. Foucault (1978) argues that because there is no outside of power, an individual will be unable to transcend universal structures. For example, Foucault states that "where there is power, there is resistance, and yet, or rather consequently, this resistance is never a position of exteriority in relation to power" (p. 95).

Ortner (2006) reminds readers that while Foucault's theory articulates that particular contexts are tied to associated power structures, people in those places have the ability to enact their available agency to challenge and change conditions (Bourdieu, 1993). However, Ortner (2006) argues, there are always possible consequences for enacting agency within a structure. One's agency is, of course, not outside of the power structures at play. So, if there is no outside of power and no concrete way to change broader universal ideas and ideals, why enact agency? The life and work of Anna Julia Cooper provide a strong example of an individual working within a structure but still exercising agency. As an African American woman in the late 1800s, Cooper foregrounded questions of gender and race in her scholarship about social justice despite tenuous social conditions.

In my current context as a woman of color teaching in a public high school, agency is significant for at least the following reasons. First, it helps me exercise a degree of wiggle room in my practice, despite the standardization of my profession and the push toward test scores and away from student needs. Second, agency affirms the fact that I have the ability to positively impact both the students and my context. That agency can be negotiated with and between existing power structures in schools (see chapter 2, 4, and 5).

Universal ideas and policies always create margins (Sleeter, 2011; Tsing, 2005). This is because universals are designed to facilitate hegemonic structures that privilege a dominant group (Watkins, 2001) and therefore are inherently marginalizing. Best intentions aside, the power structures underlying policies and programs to "benefit all" will subvert and marginalize those outside of sociocultural norms and values (Varenne & McDermott, 1998). Therefore, there is importance in social justice being particularized rather than being/becoming a universal. While universal laws (for example, those banning hate crimes) are certainly important, the process of social justice, the "what" and the "how," is highly contextualized. Perhaps more importantly, social justice is in a constant state of becoming (Pinar, 1998). As Woodson (1933) writes, "It is merely a matter of exercising common sense in approaching people through their environment in order to deal with conditions as they are rather than as you would like to see them or imagine they are" (p. 3). In other words, the process of social justice starts with connection—to children, to school culture, to oneself.

Actions toward Equity

Every day, I come to school and I sit down and just try to make myself invisible unless I'm sitting with my friends and they can, like, "get the happy out of me," but for the most part, I just try to stay quiet and act like I'm not there. I just try to get to class as fast as possible because the hall is the worst because you can hear what people say about you and see the way they look at you and the way they talk about others, about gay people … and, I don't know, then there's teachers. I think they realize they work in a school and kind of feel like they have to accept it but inside they are people who judge. … At times it makes me ashamed of who I am. But ever since the day I even thought about if I was gay, I hated the thought of it. I hated myself. And sometimes I still do.

The process of social justice is inherently affective. When social justice moves away from the theoretical, it becomes material, it affects people's bodies and minds. Whether questions of equity and access are brought to bear through personal reflection, implicit messages, or explicit lessons, the idea of social justice is necessarily about affect and its effects. In other words, people are affected by social justice as it changes the way they think and move in the world. Further, the effect of social justice can change school ecologies.

Similarly, affect is not solely about words, emotions, and connections; it is about actions, intentional or unintentional. Affect can "serve to drive us toward movement, toward thought and extension" (Seigworth & Gregg, 2010, p. 1). Additionally, an affective lens positions resulting actions of social justice in a less liminal space by "sticking or preserving the connection between ideas, values and objects" (Ahmed, 2010, p. 29). In other words, things that "make us happy," "feel safe," or "valued" are preserved as a valid emotion, movement, and thought. An affective lens therefore moves social justice to an act that resides in, between, on, and through people rather than in theoretical stasis. In sum, it is the felt reality (Massumi, 2010) that precipitates change.

As the theoretical collides with and between bodies, action should be met with intention, particularly where children's health and well-being are concerned (Apple, 2006; MacLeod, 2008; McLeod, 2008; Sedgwick, 2003). Just as the theory of social justice must have intention, so should its practice. A strong example of action without specific intention comes to mind in my own practice. A few years ago, I had a student who was quite disruptive during class and rude to his fellow classmates. Last year, he visited me at school to thank me for being a positive influence in his life and in his academics. I walked away from the conversation confused rather than flattered. Was he remembering the correct teacher? Had he completely forgotten the daily battle we fought? More importantly, I had to wonder, if I had accidentally helped this student, how many students had I accidentally harmed over the years? Realistically, what is helpful to some can always be harmful to others (Gershon, 2012). Intention matters (Ortner, 2006). It is precisely why "best practices" are not best for everyone (Henderson & Kesson, 2004) and why culturally relevant pedagogy can be essentializing and not necessarily relevant to all students' cultures (Sleeter, 2011). This is not to say that both examples do not have good intention at heart. A teacher should work to find best solutions for her or his classroom and attend to counter stories to enrich classroom learning. Rather, it is at the intersection of intention and attention that the action of social justice should start.

Redefining Knowing and Being

> I associate with primarily white people because that's been the group I've hung out with since I was little, but when you grow up with a lot of white people, you're just sorta forced to make friends with them. I do it because it's just easier. When you hang out with all the black kids, you're literally just described as a dumb black kid. Even if you don't do that stuff, that's how you're classified. But even if you hang out with white kids, you're the black kid who is above everybody [to the blacks]. [To the whites] you're the black kid who is better, who doesn't do that stuff. The one who actually has some "common sense." But you're still not as good as the white kids … but it doesn't matter. You're still looked down on, just not as much. Like even teachers talk to me like I'm dumb, like I can't keep up. That's not true. I can keep up. … Like one teacher. I was just reading quietly in study hall when she asked me what I was doing, and when I told her I was reading, she said, "Oh. You can do that?" Like what? Because I'm a girl? Because I'm black, I can't read? It's just not easy *being*.

At the intersection of intention and attention, social justice becomes a critical reflection of, on one hand, current contexts and ways of being and, on the other, a set of possibilities for a new sense of self (see chapters 3, 7, and 8). In anthropology reflexivity refers to the inward analytic focus on relationships. It can be seen as two branches from the same tree—one focusing more on power relations and knowledge production, while the other is more specifically directed inward toward the researcher (Gemignani, 2011). Reflexivity in relation to ideas of social justice is significant for at least the following reasons. First, reflexivity can be utilized to examine sociocultural ideas and ideals that have become normalized (Bourdieu, 1993). Second, the reflexive turn provokes an inward critical analysis of normalized structures that are (un)intentionally upheld through one's practice. Reflexivity is a conscious and deliberate reflection of "owning the 'buts'" (North, 2012) in practice and person. For example, consider this statement a co-worker made to me a few years ago, "I do not mind homosexuals, *but* they need to keep their sexuality to themselves." Being reflexive in this case can call into question one's deepest rooted beliefs, ways of knowing, and ways of being. It is necessarily a difficult unlearning process (Kumashiro, 2002). How can one be socially just on the other side of the "but" in her bias? Having a sense of ethical fidelity to social justice necessitates deep reflexivity and openness to questioning sociocultural norms and the normalized parts of oneself (Greene, 1988).

Reflexivity is crucial to the processes of social justice and can result in actions that create equitable school spaces because of how it affects individuals' ways of knowing and being. Knowledge is a socially created, mutually agreed upon set of understandings (Fuller, 2002; Haddock, Millar, & Pritchard, 2010; Woodson, 1933), and how one knows is a combination of social norms and individuals' reactions to those norms (Whitcomb, 2011). From this perspective, reflexivity is one possible tool for pushing against the normalized ways of knowing that is the status quo. If, in schools, a particular social set of understandings has been fostered to buttress dominant values (Watkins, 2001), then challenging practitioner ways of knowing must engage in a reflexive examination of self and one's understandings about questions of equity and access in schools. A socially just foundation cannot begin with unjust ways of knowing. In other words, how can an ideal of equity and access for students of color be supported or enacted if one views these students as in some way inferior? Without reflexivity, unexamined bias can undo even the most sincere attempt to end injustices in schools.

As reflexively analyzing ways of knowing is significant, so is engaging in ways of becoming and interacting, what Brian Massumi (2002) calls the *ontogenic*. Social justice should neither be an additive to school curriculum, nor an additive to ways of being. If social justice is affective, a part of the relationship between bodies, then it is also an ontological question, a "means of interacting with people and ecologies" (Gershon, 2012, p. 145). It therefore exists beyond lessons and into the implicit daily interactions that happen in schools. In embodying the ideals of equity and access, social justice is also performatively played out in one's daily actions (Gershon, 2012; Sedgwick, 2003). One example of such fundamental permanence resides in the Spanish language. In Spanish, the idea of being is expressed using two separate verbs, *ser* and *estar*. *Ser* is used to express permanent ideas, while *estar* expresses temporary ways of being. While *estar* articulates how one feels at a particular moment, *ser* describes personality traits that guide the way one relates with and to the world. Social justice, as observed ways of being, is a question of moving from *estar* to *ser*, the temporary to the permanent. In sum, how can students truly embody the lessons taught if they are antithetical to the way the teacher acts and interacts with students?

A practitioner's ontological approach to interactions in schools is significant to culture as it can challenge broader sociocultural ideals of students' ways of being. Mills (1998) argues that considering slavery as a starting point for discussions about ontology and race is an important historical reality of a partitioned social ontology. This is because it illuminates the general assumption that "all humans have been recognized as persons (the 'default mode,' so to speak)" (p. 7) rather than property. He continues by stating that "systemic racial privilege has been an undeniable (though often denied) fact in recent global history, and exploring an ontology of race will contribute to (though not exhaust) our understanding of social dynamics" (p. 44). In short, the way that we view Others' ways of being is socially constructed through historical and political ideologies, predefining social perception of marginalized individuals' ontologies (Cooper, 1982; DuBois, 1903). Much like the vignette at the beginning of this section, overcoming social ontology for students is a fatiguing act of fighting perception of being. Social justice serves to interrupt social ontologies, to let students "be" outside of social constructions.

Moving Forward

Teaching, the curriculum, the school culture, and the individual ways of being and knowing are knotted interactions (Nespor, 1997) in the process of social justice. At every intersection in this educational knot sit questions of equity and access for students in the current context of schools. The marginalization of students and their ways of knowing and being are historically, politically, and socioculturally constructed and situated (Varenne & McDermott, 1998; Watkins, 2001; Winfield, 2007). Pushing against these sociocultural ideas and ideals that have become so commonplace as to appear normal serves to disrupt power structures in schools and in broader cultural contexts. This chapter serves as a discussion of social justice's potential as a process resulting in action with, in, and between people.

The idea of deconstructing injustices in schools is certainly not a new theoretical concept or practical objective (see Cooper 1892; DuBois, 1903; Woodson, 1933). However, despite current and consistent marginalization of particular student populations in schools, the normalized structures that buttress injustice continue to go largely unabated in daily practice (Apple, 2006; Varenne & McDermott, 1998; Watkins, 2001). Realistically, the standardization of the teaching field makes it increasingly difficult for practitioners to analyze the foundation that underpins the structure of schools (Gershon, 2012). Yet, standardization alone does not excuse an inattention to the ways schools function. Anyone who works and lives "in the trenches" should be aware of the material of the trench in which they lie. If "ideologies are not left to chance" (Watkins, 2001, p. 2) in education, then teachers should not leave the ideology of justice to chance in their practice. This chapter is therefore an invitation to a process of fluid possibilities with the hope that an examination of self, schooling, and its structures will result in action for those living in the margins of schools. It is an invitation to (un)learn about ourselves and our schools and (re)learn a new way of being. Here are three possible organizing questions for lead-learning practices:

- How can social justice be used as a study topic or framework while retaining its fluid complexities?
- Given that social justice often calls for a degree of reflexivity, how can lead learning help teachers enter into an iterative and recursive process of reflection?
- How can teachers critically examine their own culture if the normalized ways of being and knowing are the foundation of marginalization for particular student populations?

Endnotes

1 The colleague described here is no longer an employee of the district. Additionally, the student's name used is a pseudonym.

2 This quote, like the others beginning each section in this chapter, is taken from interviews in my dissertation research project, which has been formally approved by Kent State University. My dissertation research participants have reviewed the interview excerpts quoted in this chapter and have given me formal permission to publish them.

7

DELIBERATIVE CONVERSATION: CONSCIOUSNESS-RAISING FOR DEMOCRATIC INTERDEPENDENCE

For there is, in fact, no contradiction at all between the practice of humanism and the practice of participatory citizenship. Humanism is not about withdrawal and exclusion. Quite the reverse: its purpose is to make more things available to critical scrutiny as the product of human labor, human energies for emancipation and enlightenment, and just as importantly, human misreadings and misinterpretations of the collective past and present. (Said, 2004, p. 22)

Welcome! Please, Join Me. Let Us Learn with One Another

In this chapter, I suggest we not lose sight of the humanistic and ecological essence of 3S pedagogy—the ways in which we live with one another as interconnected parts of the world. In the spirit of this interdependence, picture educational institutions advancing *liberal arts breadth* as they prepare students to be integrated thinkers, creative problem solvers, trans-disciplinary/trans-cultural team builders, empathetic listeners, and purposeful leaders. Picture the co-enactment of *democratic humanism* in our schools as all curriculum stakeholders—teachers, administrative staff, students, parents, and community members—embrace and enact deep, meaningful learning experiences. Picture learning environments where educators challenge themselves and their students to cultivate ways of life that are grounded in *ecological cosmopolitanism.*

I recently spoke with a friend, Renee, one of a group of five cosupporters we affectionately nicknamed the Ph.D. Moms. Over the past six years, the five of us have shared our doctoral journeys of coursework and research in the Curriculum and Instruction program at Kent State University. During this time, we also deliberated about many layers common in our lives, which not only included child rearing, but teaching strategies, pedagogical philosophies, and exercises in meaning-making. Each of us brought to our doctoral studies different areas of teaching expertise—early childhood, mathematics, literacy, social studies, and architecture (me). One might say we were like-minded teacher-learners who worked as critical friends, challenging ourselves through scholarly activity and discourse to pursue the aims of democratic curriculum problem solving.

During our phone conversation, Renee described an interesting, but simple, experience of collegiality at a recent interview. She related to me by explaining her immediate draw to the historical architecture as she arrived on campus by car; she was moved by the grandeur of the edifice as she approached on foot and the light-filled foyer exposed as she opened the door of the building. Upon entering her destination, Renee was astonished to be greeted by the genuine, smiling face and handshake of the Search Committee Chair who stood eagerly awaiting her with the invitation, "Welcome! Please, join me." We laughed together at the immense sense of importance she felt resulting from the value the Chair and committee members recognized in her ideas and sharing of her personal story. Later that evening, I reflected upon my conversation with Renee. We were laughing because Renee felt her ideas were valued at this institution. She was quite pleased that the Search Committee openly supported her holistic approach to education. They were willing to hire a teacher who had a vocational calling to 3S pedagogy.

I then reflected on another related moment when I made an appointment with Geoff, an associate provost, to discuss a colleague in my college, Michael. Michael is an award-winning practitioner, gifted teacher, and international scholar. Geoff was aware through previous conversations that I considered Michael a critical friend, someone who actively participated in a collegial-study initiative that we called a "Disciplined Professional Learning Community" (DPLC). The creation of this DPLC was part of a grant-supported project, led by Jim Henderson and Rosie Gornik, to create a curriculum leadership website that challenged the Tyler Rationale.[1]

During the project, I quickly identified Michael's like-minded dedication to democratic curriculum problem solving through his collaborative contributions to our college's DPLC. He was the one member truly open to discussing ways we might embrace holistic 3S pedagogy in our college's curriculum. I appealed to Geoff, requesting that he consider offering an available administrative position to Michael because our university was in jeopardy of losing his pedagogical expertise and alternative ways of thinking to another institution that was courting him. Geoff did not foresee Michael leaving, but because of his respect for Michael's research and for my work on creating the DPLC, he agreed to pursue this matter further. Geoff was unable to find wiggle room in the political climate to accommodate my appeal; and as I predicted, Michael left. Geoff shortly followed.

Geoff is now a provost at a southern university in the United States and enthusiastic about encouraging the new curriculum development discourse and practice advanced in this book. As program director of a professional architecture program at a midwestern university in the United States, Michael now fosters a democratic curriculum culture with a liberal arts orientation; and his program is thriving due to his openness, genuine acceptance, and reciprocal valuing of others' contributions. My personal reflections on Renee, Geoff, and Michael are just three small reminders of the value of recognizing our connectedness to one another.

The study of liberal arts breadth, democratic humanism, and ecological cosmopolitanism are three key ways to build personal capacities to embody and practice democratic interdependence. The study and practice of these three topics invites the cultivation of Dewey's (1930/1984) "new individualism," as introduced in the preface. Such individuals understand 'sociality' as mutually respectful transactions inspired and informed by a feel for the interconnection of all forms of life on our planet and, perhaps, even a feel for the cosmological wholeness of our universe (Gombrowicz, 2005). With this sense of social understanding, I have written this chapter as a lead-learning invitation to study how deliberative conversations on democratic interdependence informs the reflective inquiries in chapters 2–4.

3S Pedagogy and Liberal Arts Breadth

While studying, practicing, and teaching architecture to high school, community college, and university students for 20 years, I have become increasingly concerned about the role architects play in society. Architecture must regain its stance as a liberal profession grounded in ethics; and through my doctoral studies in curriculum and pedagogy, I found ways to address the professional status of architectural education in more critical, holistic ways. This is an important matter because:

> [The] architecture school remains the crucial site where the discourse of architecture is formulated and disseminated. More than the sum of its curricular components, it is the place where students become conscious of themselves as members of a preexisting community of professionals and intellectuals, where they begin to sort out the manifold identities available to them, and where the future field of architecture, in all its disciplinary and professional cognates, is collectively constituted. (Ockman, 2012, p. 32)

I am deeply concerned about the "widening separation of architecture from the humanities [which] has deprived it of much of its ethical substance" (Coleman, 2010, p. 201). I feel that professional architecture education has an obligation to renew this connection to the humanities. Though architects utilize drawings as a form of expression to represent concepts, their designing practices can reach beyond representation to construct deeper, meaningful insights into the relationship between people and spaces (Murcutt, 2009), and I suspect that many other professions can also generate and promote such deeper, ecological insights.

I firmly believe that architects—as well as other professionals such as doctors, lawyers, accountants, engineers, and educators—can address the topic of democratic interdependence through deliberative conversations. In a recent *DesignIntelligence* article, Andrea Rutledge (2012), the Executive Director of the National Architectural Accrediting Board (NAAB), recognizes that:

> NAAB has come to realize that educating the 21st century emerging professional calls not for fewer SPC "Student Performance Criteria" related to leadership, collaboration, communication and critical thinking, but instead for improved definitions, better guidelines on how these SPC are manifested in student work, and new or different types of assessment strategies for teams reviewing colleges. (p. 5)

I invite readers of this chapter to identify such policy support for 3S pedagogy in their professional fields.

I have observed how teaching and embodying 3S understanding, as informed by our Western liberal arts heritage, can encourage deep meaningful learning in studio practices in colleges, which provides a basis for architectural artistry in the community. In fact, my dissertation research focused on this topic, and it was quite a joy to discover the ways in which a school of architecture that is grounded in a liberal arts philosophy fosters holistic teaching and practical artistry. I discovered that, although the NAAB suggests that architectural leadership should be addressed in a lecture format, studio courses grounded in 3S pedagogy allow for the cultivation of democratic self and social understandings through arts-based educational experiences (Eisner, 1998). Three student-learning themes emerged from my dissertation research. I found that 3S pedagogy enhances students' capacities to make responsible educational choices, to engage in professional leadership role-playing, and to be sensitive to equity issues (Bilek-Golias, 2012). My research has convinced me that all professions would benefit from this book's synoptic study with its liberal arts breadth. My research also demonstrates that it is never too late to engage in this professional broadening. Educators, who may not have acquired a strong liberal arts background as part of their teacher preparation, can simply begin to study this book's seven topics with one or more critical friends; over time, they will experience the emergence of liberal arts breadth in their thinking and in their practices.

Because the architecture profession has slowly been losing its liberal status (Boyer & Mitgang, 1996; Hill, 2005; Tafuri, 1976), I believe that a liberal arts approach to professional architecture education is not only vitally important for "high gains in critical thinking, complex reasoning and writing skills" (Vedder, 2011), but necessary to promote the interpretive artistry that enables professionals to avoid getting caught up in a narrow technical rationality. Working with a liberal-study orientation, they are better positioned to cultivate their practical wisdom (Henderson & Hackney, 2014; Nancy, 2010; Schwandt, 2002; Schwartz & Sharpe, 2010).

The Association of American Colleges and Universities proposes a strong definition of liberal education as,

> an approach to learning that empowers individuals and prepares them to deal with complexity, diversity, and change. It provides students with broad knowledge of the wider world (e.g., science, culture, and society) as well as in-depth study in a specific area of interest. A liberal education helps students develop a sense of *social responsibility* [emphasis added], as well as strong and transferable intellectual and practical skills such as communication, analytical and problem-solving skills, and a demonstrated ability to apply knowledge and skills in real-world settings. (para. 1)

Such a liberal arts education is intended "to be pursued as an end in itself" in comparison to a technical "education whose purpose is to be practical or useful" (Miller, 2007, p. 184). Null (2011) argues that liberal arts curricula encourages student to be "free thinkers" with the ability to "draw upon many fields of knowledge, pursue truth, and solve problems. To be free means to use our minds to think independently while at the same time basing our judgments on a well-conceived view of tradition and purpose" (pp. 15–16). In short, by studying 3S pedagogy, educators are liberating themselves; they are cultivating the freedom of practicing broadly informed judgments.

Deliberative Conversations on Liberal Arts Aims

Does the core course sequence of professional architectural education (or a similar core sequence in any professional socialization) inspire a vocational calling and responsibility for graduates to embrace leadership roles in addressing matters of global concern? A liberal arts approach would foster this kind of global orientation in a way that a limited, narrow curricular focus would not. In my teaching field, I feel I benefit from the use of a pedagogical "language of invitation, offering encouragement, guidance, sharing, advice and trying-out," not a language of "requirement, compulsion, prescription, testing and assignment" (Noddings, 2006, p. 339). This enables me to teach for "a sense of common purpose connecting the practice of architecture to the most consequential issues of society" (Boyer & Mitgang, 1996, p. 13). Picture the profession of architecture (or any other profession) having such a common curricular purpose. Would not this be an exciting educational future for all types of professional socialization? We would be preparing professionals as competent workers and as publicly inspired leaders.

Regardless of the field of professional study, "our primary goal should be to produce students who have a Socratic knowledge of their own ignorance—both of other world cultures and, to a great extent, of our own" (Nussbaum, 1997,

p. 147). A worthy progressive pedagogical aim for studio work in architectural education, for example, would be to treat "architecture as a cultural act" (Sabini, 2011, p. 54). This curricular aim would not only set the stage for students to practice evidence-based judgment, reflective decision-making, and self-governance but to act with what Robert Vischer describes as "muscular" empathy, which links aesthetic appreciation to the rhythmic experiences of the body's "self-motions" (Greiner, 1909). As Vischer puts it, "[w]e move in and with the forms" (p. 101). This experience of a rhythmic continuity between self and other, outside and in, defines empathy in Vischer's view. By objectifying the self in external, spatial forms, projecting it into and becoming like them, subject merges with object. Self and world bond precisely in the way that Jen discusses in chapter 3. Furthermore, this embodiment topic connects to a broader theme of the book: *that through envisioning, embodying, and practicing holistic understanding within supportive learning communities, we can make what currently seems impossible possible.*

While presenting subject-matter learning, teaching for self-understanding can be fostered through recognizing the worthiness of others, as Appiah (2006) writes, in the delight of deliberative conversation enacted with empathy. Empathy, or *Einfühlung*, as a felt element of conversation, is an intellectual and pleasurable exchange with a sense of perception rooted in what German philosopher, Immanuel Kant describes as purposeful meaning-making (Vischer, Mallgrave, & Ikonomou, 1994). It is imperative to create meaningful exchanges between: student to student, student to teacher, teacher to teacher, teacher to stakeholder, and so on with the intention of analyzing, exploring, and questioning possibilities together towards a broader cosmopolitan understanding, which Petra discusses in chapter 8.

3S Pedagogical Design

The design studio is an exemplar of 3S learning. This holistic learning-by-doing is guided by master practitioners who serve as lead leaners coaching their students (Schön, 1985, 1990). This pedagogical model could be useful for all professional schools in a university. The environment of a studio is typically structured with a dozen or so students sitting in a loft-like space with drafting tables, paper, books, pictures, and models, which teaches the kind of place it is. Every part of the physical environment, human or inanimate, affects other components within the environment. Hopefully, the students are affected by the spatial volume, furniture arrangement, fenestration, and materiality. In effect, the studio space is constructed in such a way so that there is a strong interrelationship between its environmental components and the possibilities for a wide-range of creative responses from students.

At the beginning of the term, the studio master provides the students with a "program," or a set of design requirements for a type of building and its site. The students are to develop their own version of the design by sketching, drawing, and modeling. At the end of the term, there is a critique or "crit" when they present their designs to a "jury," which is typically a panel of architectural faculty members and professionals. Between these major events, students also learn from one another through 'situated learning' (Lave & Wenger, 1991) within their studio communities. The patterns, behaviors, and beliefs practiced during these moments together influence how students form their professional identities. Establishing a culture of democratic humanism would encourage students to consider living a fuller life through a moral way of being with one another. Honoring such a value has the potential to produce students who will become leaders immediately impacting the significance of our profession(s).

Deliberative Conversations on the Aims of Democratic Humanism

Democratic humanism is a pragmatic, ever-growing manner of thinking and "a way of personal life and one which provides a moral standard for personal con-duct" (Dewey, 1939/1989, pp. 100–101). In particular, Edward Said's (2004) democratic understanding of humanism resonates with me as a public intellectual and scholar-teacher committed to peaceful interdependence. I question if I am being appropriately inclusive in my teaching, or if am I caught up in my own 'exclusivisms' when I work with my students. Said (2004) defines "exclusivism … [as] that avoidable narrowing of vision that sees in the past only self-flattering narratives that deliberately filter out not just the achievements of other groups but in a sense even their fructifying presence" (p. 51). There is a curriculum question that serves as a basis for my pedagogical reflections: Will my students come back in the future for fostering, in Said's (2004) language, "democratic, open to all classes and backgrounds, as a process of unending disclosure, discovery, self-criticism, and liberation" (pp. 21–22)?

Picture the enactment of educational experiences where students would engage with community members on authentic needs, coming to understand through inquiry and analysis their cultures, values, and beliefs as well as their physical and natural world. Imagine how other professions could enact such a holistic, problem-based orientation—curriculum sites where teachers work as publicly engaged intellectuals (Behm, Rankins-Robertson, & Roen, 2014). How might your students assume leadership roles in their respective communities? While various universities offer community outreach as well as design/build studios, we have just scratched the surface. As recent research conducted by the American Institute of Architects' (AIA) Repositioning Initiative reports, "the public admires the profession but really doesn't know why architects are relevant" (Jacob, 2013, p. 42). Delving deeper in deliberative conversations might lead to the discovery of a host of curriculum alternatives for architecture and other professions that encourage public partnerships to meet future local and global demands. Ultimately, trans-disciplinary discourse and trans-cultural learning experiences also have the power to renew our profession and how the public views our role.

Rutledge (2012) offers five curricular concepts that could possibly support deliberative conversations on democratic humanism: lightness, quickness, exactitude, visibility, and multiplicity. Here are some selected quotations on his five curriculum concepts with my reflective inquiry additions:

- **Lightness**—"Do students demonstrate the ability to identify, explain and incorporate the needs of users/occupants according to the distinct cultural norms of any and all user groups? Do students demonstrate the ability to use multiple forms of graphic representation to explain their concepts and ideas? Do students demonstrate the ability to connect the larger needs of society (macrocosm) with the specific needs of the client (microcosm)?" (pp. 4–5) [I would add: How do students respectfully interact with the clients? Do clients express feelings that indicate the student listened empathetically to their stories, understood their cultures, and/or identified their immediate and potential future needs?]

- **Quickness**—"Do students demonstrate that they have explored multiple precedents, ideas, images, scientific information, and related discipline in the search for a solution to the design problem as presented? Do they demonstrate the use of an 'abundance of thoughts or images' rather than pursuing the most expedient or obvious solution?" (p. 5). [I would add: How do students utilize their skill sets and current understandings to communicate their ideas while considering contributions of all stakeholders involved with a given typology?]

- **Exactitude**—"Can students plan their work in such a way as to convince others of their ability to integrate all the required elements of a comprehensive design?" (p.5). [I would add: How do students thoughtfully execute their design solutions while portraying a sense of confidence and humility?]

- **Visibility**—"Do students demonstrate the ability to think, draw, write and speak concisely and to fully express their ideas, objectives and outcomes for a particular project?" (p.5). [I would add: How do students represent comprehensive design solutions clearly while recognizing their role as team members of a project?]

- **Multiplicity**—"Do students demonstrate their understanding of what it means to be a member of a democratic society and to act responsibly and with a view toward understanding the 'network of connections between the events, the people and the things of the world'?" (p. 5). [I would add: Can students demonstrate their balanced holistic learning? Can they create diverse, idiosyncratic expressions of 3S understanding?]

Through our lead-learning exchanges, my colleague, Petra, who is the author of the lead-learning invitation in chapter 8, and I have conversed and deliberated over the important ideas of Said as they relate to the aforementioned aptitudes. Said (2004) encourages us as academics (and as citizens) to look beyond the dominant paradigms in our fields and in our national consciousness. As humanists, we must be careful to try to view world events from the viewpoint of the disenfranchised and marginalized. We must question the status quo (e.g., Why is it that in other countries, citizens can recycle and compost at fast food restaurants, but asking this of Americans seems to be too demanding?). We must forge an alternative path as humanists in our present day world; it is not an easier path, but if we are to help craft a healthier planet and more empathetic world, we must act as fearless individuals, constantly questioning the way things are.

3S Pedagogy and Ecological Cosmopolitanism

Today's interdependent world calls for our professions to graduate "cosmopolitan" citizens and leaders who recognize in Appiah's (2006) words,

> "obligations to others, obligations that stretch beyond those to whom we are related by the ties of kith and kind, or even the more formal ties of a shared citizenship ... [while taking] seriously the value not just of human life but of particular human lives, which means taking an interest in the practices and beliefs that lend them significance" (p. xv).

Has our culture become one of self-absorption, and does the egregious use of the word 'selfie' in our society serve as an indicator of this narcissistic trend? Nussbaum (1997) argues that we educators need to do more to advance cosmopolitan outlooks. She writes that, "at present we are not doing well enough at the task of [cultivating interdependent] understanding, and these failures are damaging our nation—in business, in politics, in urgent deliberations about the environment and agriculture and human rights" (p. 147).

We must challenge our culture of self-absorption to educate a new generation of professional leaders to act selflessly despite a competition driven society, and one in which Judy Pearsall, Editorial Director for Oxford Dictionaries, named *selfie* as the 2013 Word of the Year (Burton & Purdy, 2013). The Oxford Dictionaries language research program collected "around 150 million words of current English in use each month" and saw "a phenomenal upward trend in the use of *selfie*" (para. 3). Is this verbal trend indicative of the value system of our current citizenship? Imagine if the twenty-first-century lessons we teach our students stifled this self-absorption and were infused with a "humble and critical attitude toward" one's self and others. Picture students adopting a domestic and global frame of reference posture that is well articulated by Noddings (2013):

> A more humble and critical attitude toward the nation and a more appreciative one for the home-place on which the nation has been built. The shift signifies deeper concern for natural resources—land, air, water, and the interdependence of all living things. This same shift of emphasis is required at the international level. Of course, we should be especially concerned about international (world) affairs, but we should be especially concerned about how these interactions affect the health of Earth, our universal world home. It is a shift toward ecological cosmopolitanism. (p. 83)

Picture building students' critical consciousness so that global citizens were not competing against one another, but working alongside each other to make our local and global communities better places to live. Picture helping students understand the impending importance of the consequences of their decision making on their personal futures, their children's futures, and their children's children's futures—the food they eat, the products they purchase, the chemicals they use to clean and maintain their possessions, how and where they dispose of what they no longer want, and more (Hawkin, 2010; McDonough & Braungart, 2009; Tanzer & Longoria, 2007). Picture a shift of appreciation and attitude where young people affirm the infinite value of a diverse and diversifying global humanity. Picture a generation of professional leaders critiquing the use of *selfie* and embracing words that reflect democratic interdependence, such as *Earthie*—words that diminish self-absorption and encourage ecological cosmopolitanism.

Deliberative Conversations on the Aims of Ecological Cosmopolitanism

Education of the twenty-first century must look at our local and global environmental conditions—air filled with pollutants, mountains formed of garbage, and rivers laced with waste. Schools need to transform critical studies in ecology, history, and geography to emphasize ecological cosmopolitanism as a way to think about place. Noddings quotes her earlier writing:

> If we love a particular place, we know that its welfare is intimately connected to the health of the Earth on which it exists. … Because I love *this* place, I want a healthy Earth to sustain it. … If the well-being of my loved place depends on the well-being of Earth, I have a good reason for supporting the well-being of *your* loved place. I have selfish as well as cosmopolitan reasons for preserving the home-places of all human beings. (Noddings, 2012, as cited in Noddings, 2013, pp. 98–99)

This shift in attitude touches on a key essence of 3S pedagogy, which Friedman (2014) writes about in a column of, *The New York Times*. He interviewed Laszlo Bock, vice president responsible for hiring at Google. Bock is looking for individuals with a liberal arts breadth of understanding as "the No. 1 thing." He is also looking for "general cognitive ability, and it's not IQ. It's learning ability. It's the ability to process on the fly. It's the ability to pull together disparate bits of information" (p. SR11). Bock continues describing the importance of democratic humanism in new hires,

> when faced with a problem and you're a member of a team, do you, at the appropriate time, step in and lead. And just as critically, do you step back and stop leading, do you let someone else? Because what's critical to be an effective leader in this environment is you have to be willing to relinquish power. (p. SR11)

He continues to describe an openness and growth towards ecological cosmopolitanism as he looks for ownership and humility. He expands, "humility" is to know when "to step back and embrace the better ideas of others" and ownership is "the sense of responsibility ... the sense of ownership, to step in to try to solve any problem" (p. SR11).

Picture a future where we are confronted by continuous environmental destruction, population booms, loss of finite resources, extinction of inimitable species, and damage to habitats upon which survival of the human population depends (Fisher, 2012). This picture compels us to become stewards of the Earth. Personally and professionally, we can make a difference through our disciplined study of the ecological cosmopolitanism topic. Within the liberal arts, we find the sort of passion and energy for "rich aesthetic experiences" wherein lie "the possibilities to develop compassion, empathy, environmental and social activism, democratic citizenship and spiritual transformation" (McElfresh-Spehler & Slattery, 1999, p. 3). This resourceful and resource–conscious, pragmatic approach finds the "end-in-view" wholly within our ability to imagine.

Going Forward with Lead Learning

We must teach for creative problem solving, which will encourage an empathetic, self-disciplined "critical reflection (that) leads to an understanding of what is beyond" (Aoki, 2005, p. 131). "The aims and ideals that move us are generated through imagination" (Dewey, 1934, p. 49). How can professions "be more effectively engaged in society's most consequential problems? Most essentially, how might schools themselves add knowledge and clarity to that mission" (Boyer & Mitgang, 1996, p. 33)?

Professionals and academics in higher education must accept leadership roles in the spirit of democratic humanism. Schools of architecture have an ethical responsibility to "prepare students to develop their own analytical framework in which to envision a better society ... [by emphasizing the] importance of ending the isolation of the architectural discipline both within the educational institutions and professional communities" (Boyer & Mitgang, 1996, p. 21). Other professional schools share in this same responsibility for encouraging democratic interdependence. As democratic agents answering to our responsibility to serve society, it is important to "model and teach habits of mind for engaged citizenship—creativity, civic mindedness, the ability to mediate among competing viewpoints and interests" (Behm, Rankins-Robertson, & Roen, 2014, para. 11).

Russell Tuttle, with a nod to pop culture, writes that "sadly, over the past millennium, Earth has become the Planet of People, ... where far too many individuals and societies behave like the omnipotent beings in Pierre Boulle's *Planet of the Apes*" (Kelly, 2014, para. 24). For this reason, it is increasingly important to embrace what "is perhaps the hardest job of education ... [which is] to produce people who will think but not give up working rationally and passionately for a better life, a better world" (Noddings, 2006, pp. 196–197). During a time of globalization, supply and demand education, environmental upheaval, and fast-paced development of digital technology, "a deep understanding of ethics can help architects [and other professionals] make decisions about how to address such challenges in as fair and effective a way as possible, and there may be few forms of knowledge more important … to have in the century ahead" (Fisher, 2012, p. 315). Can we not only accept the invitations, but celebrate the openings for DPLCs that publicly engaged trans-disciplinary, trans-cultural scholarship generates? Furthermore, as Jim Henderson encourages in the preface, can we learn and lead while engaging in 3S pedagogy toward a commitment to ecological cosmopolitanism, for our sake and for the sake of future generations? This is my calling. Will you join me?

As you consider my invitation, I hope you also consider the following questions as possible beginnings to ongoing deliberative conversations:

- What sorts of assignments with a *liberal arts breadth* can we give our students that cultivate their freethinking capacities?
- Are we encouraging *democratic humanism* and a critical and inclusive disposition toward human knowledge in our teaching?
- How can we encourage the paradigm shift from practicing 'business as usual' *and* join together across disciplines and across cultures to rebuild in the spirit of *ecological cosmopolitanism* and preserve our common home—Earth?
- Can we establish critical distance from policies and attitudes that treat education as a business, not as a vital invitation to 3S understanding?

Endnote

1 This Kent State University website can be accessed at: www.ehhs.kent.edu/cli.

8

DELIBERATIVE CONVERSATION: INSPIRITING TEACHING THROUGH MYTHOPOETIC INSPIRATION

In our concern to make the study of education scientific, we have ignored other channels.
(Dwayne Huebner, 1999, p. 2)

An Invitation

I believe as educators we are equipped to prepare our students to be fully rounded individuals—academically and emotionally. I invite you to inspirit your teaching with a belief that it is possible for us to "write" a *new* storyline for our students, ourselves, and our schools. As Alfred Tatum (2007) wrote, "pressure to meet adequate yearly progress (AYP) has led to overlooking young people" (p. 83). I assert it is time to start looking *into* the young people we teach—to kindle the spirit inside each one of them.

One of the ways we can do this is by expanding our notion of what constitutes "curriculum." Curriculum consists not only of what we as teachers are "expected" to teach, but "also a conversation among participants, one which supports and explores the possibilities of unpredicted and novel events, unplanned destinations, conversation which incorporates life history and politics and popular culture as well as official institutional academic knowledge" (Pinar, 2012, p. 217). I invite you to embolden your students to "dream of vast horizons of the soul" by joyfully connecting academic content to their lives. Those who measure learning solely by the metric of test scores may characterize joy as superfluous. Joy might not boost economic quarterly reports. Yet, there is simply no denying that students who do not have "skills" like emotional intelligence are just as unlikely to succeed in the workplace as those who have not been prepared academically. Emotion matters, no matter the perceived role it takes—as a means for justifying wonder in classrooms or for creating a competent workforce. We galvanize students when we tell them their stories figure into the curriculum. Students' enthusiasm brings joy to our practice as well. I invite you to envision schools that are imbued with delight and rigor, where we seek to reach each student through deep personal connections. I invite you to study mythopoetic curriculum theory.

Mythopoetic Dimensions of Curriculum and Teaching

In curriculum studies, mythopoetics is a broad topic that encompasses the artistry, emotion, and spirituality of teaching. The term *mythopoetics* derives from two Greek stems: *muthos*, which means "word or story," and *poieo*, which means "to make." Before the written word, humans communicated largely through stories. In these stories, certain archetypes prevailed: the hero, the mother, the explorer. Though human culture has morphed significantly since the age of mythology, these archetypes have prevailed. Teachers themselves can be characterized as "nurturing" or as "school-marmish" archetypes. They have also been characterized as tyrannical or lazy and resistant to change. Some researchers, like Nelson Haggerson, Jr. (2010), use the concept of mythopoetic research to *demythologize* cultural stereotypes like "the good mother" role in teaching. For our purposes, this study first explores the recurring human stories that connect us across cultures and through our profession, primarily the emotional nature of our work. As Haggerson suggests, schools also have archetypical characters.

Mythopoetic curriculum theory also allows us to contemplate a time when humans used language *less*—to those primal, emotional aspects of ourselves which we often suppress in modern institutions—in this case, schools (Hendry, 2011). My view is that studying the topic of mythopoetics allows educators to explore the wonder and magic of our work with children, young adults, and adults. It is difficult to capture many teaching moments quantitatively or through some numerical value system, though it appears that more and more often what is considered "good" teaching is evaluated as such (Gabriel & Allington, 2012). Mythopoetics gives us access to understandings that are not solely intellectual, instead relying on narratives to recount these experiences. Education is a multifaceted emotional endeavor filtered through each of our narratives. These mythopoetical aspects of our curricular work help us find spiritual meaning in teaching.

The Trouble with "Spirituality"

I want to be very clear that I am not advocating any particular religious tradition in my exploration of spirituality, nor am I attempting to equate spirituality with religion. As Kathleen Kesson so deftly points out, "Bringing in the mythopoetic dimension of experience is not about bringing a particular religious teaching to schools; it's about a way of teaching that *fosters the making of personal meaning*" (Henderson & Kesson, 1999, p. 98). Nel Noddings (2013), when writing about spirituality, points out that "the dictionary defines spirit as the principle of conscious life, that which connects the physical body to something felt beyond it" (p. 129) and that:

> The spirit may be thought of as a capacity for deep emotional response—a soaring feeling that carries us above routine, daily life. Or, in contrast, the response—still deeply spiritual—may be a pervasive feeling of calm, of contented peace at the end of a satisfying day. Such experiences are at least in part aesthetic. (p. 128)

Dwayne Huebner (1999) extends this idea, writing that "spirit is derived from the Latin word for breath or breathing … spirit refers to that which gives vitality, that which gives life" (p. 343). He also likened teaching to a vocation, a term which literally means *calling*, but its early origins are indicative of a *spiritual* calling:

> We are not called merely to be something other than we are, nor are we called by some mysterious force beyond us. To accept the vocation of a teacher *is to answer the call of children and of young people* [emphasis added]. Sometimes their call is suppressed by those in charge of schools or by others with power over the young. The voices of the powerful frequently dominate the channels of communication, noisily covering the voices of the young. These activities of the powerful sometimes cause some of the frustration in the work and life of a teacher. Yet, it is precisely this frustration that encourages the teacher with a vocation to journey beyond current meanings and values. (p. 380)

Thus, when I refer to spiritualty and the sense of teaching as a vocation or calling, I am not referring to a calling towards a cloistered religious life but to the ethereal tie that connects us to the young people with whom we have been entrusted—the stories that bind our lives together. In one of the narratives of teaching, we are called to be caregivers, responsible for guiding the next generation. This storyline is not new.

Pinar, Reynolds, Slattery, and Taubman (1995) write, "[Curriculum] is what the older generation choses to tell the younger generation" (p. 847). I have most certainly experienced deeply spiritual and emotional moments in my time with children and young adults. I have had similar moments with colleagues, though sadly, I think this is less common in a field where many teachers work in "private practice" (Little, 1982, 1990). Teaching is a *feeling* profession (Noddings, 2003; Palmer, 2007) as well as an *artistic* one (Eisner, 1994), as Jen so deftly points out in chapter 3. Though few would deny this, we are often expected to suppress this aspect of ourselves in the classrooms and hallways—especially when operating under the standardized management paradigm (Dirkx, 2008). Yet, our time in schools is so much richer when we can bring our emotional selves to the teaching experience (Palmer, 2007). Studying mythopoetics has brought a certain mindfulness to my practice, helping me to see my students as fully rounded individuals— spiritual beings with their own emotional needs. Developing this awareness has made me look beyond grades, evaluations, and assessments.

I realize that each student is a "custom job" (Eisner, 1994) that encompasses a complete storyline that they bring to my class. I may never know each student's narrative, but I *know they have one*; I am aware that we are currently crafting new narratives as we work together, as the teachers' stories highlight in chapter 9. I discovered this personally through my experience with the National Writing Project. I hope that by sharing my experiences, you may begin to reflect on your own. I believe Wendy's chapter 5 on navigating the standardized management paradigm serves us well as we begin our study of the mythopoetics of holistic understanding together, highlighting how our choices are not *either/or*, but a middle path—one that allows us to move forward both with spiritual and professional integrity. I hope that by reading my experiences, you can craft an understanding of mythopoetic inspiration as filtered through your own teaching experiences and stories. As you read, I encourage you to consider how your own teaching narratives have shaped your concept of curriculum and the underlying beliefs that guide your teaching. What feeds your soul in the work you do?

Mythopoetic Inspiration: The National Writing Project

The National Writing Project (NWP) was founded in 1970 at UC Berkeley. The focal point of NWP is the intensive Invitational Summer Institute (ISI), a four- to six-week program open to teachers. Teachers who have completed the ISI are considered Teacher Consultants (TCs). A basic premise of NWP is that teachers who are writers are better teachers of writing (Lieberman & Wood, 2003). In 2001, I participated in the NWP at Kent State University. Through my participation, I felt myself 'transformed' (Whitney, 2008). I was transformed in large part by writing—how it was used among the twenty-some teachers who attended that summer as well as with our students when we returned to our classrooms. While I enjoyed writing before as a student as well as an educator, using journaling to help me grow, I cannot say that the writing I did with students was particularly artful or transformative.

My notions of what it meant to 'teach writing' were disrupted on multiple levels during the summer of 2001. The first radical suggestion was that we teachers *were* writers. Indeed, if we did not view ourselves as writers, how could we imagine teaching our students to write? The very first day, we were asked to share our writing in a gallery-like setting. It could be any form of writing—from poetry to grocery lists. We were asked to reflect how writing had been a part of our lives up to that point. We were invited to walk around the room reading one another's writing, attaching our work to banners that encircled the room, responding with sticky notes to what was shared. It was a risky thing. Yet even on that first day, a burgeoning sense of community began to form when we read love letters, letters from parents to children, poetry, and childhood stories written in charming scrawl shared by other cohort members. Through this experience, I began to reconceptualize my views on what constituted writing.

The second radical suggestion was that we are *all* teachers of writing, whether art, music, math, science, or kindergarten teachers. With the advent of the Common Core State Standards (CCSS) in English Language Arts, this may not seem like such a novel idea. But this writing was by no means 'standardized' nor was it all nonfiction; we wrote in all genres in all content areas—science, poetry, and mathematical art. Boundaries between the written, the visual, and the performative were fluid. The third notion was that writing can take many forms and can be inspired by art, music, or drama. Perhaps this last form was the most jarring for most of us. We came to this program to be better teachers of *writing*. Many of us were 'language people.' Yet, we found the less we relied on language to inspire language, the more thoughtful and imaginative our writing became. Looking back, I now see that NWP encompassed much, if not all, of what I understand to be mythopoetic curriculum theory.

Writing as Teaching

It had been a long time since many of us had regularly and systematically written in the very genres we assigned to our students. When was the last time we tried to hammer out a story with well-rounded characters and compelling plot twists? If it was challenging and revealing for us, was it any different for our students? We also rediscovered there is *power* in authorship. As Glenn Hudak (2010) writes:

> Authorship addresses the human condition, however, by allowing us to creatively explore and translate painful, perhaps oppressive, moments in our lives into fiction that embodies just enough truth to help us work through the full impact of what has and is happening to us. Authorship is the beginning of our journey to what Lear (1999) refers to as "open minded." (p. 50)

We came to embrace the role fiction plays in our lives. Mary Aswell Doll (2000) alludes to the place fiction is relegated in academia:

> I insist that the engagement with fiction (prose, drama, poetry, myth, fairy tale, dream) can be a learning experience of the first order—not because students hunt down symbols or identify themes, not because they check boxes on multiple choice tests, and not because they echo the professor's beliefs: safe activities all. None of these. Rather, out of the very chimney corner from which the humanities huddle, fiction disturbs the status quo. Feelings

thought to be central get routed. Peripheral imaginings begin to take root. One can, indeed, "learn a tremendous amount" from fiction. One learns about one's self. One learns about living. But the learning is subtle. (p. xiii)

Through our experiences with writing and reading fiction, nonfiction, songs, and poetry, we discovered (or rediscovered) that teaching could be a deeply spiritual act—a source of deep *connection* to each other and to the students in our care. Pearson and Hoffman (2011) describe the South African concept of Ubuntu when discussing the connection teachers have to students in their care. They point out that "Ubuntu is a Nguni word from South Africa that addresses our interconnectedness, our common humanity, and the responsibility to each other that grows from our connection. Ubuntu roughly translates into 'humanity or fellow feeling' or 'I am because you are'" (p. 22). The notion of Ubuntu captures the notion of spiritual interconnectedness. NWP was a place where we could nurture connections to other teachers as well as to our students.

For most of us who connected through NWP, teaching was not only our profession, but also our *calling*. It was also our source of livelihood, and we had to be careful as we negotiated sharing what we experienced that summer when we returned to our schools. Stephen Brookfield (1990) writes of teachers committing "cultural suicide" when they return to their buildings energized from professional development only to be shunned by other staff members who view new strategies as a threat to their own competency. If we were to come back to our schools and announce that a method like writer's workshop was *the way* to teach writing, we would risk implying that other teachers somehow were using outdated or poor practices, turning them off and having them tune us out, which inadvertently would isolate us from the very colleagues with whom we hoped to share new instructional practices. We had to negotiate the dynamics of sharing this transformative experience with our colleagues who had not done the same. In finding the NWP community, we cloaked ourselves in the safety of it; when we dared to try different instructional strategies or utilize texts in unusual ways (picture books in high school social studies classes, anyone?), we had a supportive network available to help us navigate the standardized management paradigm in which we worked.

Writing as Transformation

After NWP, I felt liberated to be a multifaceted *person* with my students—to express emotions I had often repressed in the name of "professionalism." The veil of detachment lifted a bit. Let me be clear, I did not return to my building (in the words of Lucy from the *Peanuts Gang*) as "some kind of fanatic or something." While I think I was a caring teacher before NWP, I do not think I was a fully dimensional one. NWP gave me the space to share more of myself (often through writing) with my students. By sharing my writing with them (especially the raggedy rough drafts

I labored over just as they did) and by being granted permission to stop writing exclusively for me *as their teacher* in graded, rubric-evaluated assignments, I allowed my students to start writing *for themselves*. I began to live with my students, as Carlos Ruiz Zafon (2001) wrote in *The Shadow of the Wind*, as if:

> Every book … has a soul. The soul of the person who wrote it and of those who read it and lived and dreamed with it. Every time a book changes hands, every time someone runs his eyes down its pages, its spirit grows and strengthens. (p. 5)

I believe the same can be said of any piece of writing. After our NWP experience, TCs valued not only the "souls" of published authors, but those of our students. We gave our students opportunities to be authors by finding authentic opportunities for them to publish their writing.

We viewed each act of writing in the classroom as an opportunity for revelation, whether it was about the complexities of a math problem or the loss of a grandparent. My hope was that every student, in seeing their writing validated, would in turn be willing to share a part of their own "soul" within the safety of our classroom community. With these small changes, the very purpose of schooling and learning changed. Something else fairly remarkable occurred as well, which has been well documented in research: children who had choice in what they read and wrote became better readers and writers because they did it more frequently and more *joyfully* with opportunities for choice embedded whenever possible (Allington, 2012). Quantitative research conducted by the NWP also indicates that students who have teachers who have completed the NWP ISI perform *better* on standardized tests than students who do not (Stokes, Hirabayashi, Murray, & Senauke, 2011). Research indicates that even when using quantitative measures, mythopoetic inspiration "works."

Shaken Notions of Curriculum

In the fall of 2001, we new TCs returned to our classrooms excited, and perhaps somewhat frightened, by what lay before us. We did not have very long to focus on the mundane rituals of a new school year. On a sunny Tuesday morning that September, all of our lives changed as planes hit both towers of the World Trade Center and the Pentagon. At that point, "curriculum" encompassed so much more than state standards or district-adopted textbooks; it incorporated our lives as teachers and those of our students. Although those were the days before blogs and social networks, the listserv we created to maintain our community was flooded with responses to the events that exploded before us and our students. Our writing was not analytical, it was raw with the horror of the day—for not only did we experience the events as frightened bystanders, but also as teachers. We had to help our students process a catastrophe that left us without words. At no other time in my life was my conception of curriculum as shaken. The events that day laid bare all the nuances of curriculum. As a group of teachers who had just concluded our ISI with the NWP, we naturally turned to the safety of our community and to writing. We wrote and shared poetry with one another in our online community—pieces many of us may not have dreamed of sharing with colleagues in our buildings. We turned to writing to help us process the catastrophe, but we did not write analytical essays; we wrote poetry. Poetry became our primary means of communication—poetry, a genre that was rarely evaluated on standardized tests—because it was the way we could best use language to process emotion. Nelson Haggerson (1971) writes about the capacity poetry gives us to reach others (in teaching them) in, *To Dance with Joy* by noting, "I feel joy in finding myself, other selves seeing others discovering themselves, loving themselves, loving others in helping them discover—grow" (p. 87). My experience with using poetry mirrored what Haggerson alludes to in his own poetry—that there is a certain liberation in the genre. Huebner (1999) writes, "It is in poetry, 'the inaugural naming of being' that truth establishes itself" (p. 148). Through poetry, we had a means to help our students pour their emotions into words as well as to try and make sense of seemingly senseless acts, just as we did ourselves.

What if we had not experienced the NWP ISI? Would we have felt secure enough to abandon what we were 'supposed' to be teaching? I know I would not have. I was just as guilty as anyone else of assigning trite acrostic poems and calling it, "teaching poetry." Through NWP, my notions of what constituted real and meaningful curricular experiences for students were moved solidly out of my prior comfort zone and into a place where I could move students with words, art, and movement—my own and others.

Through writing, I came to better know myself, which in turn helped me to better connect with my students. It might be said that through NWP, I truly discovered that "questions over studying, teaching, and learning as well as understanding, reading, and intervening are profoundly ontological, epistemological, and political" (Malewski, 2010, p. 5). Curriculum encompassed so much more than state standards or district-adopted textbooks. It incorporated our lives as teachers and those of our students. It was painful to acknowledge that the workbooks so often used (or misused) in schools are easier *for teachers*—they are safe, filled with "right" answers, and do not ask that teachers (or students) offer up much of themselves to the work of learning (Allington & Nowak, 2004). Though workbooks and other means of traditional education have their place, I often found them limiting rather than inspiring.

In addition to limiting content, I found that textbooks constrain the topics teachers can broach with students. How can teachers address inequities and differing worldviews if they cannot select what stories, articles, or poetry students will read? (Boni's chapter 6 explores issues of equity far more deeply and skillfully.) Having such thoughts about teaching materials did not always make me the most popular teacher in the lunchroom. But I tinkered through my notions of curriculum that allowed me to find a balance between the traditional and motivational in a way that did not allow me to lose the heart to teach. Finding a community of like-minded teachers in both NWP and my school district(s) helped me to find a safe place to navigate the sometimes treacherous educational waters of practicing inspired pedagogy. Through these experiences with NWP and in my teaching, I was able to conceptualize for myself what constituted mythopoetic curriculum theory (MacDonald, 1995).

A Different Path

In his poem, *The Road Not Taken*, Robert Frost (1920) eloquently alludes to our ability to take a different path in life from the one most others travel. I pull inspiration from him and hope this chapter offers you the strength to explore alternative, idiosyncratic paths towards a more soulful nature in your own teaching (Palmer, 2007). My experiences attest to the fact that it is indeed easier to engage in "alternative" educational practices when you do so within the context of a supportive teacher network—whether situated within or outside of your school building, as Chris highlights in chapter 4 on building teaching communities. My greatest fear for our profession "in the time of testing" (McCracken & McCracken, 2001) is that we lose our capacity to be touched by the dignity of our students in an age where high quality teaching is often viewed primarily as raising student test scores. We simply cannot know what educational experiences might spiritually impact a student or colleague (though I am fairly certain it will not be a workbook page, yet I do use them from time to time). I find such moments occur at the most inopportune times in teaching—sometimes reassuringly and sometimes jarringly. Both serve to keep me attentive to the students I am teaching *now*—not to an idealized version of a student in another person's story. When I try to write (indeed, much as I am doing as I write this chapter), I harbor a fear of how my readers will evaluate my writing. I realize this is not so very different for the college students I sometimes teach now or for my fellow doctoral students, let alone third graders or sophomores. Writing leaves *traces* of who we are, just as Carlos Ruiz Zafon (2001) suggests. Writing is our story manifested on the page. It matters not the genre. Writing is an act we are invested in personally—especially if that writing is published. Through writing, I have been inspired to cultivate mythopoetic inspiration.

   Incorporating writing in almost any curricular area is also extremely easy, giving teachers the opportunity not only to assign essays, but also to 'get into' our student's heads. Joan Countryman (1992) encourages teachers to have students write a "math autobiography" early in the school year to see what each student knows about the subject (indeed, in perhaps no other subject is quantitative data so valued and yet there is still room for writing) and to ascertain what they *feel* about the subject. David Jardine (1998) writes,

> mathematics has become simply meaningless for some teachers and some children, producing little more than anxiety, apprehension, and the unvoiced belief that mathematics is a matter for someone else, for some "expert" who

has abilities and understanding that are "beyond me." It has become inhu-man, lacking humus, lacking any sense of directed presence in or relevance to our lives as they are actually lived. (p 53)

A study of mythopoetic curriculum theory (in my case, through writing) con-nects us to one another through *empathy*—we realize we are not alone when we recognize the *feelings* we share when we share our individual stories.

In Parker Palmer's (2007) book on courage and our teacher selves, he observes that:

> To chart the [teaching] landscape fully, three important paths must be taken—the intellectual, emotional and spiritual—and none can be ignored. Reduce teaching to intellect, and it becomes a cold abstraction; reduce it to emotions, and it becomes narcissistic; reduce it to the spiritual and it loses its anchor in this world. Intellect, emotion and spirit depend on one another for wholeness. (p. 5)

This is the value of mythopoetic holistic understanding: it can help us find magic in the mundane if we allow ourselves to be open to incorporating wonder in our classrooms through sharing our stories—*even in math classes.* The children, young adults, and adults we teach not only absorb the content we teach, they also absorb a little of us. "Teaching, like any truly human activity, emerges from one's inward-ness, for better or worse. As I teach, I project the condition of my soul onto my students, my subject, and our way of being together" (p. 2). Sometimes we repress our emotional connections to "save face." As I mentioned prior, I have repressed my feelings in educational settings in the name of professionalism—sometimes we must, as all professions do. But how are teachers different from those in the medi-cal profession? I seek out a doctor who hugs me after she gives me bad (or good) medical news. I go back to the vet who cries when she hands me my cat's ashes. Were these health care providers any less competent because they performed them with a modicum of emotion? Though different settings and individuals require different strategies, I have found most students, parents, and colleagues with whom I have worked often appreciate the fact that as a teacher, I realize the emotional implications of my work.

Emotional Literacy

There are certain teaching stories that resonate within us for years. One of my own centers on my reading the book, *Stone Fox* by John Reynold Gardiner aloud to my third graders. I warned them that someone else would have to read the last chapter aloud because it would often make me cry. This, of course, fascinated them. Teachers do not cry. When the time came, I had a volunteer read the last chapter and I focused very diligently on keeping myself together (we read aloud before lunch and the last thing I needed was to head out into the hallways a red, puffy mess.) My students listened and watched me. At the end of the book (I will not ruin it for those of you who have not read it; it is one of the books that may have inspired *No More Dead Dogs* by Gordon Korman), they began to chant, "Cry! Cry! Cry!" I am trying to remember if I allowed a tear to eke out. (Probably not. Avoiding crying in front of colleagues elicited other powerful emotions, I am sure.) It may seem like my students were being callous, but I think not. I believe it may have been the first time they saw an adult in a school setting express a visceral emotion in reaction to a book. By admitting that literature evoked strong emotions within me, my students learned the power of words, stories, and literature. As Carlos Ruiz Zafron (2001) writes, "Books are mirrors; you only see in them what you already have inside you" (p. 5). My students saw me as a compatriot—a lover of books (and in this case, a lover of dogs).

As a student and teacher of literacy, I believe modeling emotional reactions to literature is as critical as modeling the newest reading comprehension strategy. I have seen math teachers express sheer joy when they found fantastic graphing programs. The point is: all content areas are ripe for the infusion of emotion and personal stories—a venue for developing 3S understanding. Perhaps one of our most powerful tools in our children's learning is helping them emotionally connect with content—to find wonder within the school walls. Writing is one means to do that and still remain within the confines of "the academic"—in *all* content areas. Writing has the potential to allow teachers to know what their students are thinking and feeling throughout the curriculum (Harris, 2006). We lose a lot of the power of writing if we use it *only* to evaluate what students are thinking. Writing provides teachers who desire to incorporate mythopoetic elements into their classrooms the wiggle room to incorporate democratic curriculum leadership within more restrictive settings, as Dan alludes to in his chapter 2. Heubner (1999) asks:

> We might really ask if our curriculum provides opportunities for wonder—indeed is it full of wonder? Or is it dry, cut and digested, filled with abstractions and the future. We must struggle to keep the young open to the world around them—available to new, yet unknown phenomena. (p. 7)

I have experienced wonder in every content area. Have *you* ever been amazed by the way a Fibonacci sequence can be found in such diverse organisms as sunflowers and seashells? There is *wonder* in mathematics and science when these subjects are brought to life in the natural world.

In an article written primarily for Language Arts teachers, Peggy Harris (2006) highlights how a group of students studied the *Challenger* disaster through a mathematic lens. Although her article makes a strong case for the power of writing in the content areas, at no time does she point out the various opportunities to engage in an exploration of the emotional and mythopoetic domains. Here was a chance to explore the mythopoetic aspects of the catastrophe: to view the astronauts and Christa McAuliffe as heroes and warn again of the dangers of engaging in herd thinking. Yet, it was an opportunity missed. I have worked with great social studies teachers who allowed me to utilize "multigenre writing" (Romano, 2000) to explore the Holocaust and imperialism in the Belgian Congo, capitalizing on the opportunity to use emotion to connect students with history. The former resulted in an exhibit at a local college.

At the opening reception, we had the first floor of the college library filled with parents and grandparents (some of whom had survived concentration camps). When we dared to marry writing, art, and "academic content," several generations of families came together to attend a school event. Never have I seen this happen when students turned in traditional research papers. While teachers cannot always incorporate this type of creative writing, I would argue that we have far more wiggle room to do so than we imagine—especially if we can demonstrate that this type of writing gets our students to read and write *more*. These literacy experiences are the most beneficial to students because they provide authentic reasons in which to engage in literacy practices (Allington, 2012).

Although test scores reign supreme in some venues, skillful teachers and administrators have known what Zull's (2002) work on brain-based research suggests: emotion and learning are intertwined. Capitalizing on this, we as educators can seek to make our work in schools more educationally, emotionally, and spiritually meaningful for the children and adults who dwell there. Pearson and Hoffman (2011) note that "professionals do not serve institutions. It is only an accident that teachers happen to be housed in institutions. The ethical and moral responsibility for the student falls on the teacher" (p. 20). We must keep ourselves focused on the ultimate intention of schooling: the *people* (not the products or outcomes) we send forth into the world.

Mythopoetic Inspiration as Empowerment

In my study of mythopoetics, I am drawn to the notion that we will all become better educators when we first connect to that which is human within us—the stories that shape who we are. I made this connection through writing, though it will be different for each individual educator reading this text. Expressing authentic feelings such as sadness and wonder belie the fact that we are teachers, but first, we are *people*. This capacity for wonder is what connects us to one another and allows us to still marvel at the planet on which we reside (Jardin, 1998; Noddings, 2013), as Beth alludes to in her chapter 7 on democratic interdependence. These may seem like outrageous ideas in these days of evaluation and sensibility, yet anyone who has worked with children, adolescents, or adults knows that when we work with *people*, emotions often prevail *over* reason. We can choose to ignore this aspect of ourselves, or we can harness it, helping to make us more available to our students (Palmer, 2007). I think our students deserve this. I think we do, too.

Pinar (2012) writes of the unsettling times in which we teach. We can choose to be defeated, demoralized, to become automatons to scripted programs, to be disheartened by unflattering news reports or unappreciative outsiders. But the truth is this: we have the capacity to shape humanity in the way few (if any) other (paid) professions can. We can help those we teach (and *with whom* we teach) to connect to each other and to the world around them in meaningful, authentic ways through the stories we create together. We can be a person who brings wonder to others' lives, even when they may not find it anywhere else.

I believe that like the phoenix (a mythopoetic image for certain), educators will rise out of the ashes of "curriculum deform" (Pinar, 2012) by connecting to something deeper, more spiritual and soulful in our work with students. This is our calling, and through mythopoetic inspiration, we heed that call. This is what gets us out of bed and through the hard days. I found this support through the National Writing Project, but I have also connected with others in numerous educational settings who envision education as a soulful enterprise. People who do more. Who work when no one is watching, not because they are told to, but because they are doing it for that *one* student (or colleague) who needs or inspires them. One poem that was an informal rallying cry at NWP was *To Be of Use* by Marge Piercy (1973), which is a love song of sorts to those of us who harness ourselves to our work and do the "heavy lifting" required in teaching—not because we are well compensated, but for those magnificent opportunities we have to impact even one child, young adult, or adult.

I invite you to reflect back on how your stories have shaped your teaching life. How can you "write" new stories, along with your students and colleagues, as you attempt to infuse elements of mythopoetic inspiration in your teaching? I hope the questions below alongside the stories I shared above will serve as inspiration as you as you begin to infuse elements of mythopoetic inspiration in your own work while incorporating 3S pedagogy into your practice.

- How might you evaluate your teaching to allow you to include more of *yourself* in my work?
- How might you use writing so that you include opportunities for your students to express what they are *feeling* as well as what they are thinking about content?
- How can you justify/utilize this as another piece of data to more fully represent your students?
- How can you give your students opportunities to write for real purposes and audiences?
- How can you help students and parents to demythologize some of the pervasive stereotypes they encounter in and about schools?

PART II

Collegial Stories and Commentary

Part II contains three chapters. Chapter 9 is a powerful illustration and affirmation of this book's new curriculum development. Three experienced teachers who took part in Kent State University's Teacher Leader Endorsement Program share their initial experiences with this text's lead-learning approach. The chapter, which is composed in a montage format, begins with an introduction on how these teachers' narrative work was organized, facilitated, and enacted in a spirit of "sacred shared time." This is a very exciting chapter since it clearly demonstrates that this book's conception of curriculum development can be practiced, even under the most stringent standardized management conditions imaginable. There is, indeed, hope for the inspired and informed actions that this text encourages and counsels. There are a vast number of educators who have a deep vocational calling to their profession. This book has been written for these current professionals, as well as for those motivated educators who follow them. The chapter 9 teachers are powerful exemplars and worthy representatives of these present and future lead professionals.

As mentioned in the preface, this book's new curriculum development has been piloted and refined through six years of action research in two Kent State University graduate courses. A key outcome of this work has been the identification of a pattern of four persistent, overlapping moments in each educator's journey to understand this text's lead-learning approach: *customary, emerging, engaged,* and *generative*. In customary moments of understanding, educators are habitually immersed in more traditional, compliant, and managerial conceptions of curriculum development. Given our current historical context, this is the default mode for curriculum and teaching activities in most educational settings around the world. In emergent moments of understanding, educators exhibit a growing awareness of the vital importance of building capacities for 3S pedagogical artistry through the study and practice of the three embedded reflective inquiries informed by the four deliberative conversations. In engaged moments of understanding, educators express deep, long-term commitments to the study and practice of these seven topics; while in generative moments, they feel inspired and ready to informally and/or formally invite one or more colleagues to join them in the study-based practice. As the chapter 9 teacher leaders completed their narrative expressions, they all felt that they were now mostly centered in generative moments of understanding, and this will be readily apparent as you read their montage.

A highly experienced educational administrator with a strong background in leadership studies has written chapter 10. There is an interesting historical symmetry in including this educator's voice. Franklin Bobbitt, who was an educational administrator and a leadership studies scholar at the University of Chicago, published *The Curriculum* in 1918; and his book was the first curriculum development text published in the United States. As we approach the centennial of Bobbitt's text, it is symbolically significant to counter Bobbitt's scholarship—and the curriculum development pathway that he pioneered—with a female educational administrator and leadership studies scholar who works at a state-supported public university. In a deeply inclusive, collegial, and generative spirit, she argues for the importance of this text's lead-learning approach. She is quite enthusiastic about this book's new curriculum development and is very committed to finding ways to support the emergence of generative lead learners. Her chapter is also a specific articulation of Ylimaki's (2011) vision for a new field of curriculum leadership:

> The need to create a new curriculum leadership field comes upon realizing that the well-meaning instructional leadership rhetoric is betrayed not only by its emphasis on professional (data-driven) procedures but also by its failure to link leadership with broader cultural political movements and critical theories required to make inclusion and democratic education a reality. (p. 179)

Chapter 11 is a simulated panel discussion that addresses the possibilities and challenges of the book's new curriculum development. As noted in the part I introduction, this text's design and rationale is grounded in a spirit of open-ended explanation, experimentation, and criticism. Chapter 11 extends this underlying sense of pragmatic fallibility to a cross-cultural examination of pragmatic feasibility. Given the current historical conditions of our world, is there hope for this text's lead learning? If so, in what ways can this collegial leadership be embodied and enacted? The chapter 11 panelists represent four continents and possess a wide range of educational experiences. Their diverse perspectives on the worth and feasibility of this book's central ideas are insightful and thought provoking. Their panel discussion ends with a provocative, hopeful vision for the future of this book's lead-learning advocacy and invitation.

9
LEAD-LEARNING STORIES: A NARRATIVE MONTAGE

You must never be fearful about what you are doing when it is right.

~ Rosa Parks[1]

Susan's Reflections – I don't have fear in my teaching as I did earlier in my career. When I'm teaching and making decisions, I act on them with confidence and clarity. It may not be something that is expected, but I have the confidence, wisdom, and skills to find the wiggle within the wiggle room. It's right to be on the side of my students, to empower them to work together and think for themselves. Likewise, I'm thinking for myself in my teaching and not following a choreography that someone else has written for me. Being told how to teach does not feel like "the right thing."

I hear and I forget. I see and I remember. I do and I understand.

~ Confucius[2]

Konni's Reflections – There's so much truth about the nature of learning in these words. The quote always reminds me of when we first started talking about the 3S understanding and including students in our classroom conversations as we teach. Our students should be the center of our classroom discussions and shouldn't need to raise their hand to get our permission to enter the conversation. Students will only remember some of what I say to them, but when they have the conversation among themselves, they remember a whole lot more. Once I began letting this happen in the classroom, I began enjoying teaching once again! Students have to be given the chance to *do* the 3S themselves to understand it, just like teachers do.

> *We need to be the change we wish to see in the world.*
>
> ~ Gandhi[3]
>
> Jen's Reflections — These words are clear, simple, and speak to the heart of being a lead learner. If not me, who; if not now, when? I've witnessed this call for self-action in myself and with my students. If I'm not going to be the change for education, why am I going to sit around complaining and not do anything about the part of my reality I can control? Change starts within you. If you don't like something, change it! You don't need to sit around waiting for permission. Getting to this space in your mind is empowering and peaceful.
>
> *And the day came when the risk to remain tight in a bud was more painful than the risk it took to blossom.*
>
> ~ Anaïs Nin[4]
>
> Jennifer's Reflections — The theme of holding back, restricting growth is not an uncommon experience for many people. We might have a deeper calling to do something, but we end up going along with how things are or have always been done. Perhaps we do this out of fear, uncertainty, selfishness, sacrifice, or other reasons. Anais reminds me that we, teachers with calling for holistic pedagogy, must take risks in order to grow. We need to let ourselves blossom, becoming living expressions of our craft.

We warmly welcome you to our lead-learning, narrative montage! Our chapter opened with a collection of quotes because they, for us, illuminate the spirit and potential of the new professionalism and lead-learning study and practice grounding this book. We, the authors, are excited to dig deeper into this book's vision with you and share our experiences as educators actively grappling with it in our pedagogies and lives. Within the pages of this chapter we are going to share how we, as a group, began working this way, and we want to encourage you to do the same. You do not need anyone's permission to engage with this book's ideas just jump right in and begin studying curriculum development. We know it might seem daunting, but we, as teachers, do not need to let ourselves be restricted by the forces around us. We can find ways to critique, resist, and even refuse to let others belittle our voices and prescribe the educational experiences we create for our students and ourselves. It is time to stop feeling as though we are alone, isolated by the walls of our classrooms. It is time to let ourselves turn inward and rekindle our connectedness with why we became teachers. It is time to find ways to foster holistic understanding within ourselves as well as within our students, fellow teachers, and even administrators and the greater community. We invite you to join us as lead professionals on a quest for a more affirming, progressive, critical, holistic, inspiring vision of what curriculum and pedagogy can become.

Before describing this chapter's organization and purpose, we want to very briefly share some background to help you contextualize the chapter and get to know us a little bit more. Konni's, Jen's, and Susan's "journeys of understanding" (Henderson & Gornik, 2007) around this book's new curriculum development began approximately two years ago when they participated in Kent State University's (KSU) Teacher Leader Endorsement Program (TLEP). The goal of KSU's TLEP is to prepare visionary, collaborative educational leaders with a strong commitment to professional integrity and emancipatory, holistic pedagogy. As you will learn, each of them came to the program for various reasons and with different teaching backgrounds. However, the one thing they had in common was an itch—an inkling inside their hearts. Their "teacher being" (Fowler, 2006) was looking for something more than being compliant bureaucratic functionaries. While in the TLEP, all three educators experienced the lead-learning study scaffolding presented in chapters 2 through 8, and they embarked on ways to practice studying with colleagues and administrators. Each teacher took the wisdom she gleaned from the TLEP into her classroom, deepening her understanding of holistic pedagogy. Jen, Susan, and Konni each experienced dynamic personal journeys in which their understandings of curriculum were complicated through experiencing the sophisticated curriculum and teaching wisdom advanced through studying and practicing. And their growth is still happening as you read these words!

The musings found within the pages of this chapter were birthed through eight months (from August 2013 to March 2014) of ongoing collegial dialogue and lead-learning engagements between all four authors of this chapter. We came together each with varied backgrounds: Konni as third grade teacher, Jen as an elementary intervention specialist teacher, Susan as a kindergarten teacher, and Jennifer as a graduate student studying curriculum and instruction. We met regularly over delicious food and great wine, communing as lead learners. We voiced frustrations, shared personal stories, reconsidered experiences, explored critical questions, and wrote and revised this chapter. Our meetings also involved reading and discussing drafts of the various chapters in this book as they emerged.

There was a sense of *holonomy* in our collegial work. We came together acknowledging our differences and wanting to create a narrative montage that embodied a sense of the multivocal, interdependent dynamic between us. We strove to embody holistic pedagogy and become more familiar with Eisner's (1994) "teaching artistry" at the heart and soul of this book. Our work on this chapter has been an experience in what Fowler (2006) describes as, a "celebration of living an extraordinary ordinary life with loving relationships, hard work, social and ethical responsibility, and creative problem-solving amid the difficulties a (teaching) life presents in the dismaying dregs … [in] the twenty-first century" (p. 31). We want you, our readers, to know such inner development is not impossible; it is doable and not just an abstract, intellectual exercise. Our chapter has placed great effort on bridging educational theory and practice (Schwab, 1971) in light of the current policy management terrain in education. We want you to come away from our chapter connecting more deeply with the book's vision and seeing how the way of professional being at its heart is pragmatically realized through everyday lived experiences (Cherryholmes, 1999).

The *why* behind this book's rational for curriculum development was outlined in the preface and chapter 1. The book's *what*—its focus on building "human capacities" (Nussbaum, 2011) for 3S pedagogical artistry—was also discussed in chapter 1. This discussion was followed by an examination of the book's *how*—its methodology for cultivating such capacities. In this chapter, we invite you to delve deeper into the substantive part of the *how*. In short, this chapter is an illustration of how this book's curriculum development can be practiced. Although we touch upon the substantive features of the studying and practicing, much of what is to come also focuses attention on bringing to life the syntactical features of lead-professionalism, forgiveness, perseverance, and contemplation.

As chapter 1 foreshadowed, this chapter is a response to Pinar's (2006) call for the creation of conceptual montages as the new direction for curriculum development after the reconceptualization of curriculum studies. Not only does this chapter speak to the existential and phenomenological dimensions of human understanding, it is an experiment with the notion of conceptual montage as a way of "enabling teachers to complicate the conversations that they will lead in their own classrooms" (p. 2). As introduced in chapter 1, the concept of *bricolage* (Kincheloe, 2001) also shapes how this book's curriculum development is practiced. Although used as a method in qualitative research, the concept of bricolage can prove fruitful in helping to describe the fluidity of this new curriculum development approach. Studying and practicing of holistic pedagogy welcomes individual meaning making with openness for "methods to uncover new insights, expand and modify old principles, and reexamine accepted interpretations" (Kincheloe, 2005, p. 687). Moreover, the study and practice "embraces a deep form of interdisciplinarity" that not only explores differences but cultivates them with thoughtfulness and an embrace of complexity (Kincheloe, 2001, p. 685).

The remainder of this chapter is dedicated to explaining and sharing three *expressive outcomes* created by Konni, Jen, and Susan with input and guidance from Jennifer. As a reminder, expressive outcomes "are essentially what one ends up with, intended or not, after some form of engagement ... [they] are the consequence of curriculum activities" (Eisner, 1994, p. 118). The three expressions include: 1) platform contemplations, 2) currere conversations, and 3) study inspirations. These expressions are the result of Susan, Jen, and Konni practicing and engaging in bricolage study of the seven-topic scaffolding. Our hope is that the expressive outcomes we have created capture not only the methodological underpinnings of the book but also possibilities for a new professional development that comes through the study and lead-learning practice.

The expressive outcomes presented here should be taken as touchstone and not as complete or final; they should be seen as fluid, open, and evolving. As Konni, Jen, and Susan continue studying, practicing, and growing as educators, these outcomes will undoubtedly expand and strengthen over time. When the outcomes are revisited months or years from now, they will undoubtedly be richer and fuller because of the "practical wisdom" (Schwartz & Sharpe, 2010) acquired through practice and time. Also, dearest reader, please do not think these are the only expressive outcomes possible as you move forward with your understanding. We hope that if you choose to explore similar expressive outcomes, you might see your own possibilities of practicing this book's curriculum development. We hope that this chapter's narrative montage can help you tap into your own journey of understanding—your deepening vision and comprehension of this text's lead professionalism.

Platform Contemplations

The concept of platforms has been central for us in developing and reflecting on the importance of this book's reconceptualization of curriculum development in relationship to our teaching. When doing deliberations or when enacting curriculum, we know that we are always working out of platforms. Platforms are created from individual and collective,

> beliefs about the content; about the students, their needs, and how they learn; about schools, classrooms, and teaching; about the society and its needs; and images of good teaching, of good examples of content and method, and of good procedures to follow. (Walter & Soltis, 2009, p. 62)

In sum, platforms are the sets of *beliefs, feelings*, and *images* we hold about curriculum, pedagogy, and learning.

The platform we present below is the result of our contemplations and personal, social transformations during the TLEP and through writing this chapter together. Our platform not only speaks to this book's vision for curriculum development but also to our concentrated efforts towards enacting more holistic visions in our schools, our classrooms, and our lives. We decided to anchor the platform with three statements that arose and continuously resurfaced during our time together. We are aware that, in continuing our growth as lead learners, our platforms will undoubtedly evolve in richness and complexity. We hope that after encountering our platform, you might begin your own contemplations—individually and collaboratively—around your personal educational beliefs and images and how you feel you have come into such understandings.

"Our Human Potential for Growth Is Infinite"

Schools are mirrors of our societies and our values. When we reduce people and their capacities to numbers and data charts and place them in competition with each other, we are doing an injustice to generations of students and to our profession. The vision guiding our sense of professionalism and our pedagogical actions comes alive when we are studying and practicing holistic pedagogy because it allows us to strengthen our inner commitment to teaching in refreshing and empowering ways. Our teaching practices have seen tremendous boosts through embodying holistic understanding because we are gaining experience in understanding that growth occurs over time. Building our capacities from within increases with experience as we put theories into practice and practices into theory all while gaining confidence in our informed actions. We allow ourselves to be open to songs of inspiration whenever and however they come while showering, driving, napping, running, eating, or meditating. We put our sources of inspiration into action towards a fuller vision of what teaching and learning can be. We are always developing strategies and experimenting with them because we know our leadership can be the agent to move people or situations in positive directions. Through reflective problem solving and the professional autonomy holistic pedagogy cultivates, we are aware of the endless potential for growth in all people.

- How might you, even in small ways, begin to be creative with your time and think outside the boxes we often get put into through federal and state mandates?
- How might you begin exploring the ways knowledge can be freeing and rewarding for not only you but for those around you?

"You Must Be Daring to Be Different"

Lead learning is about finding ways of disrupting and being different despite the habits the standardized management paradigm perpetuates. Teachers' self-esteem wavers in the face of being told what they should be doing and to change, change again, and change some more. The study and practice of emancipatory, holistic understanding as lead learner is simple to begin. It is about being willing to start, and knowing that expertise in all things education is not necessary.

Through our studying, we have found that being lead learners creates change through self-examination and acknowledging personal growth in our beliefs about teaching. Our inner work has allowed us to see ourselves as change agents and advocates for students' holistic learning. The results of our experiences with lead learning have enhanced our confidence and passion within our teaching, and we see that with persistence, realistic changes can occur. For us, part of lead learning is a willingness to challenge habitual thinking and take risks, because as teachers we find ourselves at the heart of ever-changing and forever increasing stakes of public education (e.g., new legislation, curriculum, evaluations).

We also believe in leading by doing, not in authoritarian impositions. Leading by doing can be contagious, appreciated, and respected. It can be a lifeline to those who know—and might not yet know—they need an ally. Finding support for our development as lead learners has been priceless because we need to be learning from someone else and doing authentic, deep collaboration. We have done this by seeking out community wherever possible. When others see us working for change, they, too, may feel change is possible, and they may begin taking risks. Daring to be different in the presence of others is not always simple. We have experienced and know all too well that colleagues and administrators might not understand why we are doing what we do. Their responses and questions continue to help us articulate why development from within is so important.

- In what ways might you begin arming yourself with a toolbox full of problem-solving tools and strategies to help you with studying and practicing holistic pedagogy?
- How might you work with colleagues to build 3S visions for your school and find ways to nurture this during your career?
- How might finding ways to enact 3S pedagogy enliven your pedagogy and students' lives?

"There Are Purple Skies and Green Snowmen and That's Okay"

Teaching is about enacting artistry through our instruction, which is anchored in the self, social, and subject learning in a democratic society. We want each day in our classrooms to count, and for our days together to not revolve around checkmarks on rubrics or to-do lists. Holistic understanding is a big picture concept that should not be separated from how to solve fractions, write sentences, solve problems, and follow school rules. Reconceptualizing our standards—not just reworking them—embeds human values such as living within a community, respect, and meaning and purpose to life. Part of this also involves fostering teachable moments through meaningful inquiry and interactions (i.e., teachers with students, students with students), which promotes experiences for students to make meaning through subject matter that connects them to society.

As teachers, we must always remember we touch the future. We need to honor all students, the ways they learn, and the situations impacting their lives. With 3S understanding, we are not promoting pigeonhole thinking and being. We must be cautious not to thwart students' desires, rather, support their creativity and imaginations as we strive to be reflective and productive, not perfunctory, when with them. We are on the side of all students, and empowering them is about them working together and thinking for themselves. When we find ways to have students see and experience 3S, we feel a momentum that comes into our classrooms as our year progresses. Students are leading and supporting fellow students as they engage at their own individual levels. Students take much more responsibility when we support their voices, promote solving problems, and have conversations about their questions and ideas.

- How do the ideas we described above apply to your teaching and thinking? When do these "This is okay." moments happen for you? Have you had such moments yet? How might you realize it's okay to be different in your own pedagogy?
- Validating students' voices, their learning processes and products, and going where they want to go is something we believe in strongly because we see it work. When we dictate everything, we're not letting them make choices. How might you in your classroom step back from controlling what students need to do? How can you respect their individualities and contributions?
- What are the results you experience when this occurs, and how do those feed into your understanding of holistic pedagogy?

Currere Conversations

Seeing how as part of our collegial dialogue we always shared stories about our journeys, Pinar's (1994) articulation of "curriculum-as-currere" informs our second expressive outcome. Currere is vitally important for exploring questions around selfhood, difficulties, successes, voice, professional being, and teaching practice (Miller, 1990). Currere was a way of letting us view curriculum not as a static document or material, rather as a process of *working from within* through reading, writing, and processing our subjectivity in relationship to the world alongside our pasts, presents, and futures (Fowler, 2006; Pinar, 1994). Our various collegial conversations were recorded, transcribed, questioned, and edited. We used the editing and refining process to try and capture our vocational calling for emancipatory, holistic pedagogy alongside the cultural and existential challenges of living democratically we have faced, which were broadly touched upon in chapter 1 of this book. During our discussions, Jennifer also kept detailed notes. We found that an emergent set of themes arose over time, and as a group, we decided to use eight themes, which we called prompts, as guidance for composing this expressive outcome as a dialogue between us.

Prompt 1

Since an educator's "journey of understanding" (Henderson & Gornik, 2007) is central to understanding this book's new curriculum development, can you share a little bit about how you came to the teaching profession, and how would you describe your "teaching being" (Fowler, 2006)?

SUSAN: Although my childhood was spent playing school like so many children, it would appear to be a series of accidental circumstances that led me to a degree in teaching. I can see in retrospect that it was my calling. Thirty years ago, however, when I left high school, I did not foresee this career. Now in the second half of my teaching career, there's no doubt that the classroom is where my passions lie and where I am supposed to be.

In my teaching, I always come back to the child and ask myself if I am being effective with a given child. I worry about how this child is being affected by what I'm doing. If the focus is on the mandates we're asked to function under and we're more worried about procedures, forms, and the endless list of bombardments, the well-being of the whole child is easily and frequently lost. The child's well-being then becomes a back-burner focus and can be forgotten at the bottom of the list that we must meld and filter.

KONNI: In my high school years, I started out knowing I loved children and always wanted to have them in my life, but I thought that meant being a mom, not a teacher. I didn't realize that my love for children meant I also had a gift that

I could give back to children. The experience of raising my two children led me to teaching. They're very different learners, and this left me wondering how I could help them. I started volunteering in schools so that I could get a feel for what I could do better as a parent to help my own children. I realized I loved being around multiple children and that's when I was hired as a teacher's aide for fifth and sixth grade special needs students. It was here that I thought I'd found my calling. I was so in love with what I was doing, I never thought about doing anything else. That was until a move to Ohio was necessary for our family.

One evening over dinner after my family had moved, I shared with my family how I was having a hard time finding a job. My nine-year-old daughter asked, "Well, why can't you find a job, Mommy?" I told her I didn't have the education to teach. Her words were, "Well, go get it, Mommy." I did just that! Four years later, I finished my master's and started teaching in a second grade multi-age classroom.

At 51, I feel like I have definitely found my calling, but it wasn't always easy. The first few years were spent trying to get the hang of things and trying to do what I thought I was supposed to do. After a few years, I began feeling comfortable with what I was doing. But then it got to a point, I want to say maybe around my eighth year of teaching, where I began feeling a disconnect with my teaching. I wasn't sure why, I just knew I needed to change what I was doing. That's when I was told about the TLEP and decided to enroll.

JEN: I grew up with a pretty picture perfect background—two working parents and a happy home—but growing up as a child in the 1980s and the early 1990s seemed like my life experiences revolved around learning about people that were not as privileged as I. My parents were heavily involved in the Jaycees (i.e., a civic organization) and one of their charity community events was to work with the Association of Retarded Citizens. That word was okay to be used then. Where my high school was, we had a residential facility for adults that had physical and mental limitations, and my school was heavily involved with that group. I also recall that the 1980s seemed to have every made-for-TV movie about racial segregation. I learned my privilege and how people that were discriminated against in any way, shape, or form needed to have their voices heard. I somehow became a cheerleader—a person who wanted to stand up for people's voices.

I've found this benefits me in teaching; teaching is about different perspectives and different ways people can communicate their perspectives, thoughts, beliefs, or desires. I am now in my fifteenth year of teaching students with special needs—mostly kids with autism and others with pretty intense special needs who don't always have that physical voice to share what they know and what they want to do. It's been my undertaking to help do this with them. When you are a person who is a believer in the underdog, things aren't always easy. Not only do you realize it's not easy for them, but it's not really easy for you as the person who is their cheerleader, defender, and promoter. It's taken me on quite the journey.

Prompt 2

In keeping with your journeys, what do you think brought you to teacher leadership, and why do you find resonance with the lead-learning conception informing this book?

SUSAN: I've been a leader for over a decade, serving on building and district committees and assuming leadership roles. I was led to the teacher leadership program by a pamphlet's invitation to "become a leader." Although I was already established as a leader in various capacities, this invitation spoke to me as an opportunity to become a better and more effective leader.

The lead-learning conception resonated with me because with it I gained greater confidence in my practice and a realization that I am not dependent on a "manager" to dictate my methods, choices, approaches, or tools in my practice. I feel less hindered by mandates than I feel some of my colleagues are. The other component that really resonates with me for this style of lead learning is respect for the artistry and professionalism that it recognizes. That's pretty unique to anything that I've studied or practiced in the past in terms of professional development. I didn't want to become an inadequate educator or a hardened teacher just putting in time.

My calling is to work with children and to work with my colleagues in a leadership position. I am motivated to be creative in reaching students and feel obligated to be effective and to make a difference. Leaving students behind is just not acceptable to me, so I feel like this practice is exactly how I teach. As I gain leadership skills and lead-learning practice, I do not intend to leave the classroom or switch hats to become an administrator. I want my teaching to count, and I want to be a resource for teachers, parents, students, and even administrators; so I will remain in the teacher ranks to lead and support others.

JEN: What resonates with me is that everybody has a voice and can do everything to the best of their ability. We're all here to make the world a better place. Although I was raised to be confident in who I am and what I do, I often feel a little different. I was always doing something different than my friends in my undergraduate teaching development, like extra classes or extra certifications. With this lead-learning journey, I've learned to become okay with my confidence instead of doubting if I'm doing the right thing or if it's ok to be different. I've also learned it is okay to be a leader and to continue to help people with their voices. Especially in my teaching position, people are always shocked when they come into my classroom. I always hear something like, "Oh my, your students are reading, learning, doing, and participating." I think, and sometimes say, "Well, why wouldn't they?"

When you're a teacher, typically any time you start getting into lots of leadership positions, everyone just assumes that your next step is going to be to go into administration, and that's not always the case. You can be a great teacher and a great leader. I don't ever want to be an administrator. I don't want to leave the students. I love what I do, and I love watching them learn, succeed, and grow. Being a leader and doing this type of lead learning allows you to have the best of both worlds.

KONNI: I came into this lead learning without much confidence that I was a leader. I knew something was missing from what I was doing in the classroom, but I didn't know what it was. The TLEP was a life-changing experience for me, a career-changing experience. I found others that were very much like me with a desire from within to teach and to share that with others.

My journey has definitely brought me to a point where I feel confident as a leader. I now take that into my classroom with my eight- and nine-year-olds and teach them to be that same kind of lead learner; it doesn't have to be an adult that's doing that type of holistic learning.

I think what resonates most with me about the lead-learner idea is the value it places in the learner and the trust and confidence that's given to the learner to lead their own learning. As a learner myself, I had never felt that before. Until I was given that trust to lead my own learning, I don't think I truly knew what learning was about, or what teaching was about for that matter. The idea of giving value to all the voices within the classroom was an eye-opening experience for me. It was such a small change to make, but one with tremendous impact.

JEN: So many teachers, myself included, after student teaching and graduating college, hit the ground running with idealized thoughts like, "I am going to change the world." Then, somewhere along the road, that enthusiasm gets lost.

KONNI: I felt that, too. I'd say it was probably around my eighth year where I started going, "What's missing here?" It didn't feel as good any more. I was wondering what was missing. I think that what was missing for me was those around me trusting in me.

JEN: Maybe it doesn't get lost, maybe it just gets subdued.

SUSAN: Pushed back.

KONNI: Pushed under all the paperwork. You can get really beat down.

JEN: Yeah, this and that take priority. Then, somehow you lose that passion. In any teachers' lounge, in any lunch room, any mail room you get complaining, complaining, and complaining, and to be the cheerleader or the one who puts the positive spin is hard.

For us, I think it's all been awakened because of the TLEP and the lead learning it prompts. I certainly needed the whole revival of teaching or revival of the passion. We teachers need to know that what we're doing is good and it's okay. Everybody needs their fire sparked again! Everybody needs to throw another log on it and get it going again. For us, we've had this opportunity to take that inner fire back and try to help others reignite.

Prompt 3

Having had experience now for a couple years with this book's lead-learning conception and being teacher leaders in your schools, how would you describe yourselves as learners and as leaders?

JEN: The word *perpetual* comes to mind, a perpetual learner. When we're very honest, and I think we are in this group, I think every good teacher is a perpetual learner.

KONNI: There's so much you can learn from each other even if it's a short conversation in the hallway, something you hear in a classroom, a book, or a quote. Learning is about how you can apply that information. I think that's what a learner does. If you're open to learning, that's huge because you have to be open before you can be a lead learner. I think I've learned to be the support system that I wished I had.

SUSAN: I concur with you both. We're learning from many different sources. We're learning from our kids, from our opponents, from colleagues, from instructors, from books; sources are endless if we're open to learning. To risk defining 'leader,' I think we could define it as building partnerships and being partners with our colleagues. We can lead by example when we initiate the partnerships. However, they need to feel that we're with them and not trying to be superior.

KONNI: I like that, leadership as a partnership.

JEN: It's really about relationship development. You have to be partners with your parents, colleagues, and students.

SUSAN: Yes, being a leader is about that interpersonal relationship, and it's also about caring and letting others' voices have value in the classroom. It's a lead-learning partnership; we're lead learners, but so are they. I wouldn't have thought to put it that way before now, but I see how we're learning from each other in this group and in our schools. It's all about the relationships that we build.

JEN: Being a lead learner is being open to all of this, and possibly more. It's that idea of continued growth inside yourself with others.

Prompt 4

Can you describe the inner growth you've experienced as a result of engaging in this new curriculum development's study and practice? How has it helped you in cultivating decision making and practical wisdom capacities as lead learners?

KONNI: When I look back at my growth, I have to give Dr. Jim Henderson credit from the beginning in the course we took in the TLEP called, *Curriculum*

Leadership. In that class, he gave us parameters of what he wanted but really didn't give us any set way to go about doing that. I recall thinking, "What kind of trick is he playing on us?" It took me a couple of days to realize he truly believes in us as learners and gave us that trust to go for it. I think it took all of us a good two or three days before we finally got into the groove and believed what we were doing was okay. Every time we would ask him a question like, "Are we on the right track? Are we doing what we need to be doing?" He'd say, "Are you learning?" or "What do you think?" We'd respond with, "Well, yes, we're learning." He said, "Then you're on the right track." It was the first time in my entire education that I'd been given that value as a learner and told I could learn without exact outlines or very specific criteria for a passing grade. That experience made me want to do more; it made me want to dive in to learn more. I didn't want the class to end. Believe me, I never felt that way about a class before, ever!

I recall our final presentation in Dr. Henderson's class. There were no detailed checklists, no rubric; we just presented what we learned. It was fabulous! I'd never felt so good about giving presentations before because I didn't feel like I was going to be judged about what I did or did not do. The experience was the epitome of lead learning. We were leading our own learning. As we would come together and share what we read the night before or suggestions that we had, we'd all go off ordering books and excited to come together again. Students at any age can do that, too. One reads a book and does a project on it, and that really piques everybody's curiosity. All of a sudden, they want to learn more about a topic. That kind of 3S learning is contagious.

I brought that same attitude back to my classroom. I realized that I can also value my students as learners in the same way. I don't have to stand up in front of the classroom doing all the talking. I started letting my students talk to each other more and more; it was a really different atmosphere for them. It took showing them how to disagree with each other and that it's okay to have your own opinions as long as you could back them up with why you felt that way. I modeled how to have this type of discussion with respect to others' opinions. They began seeing how they could then have a conversation with one another without me being involved. Gradually, over the course of a couple of months, conversations started happening more naturally. It took a couple more months for the students to trust in the freedom they were given and take their conversations deeper into the topic than what I had asked for. Watching this happen is invigorating!

JEN: I'm glad you brought up the course with Dr. Henderson, Konni! While you can talk to the level of giving your students the opportunity to do that, I come at it with a little bit different perspective. I teach kindergarten through fourth grade, so I have the opportunity to have students for five years. I have a lot more time to allow them and help them understand the experience of learning and growth. As teachers, we all have control issues whether we want to admit it or not, myself included. I have three aides in my classroom; that was a huge adjustment as a teacher. I went to school to teach kids and now I'm teaching grown-ups, too. It was an awkward adjustment; I tried to control every aspect in every corner of my classroom. And I've always worried about wasted time. With time and experience with lead learning and the opportunity with Dr. Henderson, I came to understand that it's okay to be with the learning. It's okay to be learning, to be becoming.

I think these opportunities have allowed me to be more comfortable with taking the time for learning versus always being constrained by lesson plans and rules. I find myself doing more of just sitting and watching my students, or allowing them the time to learn. I do the same thing with the aides I have in my class, too. I feel like they all have a bigger voice. I even find myself now dealing with other colleagues like art, music, or gym teachers in the same way. For example, when the aides ask me, "What do you think about this?" or "Hey, I have an idea." I'm okay with their ideas. The same goes with my students. I try more conversations and ask more questions like: What do you think about it and why am I expected to have the answer? I'm okay with not knowing the answer and going about trying possibilities and seeing what happens. It's okay to take time for this, and it doesn't matter if what unfolds followed a detailed lesson plan or followed some rules. What occurs is a learning opportunity for all of us—the kids, the other adults, and myself. Some of the greatest things happening in such a learning space. Then, we can share with families and others in the school.

SUSAN: When we talk about learning from adults or other adults having an effect on you, it speaks to part of Dr. Henderson's preface to the book when he talks about how we need to be open to hearing. I can expand this to say that in being open to others, we can know our possibilities as well as our limits. We are open to knowing those possibilities when we are open to all of those around us. For example, I have an aide in my classroom who is a trained paraprofessional. She is there primarily to assist my special needs students. As an adult who is present in my classroom every moment of every day, I extend a sense of professional autonomy to her and respect that she can see things that I miss. I find her invaluable, and I really think that it's great to have her as part of my classroom team. She is another person with another pair of eyes who has developed relationships with my students, who can be effective and offer a different perspective. To her advantage, she is not always caught up in all of the rules, constraints, forms, and all of the things that teachers are required to do, and therefore a more casual observer than I.

KONNI: I agree with your comment about finding the paraprofessionals in your room invaluable. Just like my eight- and nine-year-olds, they are always being told what to do. They haven't been given the opportunity or trust from others to make those decisions and feel comfortable with that lead-learning process. Just as it took us a little while to go with the confidence and trust

Dr. Henderson gave us to lead our own learning, I believe it will take others time to adjust and believe in themselves. I think more learning and more growing can happen when we allow that decision making to happen.

JEN: It's a team rather than the one person directly in control. You, as a teacher, might be the coach of your team, but you're still on the same team. I try to talk about that a lot. I can't do my job without my aides, my students, and their parents. If we're playing on the same team with the same goal in mind, how much better we are instead of everybody looking at me going, "What to do? What should I do? What are the rules? What is this?"

SUSAN: In speaking to the changing within, I see the evidence of my growth. I trust my judgments more because we've been exposed to a lot of reading and a lot of theory. A lot of it was new to me, but the ongoing studying is priceless. I wear my "3S glasses" and try to look at everything through them. I use my 3S glasses in teaching a lesson or to determine direction. When my judgments are grounded in theory and in my practice, I trust them. I know that the decisions are being made with sound judgment that are defensible.

Another evidence of my growth is my confidence to engage in dialogue with perhaps an opposing parent, colleague, or administrator. In fact, I feel led to invite others into lead learning. This invitation always comes through a kid focus or a focus on purposeful change, so I am confident to invite others into dialogue to enact change. Also, I know that confidence overflows into making me less motivated to be a hoop-jumper and more dedicated to being an effective and caring teacher looking to find that wiggle room to execute meaningful instruction and to execute change where it's needed. I am also more receptive to student input now more than ever before, and allowing their input to guide instruction.

KONNI: Self-reflection has definitely supported me along this journey as a lead learner. I think having colleagues around me like Susan, Jen, and others believing in you and being willing to sit and listen to you has made a significant difference in how I see myself. They had the confidence in me, and it made me feel better about the process, the journey. Reflection provides the opportunity to realize the importance of each personal interaction within your day. I know that over the last couple of years, I definitely have started journaling more on my own. I'm finding those positives in my day and continuously reflecting back on what could be changed.

Students now have more of a voice in the classroom community and those voices when listened to make a difference in how the lesson plays out. As I have progressed through this journey as lead learner, I have gained the confidence in myself as a teacher and I give myself the "okay" not to follow the plans I had originally mapped out for the day. Immediate reflection on student learning helps me to evaluate and adjust what still needs to be done. Reflection helps me to grow and it helps my students to grow as learners. I find it to be an invaluable tool for being a lead learner.

SUSAN: When I think of the reflection in this new curriculum development, I don't consider it something that's finite with a beginning and an end. It's not like, "Okay, I reflected, and now I'm done." Reflection is continuous, and it's happening in the moments we're in front of the classroom and when we're sitting at our desks in an empty room. I find that I'm continually reflecting and responding. Responding to the reflections is key because that's where action enters the picture.

KONNI: That is such a good point! In doing this, lead-learning reflection is happening as you're listening to what your students say and adjusting what you're going to do next because of what they're saying, which can be unpredictable. That's an example of the reflection in action.

SUSAN: Yes! That reflection is not just going to drive *future* instruction, but it's going to drive the direction of your instruction in a particular moment in time.

JEN: I think as I've become more and more reflective through this whole process, I've started to feel a little bit different, especially when I know it influences my actions, which it should. I've found myself in different leadership positions or on committees, and people start looking at you differently, too, sometimes. People start to change their vibe around you, which might make you feel less confident. I think the biggest reflection piece for me is that instead of listening to negative voices, the voices that I've learned to listen to are my students. It's about helping my students have a voice, and I'm going to listen to those voices because that's what it's about at the end of the day.

Prompt 5

The fifth theme that shows frequently when we meet is the idea of holistic understanding in action. Through 3S, you're honing your pedagogy, breaking from habitual patterns of teaching, and building relationships between you and your students. Could you speak on these ideas a little bit?

KONNI: Conversation with my students is crucial. I don't mean just listening to whether they had a sleepover or it was their mom's birthday—which is personal conversation and important because you're making connections with your students—but what I am talking about is the conversation about learning, allowing them to question you. But why? But what if? It is this inquiry that takes them one step further into the learning process. Also, as I've mentioned before, letting them talk to each other. It shouldn't always be the teacher talking to the students, but letting them have the conversation. It's amazing what happens when you get conversations started and then sit back and trust in your students' ability to learn.

In addition to the change in conversation with the classroom, I have also changed the way I plan out my week. I no longer use a plan book to write out a week's worth of plans. Instead, I draw up an outline of what standards need to be covered and allow my students' learning to dictate how I move through that outline. I do very little whole group instruction. I prefer small groups for a more intimate discussion. I will admit this change was a bit scary at first, but now find it very freeing. I enjoy the time I spend with my students instead of worrying about what part of the lesson plan didn't I get to.

SUSAN: For me, an example is when I read the new, *Pete the Cat* book to my kindergarteners, and they were sucked into the story. Then, when the book order comes in a week or so later, all of the parents are ordering, *Pete the Cat* because their kids have asked for it. That excitement around learning is contagious. Sure, we are helping to sell the book, but we are really selling enthusiasm and the learning—the inspiration.

KONNI: I know what you mean about seeing the enthusiasm for learning coming from the students. I love to hear the students' comments when you say to them, "Okay, we have ten minutes, let's get ready for dismissal," and they respond with, "The day is over already? That went by so fast." When they look at me and go, "It's already time to go home? Did we even have lunch?" They were so wrapped up in learning that they didn't even realize the day was passing. What paycheck can give you that kind of reward?

Another thing I've learned along this journey is to become part of my students, to become one with them and not separate myself as the authoritative figure. Just because I'm the adult doesn't mean that I always have the right way of doing things or the right decisions. One way I do this is by avoiding my teacher desk. I sit at a table with the students or I sit on the floor with them. Why sit at my desk? It's like building a wall saying I am better than you and have more authority. I find I can connect better with students, and they've taken me in as one of them. I'm sitting right there on the floor doing the same work that they're doing.

SUSAN: 3S understanding is something you can't script. We have to rely on ourselves to deliver appropriate instruction through caring methods, which will look different from child to child, from year to year, from class to class. In order to have quality differentiated instruction, you do need to have a gifted person who can do that and who's not going to serve up the one-size-fits-all menu. I always get frustrated that this isn't understood by policy makers. We focus on individualizing for students' needs, differentiating based on who they are and where they are, and then we give them a standardized evaluation at the end. It seems so contradictory.

KONNI: I agree, Susan. 3S understanding can't be taught in a textbook. Sure, you can read about it, but bringing it into our classroom—that's where it comes alive. I constantly tell my students that everyone's brain is different. I do not expect you to know the same thing. You're all different individuals, and then, we turn around and give the standardized test to everyone. My students believe me, trust me, and boom, this is what I give them. I give the same test to everyone, and everyone has to take the same thing. Although, all year long I've been there to guide you and listen to you and let you lead your learning.

SUSAN: It's like we hand out that test with an apology.

KONNI: I do. I'm not kidding. I say, "I'm really sorry. You're going to hear my voice sound like a robot. I'm not going to sound like a teacher that you've had, but this is what I have to do, too." It's hard, though. I want those people in the state or federal governments who initiated these mandates and tests to come sit in my classroom and watch these eight-year-olds take this test. They're disconnected from those of us doing the teaching. Policies totally contradict the individual situations of teachers, students, and community—I think in part because of the money game.

SUSAN: It's all about business and politics. They're motivated by a different set of values than we are.

JEN: I'd add that it's also tied to the idea of capitalism and business. I think that one of the greatest benefits of being a veteran teacher, and one that knows her curriculum and students well, is that you have the opportunity, at times, to give yourself some "wiggle room." When you get to this spot, you can set the curriculum aside or "on hold" for a day or two in order to do something more meaningful that will reach your students and allow you to make real-world, authentic connections with them. For example, as I prepared for our school's Yoga and Mindfulness Week, which was my initiative, it allowed me to involve my students in authentic life skill and responsibility activities. They were able to harness work and organization skills by sorting, counting, putting things in sets, making copies, putting items in mailboxes, making physical deliveries, working together, and the list goes on. As a result, my students were seen being productive and useful, and then were able to share in seeing the results of our school-wide project that they had a big hand in It was incredible! *That* is what makes connections for 3S understanding. *That* is what it is all about. *That* is taking a teachable moment and making it real. *That* is why I teach.

Prompt 6

The theme of surviving versus thriving repeatedly arose in our dialogues. Can you speak a little on this point and consider how you feel this lead-learning approach helps you thrive rather than simply survive? How does it enliven you and your practice despite the very pervasive management and control in schools?

JEN: Surviving is just doing the bare minimums to get by. It's limiting who you are—and can be—as well as your students. When you're a fairly new teacher, it's the Sisyphus analogy. You're pushing the rock up the hill, and then it rolls back down, and then again, again, and again. You're never going to walk out of college with all of the wisdom and knowledge. We still don't know it all despite our years of experience.

Thriving, on the other hand, comes from experience, trust, and confidence in yourself. Open-hearted conversation is also important. We could sit having conversations and there is always something new or different to think about. You have conversations with students and gain confidence in what will work or won't work with them. If something didn't work, it's not the end. Having enough confidence in how your classroom works and your teaching and planning abilities, you say to yourself, "Okay, so I'm just going to try this now." Or you consider maybe doing some differentiation, changing it all up, or re-teaching so that students connect and learn. Thriving as a lead learner will just take you some time.

KONNI: When you're just surviving, you feel like everything just keeps piling up, and there's never time to do what you need to do or want to do. I take thriving as believing in yourself and your learning. You believe in the decisions you're making as a lead learner and as a teacher, because those decisions help you put things in perspective. Believing in who you are as a learner helps you to settle in your classroom.

I've become a better listener to not only my students but to my colleagues, as well, in not so much what they're saying but what they *aren't saying*. That is a big change for me because as teachers, we hear so many complaints. If you take those at the surface level, that's what they are saying, but what are they *not* saying? What's inside? What's underneath it all? I feel that I have become a better listener of those things both from my students and from my colleagues. I think that's helped me thrive as a lead learner and not just survive as a teacher. I think that's a huge difference for me.

I agree with, Jen, too. Conversation is crucial, and allowing that to go both ways—from you to your students, from the students to you, from you to your colleagues and your administration and back again. You can't sit back and do all that complaining without having a conversation with your administration, and you have to believe in yourself to be able to do that. It's taken a while. Goodness gracious, I'm 51, and I can finally say maybe I'm at that point in my life that I believe in myself enough to have these productive conversations and to be a good listener after all these years.

SUSAN: I think surviving has to do with not looking at the bigger picture of education. In reality, teachers today make a lot of decisions from a self-preservation view. We have all kinds of duties alongside pressures from mandates, requirements, and procedures all which go into some appropriate place of rank and order that structures teaching. If we only approach teaching as self-preservation, that's going to impact how we are going to respond to colleagues, mandates, and, scarier yet, how we will respond to students.

As for thriving, I go back to the 3S approach. When we use that 3S learning, it's defensively faultless because the reality is that we're with students developing best interests—the growth and the development of the student's self as a learner and as a member of a democratic society. With this as a priority, the propensity to just automatically sort and classify falls aside. In thriving, we have a balance between required 'to-dos' and looking for and acting upon wiggle room. I think wiggle room is the glue that marries these opposing forces. We just have to have balance; we always have to be looking for how to make 3S pedagogy work and how to wiggle it; it can make everything cohesive.

KONNI: That wiggle room concept is so important to thriving. At first, I didn't understand the meaning of wiggle room, but I do now. It's about finding inroads in my teaching or with colleagues or administrators. Wiggle room is also knowing how to keep a critical distance from top-down management telling you what you have to do, but at the same time being able to acknowledge what needs to be done. There are certain requirements the state, your district, and your administration has, and as teachers, we're taught how to do lesson plans, how to plan a unit, and what steps it takes to get through that unit, but sometimes we just need to slow down and listen to the students and the conversations they are having. I think the biggest change I've made is not letting others dictate how I'm going to run my day. It's my students dictating how I'm going to run my day. I don't mean that my kids run my room; I mean it's their voice that speaks about what will happen next.

SUSAN: You can go about this lead learning individually, which is great, but it's also about building a community. Teachers can move past the roadblocks of the current management of teachers slowly and in small groups until our effect and productivity become apparent and contagious. We will lead by example, not force. This is part of how to thrive too.

Prompt 7

Our dialogues have frequently acknowledged the challenges and messiness that accompany this book's new curriculum development and lead learning. Could you provide some of your insights around this theme?

KONNI: I think it goes back to the reflection piece. One of the things, not only have I become a better listener, but I also think I'm a better questioner. When something is asked of me, I no longer just accept the task as something I am supposed to do and never ask the purpose for the activity. When we do that as teachers, we build up negativity without knowing it sometimes.

What's the reason behind it? What's the priority? Do you agree with it, and why or why not? I never really did that before my lead-learning exposure. Someone was the authoritative figure telling me to do something, and I did it, which means something else had to go in my schedule, and that built a lot of frustration. As teachers, we tend to let other people's uproar become ours. This leads to a lot of discontent and a lot of mistrust, too. We have to learn to question, and teach our students to question. That's part of a healthy democratic vision of life.

I will add, too, that through this journey, something does change within you. As Jen mentioned earlier, you become different. The change in you is sensed by others—sometimes feared—because they don't understand it. You've changed, and they don't always give you the opportunity to have that conversation, to invite them into your learning. I have noticed there are people that before I embarked on this particular part of my journey would have conversations with me but now almost avoid me. I want to share with them why and how I have changed and why certain things aren't bothering me the way they used to. But they are not yet ready, and I think you have to be ready and willing to accept the process of being a lead learner to understand it. This lead learning is not something you can be made to do. You have to be ready for it. It has to be within you, and if not, it's not authentic.

JEN: I can see certain people falling away, too. I think it's important to add that in our lead learning, we need be okay with what you're describing, Konni. If somebody disagrees with you or isn't going to jump on the bandwagon, that is okay. So many things might be behind that unwillingness, and just like with our students building conversation can take time. As lead learners, we have to always remember the forgiveness and perseverance of the lead-professional way of new curriculum development.

SUSAN It's hard because not everyone is ready to take that journey with you, and I think that's the frustration. What propels me in such times of tribulations is to remember it's not all about me. It's about the kids and wearing those 3S glasses. Change is going to happen slowly. If we affect a few people at a time, then growth is going to happen. Maybe there'll be an explosion of growth some day, or maybe it'll just be a baby step at a time. If we're consistent in the change that we seek and the methods that we employ, consistency can be powerful because a bucket is filled just one drop at a time.

KONNI: I like that idea of consistency and not changing just because someone's not on the same path that you are on right now.

SUSAN: We need to approach others with respectfulness because that's going to be the attraction. People will be pushed away if we're not respectful. Also, the moves that we make in seeking change or enacting wiggle room must come with results, too. The results we get can negate the criticism that other people might have about us, which can affect subsequent change.

JEN: Yes. It takes that relationship building. If we want them to see what we have and what's making us happy, then we also have to be ready to accept them for who they are and their views. A lot of this new curriculum development is fresh to a lot of people, even if you've had intuitive feelings about deeper learning and professionalism.

SUSAN: Are we trying to make a difference, or are we trying to make a point? I'm just trying to make a difference. I'm not trying to make a point of being different. I'm not trying to see if I can do it my way. In the end, I really just want to make a difference that will benefit students.

JEN: I agree with you. I always will share with my circle of friends whenever problems come my way. I always give it this test: Is this something that's going to matter tomorrow? Will it matter now or will it matter tomorrow, will it matter in a week, will it matter in a month, will it matter in a year? I'm not on a committee or doing this just because I want to be different. I want to continue to make that difference. The decisions I make as a teacher today, or this school year, I hope affect me and bring positive things next year and the year after. I hope my decisions make me a better person, make me a better teacher. It's about longevity. I also think this new curriculum development is not just about a way of teaching; it's a way of ongoing professional development from within. It's understanding how we live and who we are as people, and in turn how those influence our teaching and schools.

KONNI: Another challenge is knowing you have chosen to use 3S learning with the hopes it will affect the future, but you just don't know. We never get to see the future, but the whole plan is for us to develop these little people to be successful people in our society. We want them to make a difference. So that's another way to think about the longevity of this work.

JEN: That's so true! It's about the after light. You don't see the stars, but you see their after light. Whether it's exercise, teaching, or whatever, you don't always see what you do in that present moment. What you're wanting to do is to see it later. The impacts of your workout aren't going to be seen tomorrow. The effects of teaching somebody to read might not be seen tomorrow or the next day. Isn't that the true gift of being a teacher, though?

SUSAN: I agree. We plant seeds and that's longevity; it's unpredictable.

KONNI: I think another part of the messiness of this book's ideas is that, if we're all honest, I think it can push at your comfort zones. I ventured outside my comfort zone with this work. It didn't feel comfortable at first. Now, it definitely feels good, and I feel good talking about it. I haven't forgotten that feeling, and therefore, I can understand why others are almost hesitant to take the steps that I've taken. I constantly get the question of why did you do that? What is in it for you?

SUSAN: I know. Those first steps didn't feel good, though. That's an intimidating experience. But that internal self-fulfillment is what makes you radiant and other people are wondering what that's about.

> **Prompt 8**
> The idea of building relationships was touched upon briefly, but we've also talked a lot about how trust is something that's ongoing, built over time, and sustained. How are you experiencing trust as multidimensional? How is it you build trust in your teacher-self, between teacher-student, between teacher-teacher, and teacher administrator?

SUSAN: Trust is guarded, earned, shared, and it can be invitational and encouraged. One will be led to expand their trust in another when trust has been afforded and respected. Trust is a give and take.

KONNI: Yes, trust is definitely a give and take. Trust isn't a free gift; it's earned. It's something that you have to establish within a relationship. Relationships and trust, I think, go together. But I also think that it's like a spiral. Trust is that step factor that comes from others into you, which you can then pass on. One example I recall is Dr. Henderson's class in the TLEP. If I hadn't felt trust from him, it would not have been as easy to become a lead learner. The trust allowed me to do things and to take on things I probably would not have before. When I felt the trust, it was very liberating for me as a learner. I would have been very cautious and done just what I needed to do to make sure I was pleasing him as my instructor. But because of his trust, I felt like I could do even more. It felt safe to make my personal connections to the learning at hand, knowing I wouldn't be criticized.

Another example of the spiraling of trust is when I took that feeling of lead-learning trust I had in the TLEP to the administrator within my building. I felt her trust, which might not be the case for all teachers. I know I'm given trust from her; I feel I can do more in my classroom and I won't be criticized for it because of the trust. I can take the trust I have received and put it into my classroom and allow my students to feel that trust from me. I think trust needs to be extended from colleague to colleague as well. If they don't feel you're honest and trustworthy, then why are they going to believe in you or share with you or learn with you?

SUSAN: If you look at a relationship with established trust and a relationship that doesn't, obviously, the one with trust has the potential to be so much more fruitful. It goes to show that trust is of the utmost significance in widening the possibilities of collegiality, of creative collaboration, and of expanding new horizons. The potential for growth is exponential when trust is established.

KONNI: We talked about inviting people into this way of learning, this way of living. If they don't trust you in what you are doing and if they don't see you follow that through, why would they want to be part of what you are doing? Lead learning is not only a way of teaching and learning; it is also a way of living.

I had a professor in my undergraduate who started the course drawing a Venn diagram on the board and wanted to know our opinions on how we thought our private life and our teaching life interacted. I sat back—because I was the non-traditional student with a lot of life experience with two children and a marriage—I sat back just listening to the conversation and kind of chuckling to myself like, "Oh, my classmates have no idea how much they overlap." But again, how could they? They were young and didn't have the life experience to trust in. I pretty much saw my two circles overlapping with very little that would divide them. I truly felt that the person I was is the teacher I am, or was to become. There wasn't a lot of difference between the two, the person I am and the teacher I am. I live my life outside the way I do inside my classroom. Obviously, there are some things that you don't bring into the classroom, but the way you live your life is felt by students and others. There's no hiding it.

SUSAN: Speaking to the trust with the kids, I think that trusting one's teacher is foundational for student growth, and one's potential can be squelched or it can be fueled depending on the relationship and trust level with the teacher. We need to know we touch the future. When we are someone's teacher, mentor, or guide, we can build them up or we can tear them down. So the teacher-student relationship trust can thereafter determine how successful or how confident or how productive a child is going to be.

JEN: When I first got the position I have now, my classroom as it is now was not there, and the administrator I worked for at the time had been a teacher but didn't have any real experience with kids of such an intense need and background. My first couple of years, I had kids who were pretty physically involved and had a lot of physical behaviors, lots of aggression. When you're just starting out, you need a ton of support, and I didn't receive a lot from that administrator. Fast-forward a couple of years, I had an administrator who was a former special education teacher and saw how hard I was working. She was there and I had that, "Oh, I get it." She in turn put her faith and trust in me. She understood a little bit more. She had a better background, and she just understood my pedagogy, my classroom, my students, and me. Then, when I approached her with wanting to get some more specialized training, she was completely supportive and pushed me to do it. She told me to keep going and get better and be better.

This experience was really a huge turnaround point for me to have that administrator who put faith and trust in me and said, "I know. I've watched you work. I've seen your work ethic. I've seen your efforts and everything." She supported that and then the more training I received, the better things became, and the network of trust expanded. I had better relationships with my colleagues and better relationships with parents because they saw other teachers' and administrators' trust in me. So all of that has kind of continued to grow; even though I now have a different administrator, that trust is still there.

There's a trust system that's been established. Now, when I go in and approach the current principal with different things, for example, this year I was interested in doing the yoga for classrooms, and the response was, "Yes, Jen, because I trust you. I know that you're bringing something good that's beneficial for kids, and you are going to see it through." The administration knows I'm a person who follows through with things.

Once you establish that trust, you also have to maintain it. There has to be that follow through. I'm certainly not going to ever intentionally give my principal a reason not to trust me, but you have to maintain trust on your end of the bargain. As much as I want them to trust me, I still have to give administration reasons to trust me, and I also have to continue this with my students and my parents, too. Showing how their children are progressing and succeeding continues to build, keeping that foundation and building more trust. Trust is that spiral, Konni mentioned. It's a continuous cycle, a reciprocal trust.

KONNI: In terms of building trust with students, I started small and concentrated on just building a community, making them feel like we are all part of something. We have community meetings where we could either share something that was bothering us and together find a solution or share about something good that was happening. There was no topic we had to discuss. We're just having a meeting. I wanted that to be the beginning of open conversation with no parameters. From there, we went to small group discussions where they started to be the leaders and then having conversations on their own about the learning topic without me asking them to. They started doing the questioning, but again, you have to lead that. You have to show that it's okay and provide that environment for them to feel open and secure enough.

It did take a while to get that type of conversation going, and they had to trust that I was okay with that kind of conversation. I would say it took a couple of months, maybe even three, before they stopped looking at me for the okay to talk. It's such a great feeling when you are just sitting there on the floor with this group and they are having a conversation without you. I sat there and thought, this is what learning is all about. It's letting them make those decisions and have that conversation because they're going to learn more from each other than they are from me.

I think feeling safe—trusting—allows the student the freedom to think outside the box, as they say. The right environment needs to be created in the classroom community for this type of lead learning to take place. Once they start on this path of being a lead learner, you see their desire to learn more. The students begin to question; once they question, they want to come up with answers to their questions. As a teacher, you might guide them to an avenue to help them answer that question, but you don't answer it for them. That's really hard for a teacher not to do, but I think that's what builds their confidence and their trust. You're letting them know they can do it, and they'll do even more once they experience that.

JEN: You're right, Konni, trust with the students is about that safe environment. Your comment reminds me of an experience I had with one of the parents of my student. A comment from this parent got me thinking, how many times do I have to say, Parker do this, Parker do that, Parker look here, Parker listen. I thought to myself, "I'm not going to 'Parker' him all day today. I'm going to just allow him to be Parker." I allowed him to just take the time to be on the carpet or sit at his desk. I came to see that when I don't go "Parker-ing" him, it puts him in such a different mindset, a different comfort zone. I've kept this up and he's now much more confident and comfortable in our classroom. When I need him to be "on," I say, "I need you to be with me right now because this is a learning time for you." I let him know when we're done with what's at hand, he can go do something, have a five-minute break, or whatever. What a different child he's become with this approach. So, I agree that it's that safe environment that makes such a difference, but you can't give students that unless you are okay with providing that. It's also about trusting of yourself too and re-teaching yourself. What I do with Parker isn't going to work with other students.

I think this trusting even holds true for us as teachers with our administrators. How many of us get so excited to go to the staff meeting where you can sit there and you can just listen to your principal. Ta-da, put this on your calendar. Ta-da, here's the new mandate and change this. Ta-da, here are the new rules.

What I really want is for administration to give us a day where I can sit with my partner teacher to talk in-depth about our kids, our curriculum, and what we're going to do. Trust me, trust us, allow us to have that time, and we'll get stuff done. Just think about what a great feeling that would be if you had an administrator say, "Here, take that time." Instead of some teacher back-to-work day or some speaker preaching for two, three, or four hours about Common Core or whatever the new top-down trend is. I don't need that. What I want is real-time with a real person, my team, or my grade level. Maybe even just me in my own classroom. Being given that time and that opportunity to talk about what I know. What a difference and what a beautiful invitation to do lead learning.

SUSAN: Great point, Jen, on extending holistic understanding. We need to have an administrative perspective that works from a holistic understanding point of view and seeing that's what you need or what you want. Then, creating that environment in the school. For lead learning to catch wind, we've got to get this administrative point of view saying lead learning isn't just for teachers. It's for leaders!

KONNI: I think if we have more time with teachers to talk, maybe we could build each other up versus constantly feeling that someone's beating us down. I think that, too, is about building trust and holistic understanding in action.

Study Inspirations

Personal study inspirations were foundational to our third and final expression outcome. These inspirations came in the form of resources, which we feel inspire our vocational calling for 3S teaching. During our time in the TLEP and afterwards, we (Konni, Jen, and Susan) built individual collections of study resources, which we found in many forms ranging from pop culture to children's literature to scholarly books and so on. Although we cannot share all of them with you, the resources found here were particularly inspirational in terms of deepening our sense of lead professionalism and our study of the seven topics you encountered in chapters 2 through 8. These resources have also informed our actions in our classrooms and as lead learners trying to build communities for reflective inquiry. Here, we share our resources in the hopes that they reinforce for practitioners, and others, that you do not need to be experts in holistic pedagogy or the seven-topic study scaffolding. Resources for inspiration and action on the study topics are very much alive in our daily lives. You need only look for them. Each of the resources to come is an extension of our learning to you. We are inviting you to engage in studying, and we encourage you to explore the resources, be affected by them, and see how they might help ignite your own understandings of holistic pedagogy with all its joys and challenges. We hope these resources will help you feel connected to other passionate educators—we all have beautiful things to share about our craft!

Academic Books

Fullan, M. (2009). *Motion leadership: The skinny on becoming change savvy.* Thousand Oaks, CA: Sage.

- This book is inspirational for us in terms of making change happen. Fullan provides great advice in a "skinny" book to realistically start to affect change in your organization. He prepares readers for possible challenges and how to address and overcome them. His concept of *simplexity* allows one to approach change in a compelling way, i.e., to be a sensible change agent who can lead others using transparency, honesty, positive capacity building, and peer collaborations.

Klimek, K., Ritzenhein, E., & Sullivan, K. (2008). *Generative leadership: Shaping new futures for today's schools.* Thousand Oaks, CA: Sage.

- This book informed us greatly about the power of communication and how it can cultivate change. Although the focus is on leadership, we feel teachers serve in leader roles every day. We are leading through what we do, even if we are not aware of it. This book reinforces the importance of the interpersonal dimensions that are inherit in studying and practicing this book's visions for curriculum development. Through communication and relationships, we can cultivate change.

Sahlberg, P. (2011). *Finnish lessons: What can the world learn from educational change in Finland?* New York, NY: Teachers College Press.

• This book inspires us to seek change and enact leadership. The success of the Finnish education system, though not completely transferable to other nations, provides us with lessons that can transfer into our schools, including building on teacher strengths, creating fear-free learning for students, and generating a growing trust in the education system.

Greene, M. (1988). *The dialectic of freedom.* New York, NY: Teachers College Press.

• This book, although published decades ago, was a lesson for us in thinking about human freedom. It helped us feel empowered to be different and to be ourselves more through studying and practicing curriculum development. This book prompted us to think about how allowing ourselves to be different can rub off on students and how that may allow them to be more fully who they are in our classroom. Students do not often feel the freedom to learn because they have defense walls up because of the various lived experiences they have and the situation they return to after the school day ends. For so many, school is just a place they have to go every day, and little personal connection is seen to subject matter.

Palmer, P. J. (2007). *The courage to teach: Exploring the inner landscape of a teacher's life.* San Francisco, CA: Jossey-Bass.

• This book gives us courage to continue forward with self-reflection around our practice. It has concrete ways to delve deeper into who we are as teachers and why we believe what we do. Palmer's words are reminders about the deep connection we have as teachers with students and that we can make a difference. Teaching is not so much about what we teach (i.e., subject matter); rather, it is about how we teach.

Movies and Short Clips

Menendez, R. (Director). (1988). *Stand and deliver* [Film]. United States: Warner Bros.
LaGravenese, R. (Director). (2007). *Freedom writers* [Film]. United States: Paramount Pictures.
Avildsen, J. G. (Director). (1989). *Lean on me* [Film]. United States: Warner Bros.

• These three films all speak to the relationships that practitioners can develop with students, and how those relationships can make a difference in a child's life like no other person. These films highlight for us a lot of what we have come to understand about the 3S understanding in our classroom. Most pointedly, the importance of trust and building a community within the classroom. When a safe space is created and students are given responsibility and connection to learning, self and social understandings emerge and are supported by teachers and students. 3S learning in our own classrooms, like in the films, is an illustration to the world that teaching is artistry.

Robinson, Sir K. (2011). *Changing educational paradigms* [Video file]. Retrieved from http://sirkenrobinson.com/skr/

• Many of our students are being left behind because of the current structure in our education system. Great lengths are being taken to standardize curriculum and educational decisions often with little attention to teachers' or students' voices. This video clip reminds us that the many structures and habits of schools today are antiquated. As teachers, we must resist the school model of production lines and instead educate for democratic self and social understanding. We are educating for the whole child, not just the data collection purposes.

Fiction and Nonfiction Literature

Seuss, D. (1998). *Hooray for diffendoofer day!* New York, NY: Knopf Books for Young Readers.

• This short story is about a teacher named Miss Bonkers, who dares to be different and encourages students to think for themselves despite pressures around her. The combination of illustrations and words are fun and inspiring, but the story also shows the importance of students' voices and developing their inner capacities for 3S problem solving.

Covey, S. R. (2008). *The leader in me: How schools and parents around the world are inspiring greatness one child at a time.* New York, NY: Free Press.

• This book is inspirational because it describes how transformation in one school happened in simple ways. The book describes a school in which every student took on a leadership role, and the roles that were developed in the schools were very creative (e.g., a door greeter). The stories of transformation in the school are powerful because students cultivated a sense of responsibility and connectedness to what was happening in the school.

Intrator, S. M., & Scribner, M. (Eds.) (2003). *Teaching with fire: Poetry that sustains the courage to teach.* San Francisco, CA: Jossey-Bass.

• This book is a collection of commentary from teachers about poetry that inspires them. These teachers picked poems that help them rekindle their inner fire and courage to teach in times of joy and hardship. This book reminds us that we are not alone; a community of support can be found even through books.

Carson, B. (1990). *Gifted hands: The Ben Carson story*. Grand Rapids, MI: Review and Herald Publishing Association.

- This book is about the real-life story of Ben Carson, an African American male. Through parental support and commitment to learning, he was able to think big and transform his life despite the situations and challenging environment he lived in. This book reminds us that all students have potential for greatness despite the barriers that people and society put before them.

Maxwell, J. C. (1998). *21 irrefutable laws of leadership: Follow them and people will follow you*. Nashville, TN: Thomas Nelson, Inc.

- This book makes us question what we are doing as teachers and leaders, while at the same time affirming what we are doing. All the chapters led us to deeper connections with the idea of being a lead learner. The 21 laws presented have a universal feeling, and you can apply them to teaching, life, and relationships. For example, being a leader means seeking out people who might not have your strengths. We have each read this text over and over again because the interpretation changes each time.

Carson, R. (1991). *The sense of wonder*. New York, NY: HarperCollins Publishers.

- This is a nonfiction book by a naturalist who works with children. This book, for us, touches on the power of discovery through experience. The book is also an incredible illustration of 3S understanding and the power exploring our interconnectedness with other humans and our world.

Trelease, J. (2001). *The read-aloud handbook* (5th ed.). New York, NY: Penguin Books.

- Although this book has a literacy focus, there are so many stories to connect to and glean ideas from. Our big takeaway from this text is that a teacher can do so many little things that have a huge impact on kids, and we have to always remember this throughout our careers.

Endnotes

1 Rosa Parks's quote retrieved from http://www.goodreads.com/author/quotes/46053. Rosa_Parks
2 Confucius's quote retrieved from http://www.brainyquote.com/quotes/quotes/c/confucius136802.html
3 Potts, M.W. (2002, Feb. 1). Arun Gandhi shares the Mahatma's message. *West-India, 27*(13), 34.
4 Anaïs Nin quote retrieved from https://www.goodreads.com/author/quotes/7190. Ana_s_Nin

10
GENERATIVE LEADERSHIP: PROTECTING THE GOOD WORK

Generative leadership becomes a way of being rather than just a new set of techniques for doing the work of a leader. … Generative school leaders are intent on actualizing the generative capacity of their school for one simple reason: They realize that both students and staff will learn, perform, and thrive better. Generative environments are rich in stimuli, offering challenges and contrasts to existing mental models that can catalyze new ideas and new avenues for action. Generative leaders push back on the commonplace mechanistic ways of organizing and doing business to make room for generative modes of inquiry and action. (Klimek, Ritsenhein, & Sullivan, 2008, pp. 15, 48)

I am honored and grateful that Jim Henderson has offered me the opportunity to contribute to this book. I am pleased to be published among the contributions of many practicing teacher leaders whose good work has illuminated the thoughts and ideas presented throughout the text with their own professional wisdom. Jim and I have been colleagues for a number of years, spanning the boundaries of curriculum studies and leadership studies in our work together. We have been able to convince many of our colleagues that no one owns the "L" word. Leadership belongs to us all and is the responsibility of us all. So, as a former middle grades teacher, elementary school principal, professor of educational leadership, and now dean, I want to add to this book my thoughts on how important it is for teachers and administrators to become friends of each other's minds, to paraphrase Maxine Greene (1995), to promote deep, engaged learning in democratic school settings.

Having spent 40 years of my life in the Catholic Church, I slowly but steadily turned away from church dogmatism. Yet, when I discovered later in my adult life the charisma of the Dominican sisters, I found that their beautiful blend of intellect and compassion resonated within me. As I worked with these women, I found within them an inclusive openmindedness and a comfort with unresolved questions. Their charisma calls them to a search for truth, while acknowledging that there are multiple truths to be known. Likewise, the book you are reading is a call for the search for truth, or more aptly, truths, or more aptly, truths. It is an invitation to teachers and principals to study and develop together. It is a call to energize ourselves collegially to elevate our profession, public education, and the common good.

As educators, are we not committed to reaching the highest potential we can? Do we not want the same for our students? We know the answers to these questions. As quoted in the preface, Eisner (1994) writes that "We need to provide responsible leadership that embraces the possibilities of education and is willing to explore the alternative routes that can be traveled to achieve them" (p. 384). Yet, is the current state of educational affairs leading us in that direction? Of course, the answer is no; the current state is one of standardization and high-stakes testing—such as Ohio's 4th Grade Guarantee, that in theory would require a test-cut score before a child might advance to fourth grade, and the new Ohio Teacher Evaluation System in which 50% of a teacher's performance evaluation is based on the scores students make on the standardized tests. Due to its underlying unfairness, this policy approach generates much anxiety, confusion, frustration, disillusion, resentment, and retribution—a far cry from teachers (and their students) experiencing the joy of personal, holistic journeys of understanding. This valuable book seeks to sustain a discussion among educators—teachers, principals, and invested others—who care about "taking back" education from the managerial, legislative paradigm we now endure, and renewing what we all so fondly remember of our best teachers.

I remember a professor from my first year of college. He was a very large, professorial, serious-looking man who moved me to tears when he read aloud the Romantic poets. He evoked from his students multiple interpretations of poetry that promoted dialogue and caused me to love verse, which I learned was so much more than the beat of iambic pentameter! I also will remember always my high school Latin teacher. Because of her deep passion for her subject, her students, and teaching itself, my 15-year-old self became intrigued with Roman history and signed on for three more years of studying Latin. And, interestingly enough, in those days before high-stakes testing and metrically determined teacher evaluation, I was still able to 'test out' of two years of college-level Latin. Amazing, isn't it? If we all think back to our favorite teachers, do we not remember them as the ones who inspired us to learn more, to play with ideas, to open our minds, to grow in interdependence, and to find joy in the subject we were studying, whether it was poetry, chemistry, history, or even Latin?

The teachers who have contributed to this book are also some of these best teachers, committed to reenergizing themselves and their profession to promote dynamic engagement in student and adult learning in their schools. They tell stories of teaching and learning attained through disciplined personal, professional growth. Their practices of inquiry, reflection, and envisioning advance the democratic ideals of freedom—ideals that can neither be mandated nor statistically assessed. *They have truly centered their work in generative moments of being.*

Woeful Challenges

Yet, here we are, in the midst of what Waite (2010) refers to as macro trends that constrict our search for meaning and purpose in such a black-and-white, concretized, and polarized educational world. Scripted curriculum, high-stakes standardized testing, and professional life-and-death teacher evaluation are consequences of corporate demands for efficiency, compliance incentives, and punition via rules, regulations, and legislative mandates. These consequences have not only produced anxiety and fear but have led to teachers and administrators to "game" the system in many places around the country, where they now face charges of manipulating students' test scores. But, when financially desperate districts are incentivized with astronomical levels of funding through *No Child Left Behind* and now *Race to the Top*, they often swallow their beliefs and values and "sell out" to the corporate mentality of competition and compliance. What a very sad state of affairs for our noble profession and the students we serve. We seem to have foregone the long-term goal of promoting the love of learning for the short-term goal of making cut-scores on standardized tests a particular "achievement," which does not necessarily reflect deep and engaged learning.

To make matters worse, our society has suffered from years and years of anti-intellectualism. In a recent *New York Times* commentary, Nicholas Kristoff (2014) portrays this socio-cultural trend as a "stealth war on wisdom." He recalls President Obama being called a snob when the president advocated for a college education for every student. Moreover, in the news nearly every day is somebody without credentials disputing the science of climate change, the effects of population growth in third world nations, or the devolving health of our planet. It is almost as if our society is operating on myth and misunderstanding. When we believe that forces beyond our control are in play and we cannot do anything to help ourselves, we abdicate our responsibilities to each other, to our planet, to the preservation of democracy.

Embracing Collegiality

Yet, we must live with hope. What if we were to "envision students and teachers [and principals] enthusiastically collaborating in critical thinking and creative problem solving activities" (preface). As educators, it is our challenge to "remember that [we professionals] above all others are consecrated servants of the democratic ideas [of our society]" (Dewey, 1980/1916, p. 210). Meeting Dewey's challenge will require teachers and administrators alike to order our priorities alongside democratic ideals as "critical intellectuals" (Torres, 2010, p. 339).

Just as the assessment world has overrun the lives of teachers in our public schools, the managerial world of compliance has highjacked the lives of school administrators. In the quest to control, reward, and punish, and to standardize leadership with legislative mandates, state departments of education now function as compliance offices, thus exerting extreme pressure on principals. Principals suffer from what Reitzug (2010) calls the "impoverished nature of the current vision for education" that snuffs out all other visions beyond the quest for higher test scores (p. 319). Principals are now expected to revert to being managers rather than collegial leaders.

This reminds me of the story of the principal who was mandated to administer standardized achievement tests to five- and six-year-olds. Knowing well that the reliability and validity quotients of such testing were extremely low and that asking young children to fill in bubbles next to the "right" answers was ridiculous and developmentally inappropriate, she met with the teachers to discuss how they would shape the culture of testing in their school. Disgruntled about what they had to do, the principal asked them how they might reduce the anxiety around these tests with families and children. In the past, the school had sent alarming letters home to families urging them to ensure their children had a good night's sleep and hearty breakfast on testing days. Also, teachers had been accustomed to spreading the students' tables around to prevent children's "copying." The principal and teachers wanted to discourage these practices only to discover that when the testing zealots heard of their plans, they accused the principal of requiring teachers to "cheat" on the tests. You can only imagine how demoralizing this was to her and the teachers whose visions of educating young children extended well beyond their standardized testing. Though many critics of public education, particularly those from the corporate world, promote "training" principals in efficient data management, and though so many school districts revolve around test scores, imagine what would happen if we "educated" principals for collegial inquiry, reflection, and public advocacy. Imagine what our schools would be if teachers and principals embraced those possibilities about which Eisner wrote.

Though in a quiet minority, some educational leadership scholars have envisioned school leaders as professionals who nourish and nurture human hearts and souls. Especially in the 1980s and 1990s, before our obsession with standardized testing was out of control, and when William Foster, William Greenfield, Thomas Sergiovanni, and Spencer Maxcy were writing prolifically, we turned our attention from the principal as manager of the building to the principal as leader of a rich educational culture in support of students' and adults' deep learning and well-being. Maxcy (1995) writes of such principals as contradicting the rigidity of traditional leadership frameworks and becoming thinkers who listen "to all voices" so as to promote an inclusive feel for leadership initiatives and activities (p. 479). In other words, he advocates collegial inquiry into what "leadership" means and how it might support deep and engaged learning.

Foster (1986), whose work was influenced by Greenfield, writes of principals who focus on the "promises" of their work, the hopeful possibilities. Foster states: "Each administrative decision carries with it a restructuring of a human life. ... In a special edition of the journal *Educational Administration Quarterly*, which honored the late Foster, Lindle (2010) reflects that Foster encourages our "striving for the ideal in schooling," creating spaces that are safe for thinking creatively, but even more so, for thinking "aloud" (p. 170). Moreover, Jenlink (2010) supports the notion that principals might "facilitate an alternative discourse" and be "socially engaged in the pedagogical work of democracy ... public pedagogy" (p. 307). Torres (2010) advocates for principals as "critical intellectuals" (p. 339) who embody the disposition that there is "never a perfect, definitive, or comprehensive understanding that cannot be challenged, debated, or critiqued."

These ideas challenge principals and teacher leaders to join collegially to study the context and culture of our schools and to explore together what generative leadership should look and act like—since "leadership is ... frameless, polyglot, and fluid" (Maxcy, 1995, p. 479). The values we place on one another, and the practical judgments we make on a daily basis as "critical intellectuals" (Torres, 2010, p. 339), have the power to shape an educational culture grounded in the intrinsic motivations discussed in the preface: *inspired lead learning, caring pedagogical artistry, nuanced curriculum understanding*, and *responsible professional autonomy*. This book has given us a rich guide to do so. We now need to make a commitment to learn together in the pursuit of wisdom—to be generous and generative with one another!

"We *Are* School Reform" (Greene, 2013, p. 12)

When we do not take charge of ourselves, our profession, our public schools, we experience what is happening today in American education: we are expected to follow others' scripts and notions of accountability, keeping our good thinking to ourselves. As Greene (2013) writes, "thinking originally about the way teaching practice affects society is an important skill to have as a teacher" (para. 15), and also, I might add, as a principal. Nicholas Kristoff (2014) recently published a column in *The New York Times* that encouraged professors not "to cloister [themselves] like medieval monks" (p. 11) because society needs them. Again, I think this message is for all of us! Society needs *us*. Using the "power of collaborations" (Behm, Rankins-Robertson, & Roen, 2014, para. 11), we can "foster dynamic, engaged student learning" and "turn [our] educational vision into daily reality" (preface). As a profession, we need to take on the challenges facing education today and deliberatively explore alternatives to the restrictions and limitations of the status quo. And then we must educate our publics.

Our world needs wisdom to make the right decisions, shape healthier cultures, and promote all human beings to flourish. If we honor the plural wisdoms among us, we will grow together as an educational community. When I was first assigned as a principal of a K–5 building, having been a middle grades teacher, I knew next to nothing about early childhood education, but my experienced, knowledgeable kindergarten teachers did. So, whenever I had a spare moment, I helped in their classrooms and learned so much from them. We read professional materials together, engaged in lively dialogue, deliberated over decisions. They helped me develop as an early childhood educator because they shared with me their wisdom.

As we grow, we stumble, we make mistakes, and we have regrets; yet, if we have created a culture of collegial caring, appreciation, and support, we will mature in our collegial wisdom in spite of ourselves. Just as fishermen who return from the sea must mend their torn nets with new rope to produce even stronger ones, we too must mend, reinforce, and support each other in our search of wisdom. We must practice *connected knowing* (Belenky, Clinchy, Goldberger, & Tarule, 1986) that cultivates an environment of reciprocity, humility, and generosity toward others. We, as teachers and principals, must muster up the courage to promote and "protect our good work" (Schwartz & Sharpe, 2010, p. 287), for our profession, but most especially, for all of the students we serve. Taking the long view, we educators must become generative, democratic leaders for our organizations and for our societies.

11

BUILD IT AND THEY WILL COME: A CROSS-CULTURAL CONVERSATION ON LEAD-LEARNING POSSIBILITIES AND CHALLENGES

It is hard. It's supposed to be hard. If it wasn't, everyone would be doing it. That's what makes it great. (Tom Hanks as baseball coach Jimmy Dugan, talking to his female ballplayers in *A League of Their Own*)

If we are serious about nurturing students' academic skills, then we need to keep them wrestling with ideas that speak to themes in society and in their own lives. (Linda Christensen, Rethinking Schools)

Trust each other again and again. When the trust level gets high enough, people transcend apparent limits, discovering new and awesome abilities for which they were previously unaware. (David Armistead, Professor)

Round One (R1)

Resonating with Jimmy Dugan and John Dewey, I unequivocally believe that Jim Henderson and his colleagues are engaged in an immensely challenging and supremely significant project—educating for democratic living and being. In this first of four rounds of interactive commentary, I have the delightful privilege of initiating a dialogue with an international group of distinguished educators around the promises and challenges associated with this book's major themes. It is our sincere hope that the ensuing conversation will further highlight the compelling nature of *Reconceptualizing Curriculum Development (RCD)* and additionally animate readers' interest in the disciplined, yet open-ended, collaborative study of democratic practice and personhood that is the book's core invitational call.

Over the last 20 plus years, I have engaged in somewhat similar efforts in teacher education. Working mostly with undergraduate teacher education candidates, and increasingly influenced by my involvement with Jim's ideas of RCD, I have attempted to embody and promote a holistic 3S pedagogy that, following research on my teaching candidates, centers on an open set of study topics that collectively, as a provisional heuristic, I've come to term critical democratic pedagogy (CDP). These overlapping, transacting, and recursively studied dimensions include but are not narrowly limited to: (1) promoting opportunities for responsible student *choice*, voice, and decision-making input; (2) nurturing a classroom *community* where a sense of belonging, trust, care, holonomy,[1] expressive experimentation, and constructive conflict negotiation thrive; (3) encouraging a *critical consciousness* that carefully scrutinizes personal and social issues of justice, power, fidelity, purpose, and inclusiveness in matters of educational policy and classroom practice; (4) fostering resourceful and courageous efforts of *advocacy* where candidates and their students engage in community problem solving designed to address perceived injustices and promote priority values; (5) sponsoring *authenticity* regarding student performances of real-world tasks directed toward meaningful concerns and audiences; and (6) supporting sound *accountability* to high standards of subject matter, self and social understandings, ones rooted in authentic work and compatible with inspiring predetermined *and* expressive outcomes.

In all, integral to the fidelity-rich, walking-one's-talk theme of embodiment addressed by Jen in chapter 3, the holistic and synergistic vision that permeates my exploration of CDP and its related dimensions is, in my mind, quite consonant with the personalized, egalitarian, civic-minded, disciplined, and open-ended spirit of RCD.

It has been my experience that while teaching candidates report that as students they have had little personal classroom experience with 3S pedagogy/CDP, in general they find its goals appealing and its artistry achievable, if challenging. They wonder, though, whether in the current high-stakes testing climate, they will be free enough to wedge out the wiggle space to practice and refine such artistry.

As the preceding chapters have well illustrated, the standardized management paradigm indeed represents an imposing challenge to the robust flourishing of 3S pedagogy. In this introduction to an international dialogue, I would like to address two themes related to lead learning engagement: (a) selected artistry and recommended activity associated with cross-paradigm critique and negotiation, and (b) meaningful and motivating schoolwork and its potential for moderating vicious cycles of student underperformance, public distrust, and intrusive surveillance of educators.

Cross-Paradigm Artistry/Activity

Underlining and extending perspectives shared by Wendy in chapter 5, I emphasize three points in this section. One is the nuance-enhancing, false dichotomy-disrupting power of "methodological believing" (MB) and "methodological doubting" (MD), as defined by Elbow (1986). These two inquiry processes are disciplined, complimentary, exemplary, and broadly applicable approaches when seeking to understand new and diverse ideas.

Assuming, as RCD commendably does, that one of the most legitimate goals in all inquiry endeavors is to develop an informed, empathic understanding of the relevant issues—an understanding that can serve as a prelude to the refined formation of one's own position—MB and MD are particularly instrumental in achieving this goal. MB represents a mindset wherein inquirers discipline themselves to look generously at focal ideas with the spirit of identifying the best reasons why someone would value those ideas. If confused, the inquirer further explores with an attitude: "I undoubtedly am missing something important. I need help in seeing more clearly the virtues of these ideas." As the yang to the MB yin, MD represents the open-minded skeptic's respectful but probing exploration of the possible distortions, unexamined premises, and potential unfavorable consequences adhering to the ideas' claims. In all, figuratively speaking, as evidence of achieving deep, embodied, holistic understanding, inquirers would be deserving of an "Oscar nomination" for their capacity to vividly portray the essence and implications of the studied ideas.

A second point constitutes a recommendation that, beyond initiating the vital network-supporting task of connecting with like-minded colleagues, lead learners deliberately s-t-r-e-t-c-h out to perceived adversaries and non-allies (including union representatives, if pertinent) and develop artistry in engaging them in sustained dialogue and meaningful study. Polarized and secluded in enclaves, too often we fail to develop comfortable, discerning relationships with those we see as our ideological opponents. When relatively rare dialogue does occur, it tends to be marked by the dogmatic, the demeaning, and/or the dismissive. Educators need to be lead professionals in breaking this alienating cycle, approaching these interactions as rich opportunities for deepening understanding, exploring common ground, voicing principled objections to perceived oppressive practices (as illustrated in Dan's gripping narrative vignette, see pp 2–3) and, wherever possible, forging strategic collaboration.

As a promising reflective practice, I would recommend that lead professionals engaged in cross-paradigm critique and negotiation preserve time at the tail end of their complicated conversations with ideological non-allies to discuss several prompts that might be framed "**d**eliberatively **d**ebriefing our **d**ialogue." This "3D" moment might address such considerations as:

- Where and why do you think we significantly agree/disagree?
- Must our differences preclude respectful transaction and/or strategic cooperation?
- How can our sense of integrity, our heartfelt personal identities, our evident and potential common interests, our best selves be enriched by such transaction and cooperation?
- Based on our deliberations, what new perspectives and previous standpoints do we each want to further consider? How might we proceed in doing so?

- To what extent did we converse with an optimal blend of candor *and* sensitivity, generosity *and* challenge? Were there moments when we felt unheard, shut down, dismissed?
- Do we want to continue this conversation? Why? Why not? If yes, then when? (Kelly, 2010)

My third point is this. As lead professional educators enact such communicative artistry, they are making a quintessential democratic investment in overturning our current divisive political climate. They are engaged in what Pinar (2007) terms their "professional calling," one marked not by passive consumption and delivery of knowledge but by courageous and pragmatic engagement in the "intellectual reconstruction of the public and private spheres." Could the work that Dewey called the supreme art in a democracy, the task of educating, entail anything less ennobling and demanding?

Insufficiently Meaningful Schoolwork and Vicious Cycles of Underperformance and Distrust

As Jim well articulates in the preface, RCD is grounded in the compelling research findings on motivation which indicate that the dominant system currently prevailing in business and school settings actually works against enhanced productivity, creativity, work satisfaction, and intrinsic motivation. Based on counterproductive regimes of external rewards and punishments, this system needs to be replaced by one which emphasizes the three key intrinsically motivating dimensions of Mastery, Autonomy, and Purpose (Pink, 2009). As Pink notes, "The science shows that the secret to high performance isn't our biological drive or our reward-and-punishment drive, but our third drive—our deep-seated desire to direct our own lives, to extend and expand our own abilities, and to make a contribution" (pp. 144–145).

In this light, one critical public intellectual task for lead learners is to help stakeholders understand the highly problematic dynamics of external control and rigid surveillance. A corollary to this task would be engaging with union leadership to insure that it viably and visibly supports the credible supervision of teachers. The public has a very legitimate interest *in trusting* that educators are responsible professionals who genuinely value and seriously engage in systematic processes of monitoring, critiquing, and improving each other's work. Presumably, such processes would result, on occasion, in the eventual dismissal of individuals seen not to be fulfilling their duties. Whether it did or not, it is imperative that the public palpably understands that the education profession reliably supervises itself.

A related urgent task for lead professionals, one embodying the recursive problem-solving and public-directed processes Chris addresses in chapter 4, is to carefully educate the public on how high-stakes testing significantly narrows the curriculum and undermines students' experience of meaningful work. Critics such as Debbie Meier (2002) and Bill Ayers (1993), among many others, provide compelling arguments how such testing is characteristically inauthentic, uninspiring, superficial, ambiguous, culturally biased, and alienating.

With students exercising their veto power on exerting effort in the face of uninspired work, public educators are caught in several vicious cycles. Intense external accountability, its often felt punitive quality, and its associated high-stakes testing regime reduce the meaningful nature of the curriculum. Consequently, students are less engaged, less affirmed, and underperform. At one level, students' underperformance frustrates teachers, depresses their expectations, and has them more inclined to be blind to what Boni, in her inspirational vignette at the beginning of chapter 1, distinctly does *not* overlook, i.e., students' inherent 'beauty' and limitless potential. At another level, students' underperformance and educators' failure to decisively counteract it diminish the trust the public invests in education. Growing distrust in educators and students intensifies the perceived need for more external accountability and surveillance. And so it goes.

Besides effectively educating the public and themselves about these vicious cycles, and the motivational and structural dynamics that deeply contribute to student underperformance, it seems vital that lead professionals practicing RCD also provide multiple stakeholders with compelling images of curricula that stimulate meaningful or authentic student work. In this regard, I find the work of the Coalition for Essential Schools particularly promising (see Meier, 2002; Meier, Sizer & Sizer, 2004). Effective across a broad range of student demographics, this work demands from students demonstration of credible mastery on life's enduring challenges—basic and exemplary intellectual, moral, and practical capacities that a democratic society should expect from maturing youth, future neighbors, and informed voters. These demonstrations typically involve such capacities as formulating a clear, personally meaningful research or action project, understanding competing perspectives, analyzing patterns of personal, institutional, and historical power, making connections across disciplinary boundaries, advocating social justice reforms, contributing to the local community, negotiating conflict, dealing with adversity and 'bad habits,' using multiple media, and displaying insightful self-understanding and critique. Evaluated by panels of peers, educators, and community members, at their best, these public exhibitions, evident also in the field of architecture (see Beth's chapter 7), evoke the kind of purpose-driven, mastery-oriented, self-directed explorations that Pink (2009) indicates represent the natural, defining motivational state of humans. Seeing these performances, so the hope goes, the public would more enthusiastically endorse the compelling authentic work of education—work that Petra reports in chapter 8 also supports impressive student performance on standardized tests.

It is my optimistic expectation that RCD with its lead-learning initiatives will nurture educators' capacities for energizing students' meaningful explorations of their world. 3S pedagogy is a form of teaching artistry that advances transactional, holistic relationships not only in the classroom but in the broader global community.

So, fellow chapter 11 participants, how do you react to the major themes in the book and/or my comments, in light of your own experiences and perspectives? I look forward to responding to your ideas in Round Four of this chapter.

Round Two (R2)

Tero's R2 Contribution

I am very grateful to Tom for his insightful observations of this significant and challenging RCD project spearheaded by Jim Henderson and his colleagues. In my brief comments, Tom's introduction works as a springboard for articulating my understanding and concerns about the current state of the curriculum field and this book's responsiveness to those concerns. Put succinctly, I believe Jim's project vitally addresses many serious shortcomings in the present practice of education, curriculum, and teacher policy, practices that have spread like a world-wide malign virus to which Pasi Sahlberg (2011) refers with his GERM concept (Global Education Reform Movement).

The logic of the GERM can be framed as follows: Accurately measuring the fever is fully equivalent to curing the disease. Education policy is seen as equal or reducible to assessment, without any need to refer to bigger political vistas—like what democracy could/should mean in our intensely interconnected world where the traditional sovereignty of the nation states has politically atrophied to regional territories of the global economy.

Democratic politics as a comprehensive public space for the complicated con-versation between consensus and dissension has been colonized by the economy with its strict norms of the 'liberalized' market. Resulting from the neoliberal and neoconservative revolutionary alliance since the collapse of the Soviet Union and its satellites, this development is arguably eating her children—like so often is the case in revolutionary historical turning points. The present social and politi-cal hegemony by the totalitarian market logic is in serious crisis. In my view, related to the unfolding of modernization at large, we are witnessing a further radicalization of the concept of rationality in terms of excessive instrumentality. Now, arguably, *economic thought is coterminous with rationality*. The only social and communal tie that is available on political agendas is calculative instrumentality. In all spheres of life, economic thought is setting the parameters for civic and rational action. The trajectory of rationality since the dawn of modernity has been characterized by the increasing abolition of existential questions from the agenda of rationality and, by implication, from the legitimate focus of education. The prevailing Cartesian rationality has reduced existence to thinking: *to be is to think* (methodically) and closer to our days: *to think is to calculate*.

In my genealogical big picture, this theoretic-historical-political background is echoed in this book's groundbreaking counter-efforts. The project is one among very few—if not presently unique worldwide—both to understand the complex horizontal and vertical forces creating the current educational crisis and, consequently, to forge an intellectually, organizationally, and pedagogically appealing attempt to effectively address the crisis.

From my perspective, one of the key progressive initiatives needed is the effort to relativize and dethrone what Bill Doll and I have named the Culture of Method. For far too long, and now inscribed in certain legislation, this Culture of Method has become the index of valid education research and teaching practice. This particular double bond to understand and practice education has been instrumental in de-intellectualizing both research and practice. In order to understand curriculum theory and practice through their defining characteristics of complexity, we need bigger visions than Method and assessment, ones that would situate our increasingly international education strategies, policies, theories, and practices in terms of horizontality and verticality. To position the teacher intellectually and—through teacher education curricula—as the center of these flows of knowledge would create the space for cultural, counter-hegemonic, transnational movements and sensibilities that may extend the professional competence of teachers and provide them with the knowledge and skills needed in negotiations for their public recognition and appreciation as professionals and intellectuals.

Consistent with this compelling quest for public recognition, Finnish teacher union texts that I've recently reviewed from the 1970s to the present strongly defend teachers' professional status, their freedom, and their distinctive competence to decide what policies should guide educational practice. The political efforts to shift the nation state toward the neoliberal *market state* have found no resonance among Finnish teachers. Rather, teachers across the party political spectrum are very consensual in their strict opposition to any efforts to privatize education, introduce other than teacher-driven tests, narrow the curricula to drilling for international comparisons, or endorse the extensive use of educational technology because of the "restricted curriculum notion inherent in computer programs" that may divert teachers' professional freedom and pedagogic judgment.

In the last instance, education is a political project, one between "science, ethics and politics" (Schleiermacher, 1983/1826). It is best viewed as a project preeminently about and for democracy. Despite its contested fame, "democracy is the best option among all the even worse alternatives." In my judgment, educationally, democracy has proven the most viable alternative to actualize human talents and potential. In that sense, the Finnish saying "equity is quality" resonates with the instigating idea of common schooling, *allgemeine Bildung*. Education is meant to help every single individual optimally flourish. Education is to be passionately supported not as a benevolent gesture from those in power but because it is a basic human right, fundamental in its nature as a prerequisite for fostering subjective transformation and social restructuring. It is this vital holistic integration of the self and the social combined with the academic subject that makes the 3S RCD advanced in this book so essential and inspiring for democracy projects around the world.

Aboudou's R2 Contribution

As a response to Tom's introductory comments, I definitely agree with Henderson and Gornik (2007) when they warned us not to expect congratulations for our efforts in leading the change for holistic 3S pedagogy. They advised us to be ready to be challenged. Thus, with much appreciation for Tom's insightful introduction, here I'd like to focus on RCD's leadership possibilities and challenges, viewed from a beginning African teacher's perspective. I hope that offering my colleagues an example of its potential application in an African setting might provide them fruitful food for thought.

As background, the education systems in most African countries fall into what Null (2011) refers to as the "systematic curriculum tradition" (p. 37). In Mali, there are two National Ministries of Education. One is in charge of primary and secondary education and the valorization of our national languages, and the other is in charge of higher education and scientific research. These two departments decide what, when, and how students must learn and how they will be assessed. In effect, "teachers are obliged to administer the latest drugs (or curriculum) efficiently, not question whether these drugs are appropriate with their students" (Null, p. 40). Given that teacher education programs in Mali have historically placed little emphasis on building the capacities to conduct the kind of reflective inquiries or deliberative conversations discussed in this book, it is not especially surprising that many Malian educators seem to appreciate the guiding, if inflexible, structure imposed from above. However, educators' relatively compliant acceptance of this top-down structure is certainly problematic when we know that for teaching to be meaningful, "teachers should be able to transcend everyday experiences to imagine the possibilities of what ought to be rather than the way things are" (Henderson & Gornik 2007, p. 68).

As I consider confronting this authoritarian culture, problems I foresee facing include teachers' lack of time and compensation, skepticism toward change, fear of the decrease in standard test scores, a strong cultural deference to elders, and teachers' union resistance, in the latter case particularly associated with the perceived problematic precedent of teachers engaging in unpaid study.

Reflecting on these challenges, I believe it's imperative to start my lead learning initiatives by discussing the aims of education with colleagues and interested stakeholders. Working with educators who don't share the view that education is meant "to turn students into free thinkers who can draw upon many fields of knowledge, pursue truth and solve problems" (Null 2011, p. 15) will be complicated if we do not start from the basic beliefs in which RCD is grounded. A key study resource on aims talking is Noddings' (2009a) work. According to her, "Aims-talk is to education what freedom is to democracy" (p. 332). She notes that "failure to engage in vigorous discussion of educational aims has marked the movement toward standardization and high-stakes testing" (p. 334). Thus, how can we shift the paradigm without discussing the things that lead us to where we are?

In Mali, a great place to start conversations and incubate ideas about RCD is in our 'tea groups.' Workers usually meet during weekends to have tea together and share their joys and sorrows. It would be promising to start a conversation about RCD in these relaxed and informal settings. During the tea group meetings, people characteristically expose their concerns and thoughts on reform and seek candid feedback from different and often interdisciplinary perspectives. These tea group settings are stimulating, expansive places where domestic and international news is discussed and where new possibilities and opportunities are identified and critically entertained. For all these reasons, I believe that exposing RCD in these settings will permit the lead professional to hear the broad range of individuals' genuine support, honest concerns, and constructive criticisms regarding RCD principles. In so doing, the lead professional is simultaneously simulating and promoting the democratic spirit and processes of cross-paradigm critique and strategic negotiation at the heart of RCD. In my mind, there may be no better natural setting for the RCD lead professional to receive constructive support and criticism.

Based on the cultural generation gap I stated above, I'd propose additional ingredients for successful RCD initiatives. These include acting humbly, not self-righteously, as youthful lead-learners; showing respectful, empathic understanding toward those who might question the wisdom or feasibility of RCD efforts; highlighting—through sharing and evoking personal stories—the intrinsic drive toward mastery, holonomy, and purpose that are core motivational features of human beings and of RCD; and having the first influential older people who find RCD compelling act as potential ambassadors when talking to their peers.

Afterwards, I foresee PLCs (Professional Learning Communities) being established based on the belief that "Collegial interchange, not isolation, must become the norm for teachers" (Henderson & Gornik 2007, p. 200). As critical friends, we will provide constructive feedback on each other's classes, drawing on the supportive but gently nudging ethos characteristic of the tea group setting. Additionally, we will incorporate the spirit of bricolage and collaboratively explore a wide range of available materials for their particularized 3S applications to our classroom practices and cultural norms.

Further foreseeable initiatives include giving talks at "ENSup," the teachers' training college, and making video conferences with Dr. Henderson, Dr. Kelly, and other RCD resources, assisted by the U.S. Embassy in Mali.

I conclude with enthusiastic optimism. I realize that for RCD to be successfully implemented in Mali and other African countries, teachers' practical wisdom capacity-building and their willingness to embrace this holistic pedagogy are essential. With dynamic leadership from lead professionals, I believe these criteria can be met. I envision that African educators, despite bad working conditions, will be highly motivated to turn this educational vision into actual classroom practices for the benefit of their students and the future of their countries.

Donna's R2 Contribution

In an era where so much of what happens in schools is rooted within "scientifically based" prescriptive models, it is a challenge to engage our imaginations to promote conditions for the greater discretionary space for teachers and administrators needed for RCD. Yet, how can we not? As educators work toward images of "career and college readiness" within the Common Core (CC) curriculum, they work toward promoting inquiry within that curriculum. Technically, the shift to the CC opens the door to increased focus on inquiry and deep understanding of less content. Consequently, teachers and administrators should be able to focus more deliberately on building meaningful experiences, and this should, in turn, promote greater discretionary space for teachers to promote meaningful learning. After all, how can we expect students to engage in meaningful inquiry if we deny teachers the opportunity to do so as they plan? To this end, I challenge myself and my colleagues to reconcile the promise of 3S pedagogy with the current reality of the CC.

Sadly, the tensions between foolproof (a.k.a. scientifically based) models of instruction and the potential for 3S understanding within the CC are irreconcilable under current conditions. Any efforts to reconcile the two will require third-order change within our schools. It will not be enough to simply change practices (particularly if the primary justification for such new practices is the designation of "best" that precedes it). Rather, it will require teachers and administrators to change the very way they see curriculum and teaching (Bartunek & Moch, 1987). While first order change involves making technical changes and second order change involves more ideological changes, third order change entails changing the capacities of stakeholders and the very culture in which they work based upon a clear and significant ideological shift. These changes represent what Seo and Creed (2002) identify as institutional contradictions.

For years now, under the cloud of NCLB, teachers and administrators have been monitored for covering as much content as possible in order for students to respond well on standardized tests, but the new standards require something altogether different: deep understanding of texts and complex problem solving. Ideally, these contradictions should, in and of themselves, create the conditions in which schools will change and through which teachers and administrators will acquire more discretionary space (Hlebowitsh, 2004), or as Tom notes, the "wiggle space to practice and refine such artistry."

The institutional ruptures created by the Common Core Standards (CCS) include the nature of work for both teachers and students. First, teachers shift from focusing so heavily on instruction to focusing instead on curriculum, and seeing curriculum as meaningful experiences that lead to deeper understanding instead of merely content coverage for the purpose of a test. Such refocus is a critical precondition for 3S pedagogy. Second, students' work shifts from accumulation of a large body of content covered on a test to analysis and problem solving for deeper understanding.

I realize optimism is rare in curriculum studies. Nevertheless, I believe optimism, or perhaps more to the point, *hope*, is necessary in order to move toward greater professional autonomy. That said, I believe the Common Core Standards introduce a critical junction for schools and for society—a juncture that necessitates images of inquiry inspired by Dewey (1916, 1938a). By articulating broad aims, such as career and college readiness, the standards have the potential to reengage the vital connections between school and society and point to curriculum as the engine for that engagement. How we imagine our society and ourselves will profoundly influence the form and function of the CCS. For this to happen, we must fight for a new image of "career and college ready"—an image that returns us to our democratic roots. This shift would evoke Ayers' (2013) image of a "dialectical push and pull" (p. 147) where the individual growth of students in schools is inextricably linked to the growth of society. To ensure this right direction—moving away from a market-driven school system and toward schools as agents for democratic living—we must have a faith like Dewey's. He believed in the potential of individuals to work toward something greater than themselves, and he believed that people working together could bring about progress. If we can work toward this "less competitive and more cooperative ethos" (Fishman, 2013, p. 128), then the CCS can have a far greater impact on students, teachers, administrators, and the curriculum than most of us might currently imagine.

Rosie's R2 Contribution

Thank you, Tom. I, too, have been influenced by the notion of holistic 3S pedagogy. Since 1995, my work with Jim has refined my teaching/learning beliefs. My contribution will be the intersection of our 2007 collaborative text, *Transformative Curriculum Leadership*, 3rd ed.; the development of the *Curriculum Leadership Institute* we established in 2009 at Kent State University; the development of the *Teacher Leader Endorsement Program (TLEP)* in 2010; and my years serving as assistant superintendent and superintendent in suburban public school districts from 2005 to 2013. I will build upon your two themes, and seek to leave the reader with legitimate, hopeful news of 3S teaching in practice.

"Culture eats strategy for breakfast" is a remark attributed to Peter Drucker and popularized in 2006 by Mark Fields, president of Ford Motor Company. Research indicates that no matter how far-reaching the vision or brilliant the strategy, neither would be realized if not supported by the culture (Fullan, 2001). Organizing for 3S education requires us to think differently about the culture of schools and how we have been affected by the schools we have created (Wheately & Kellner-Rogers, 1996). As assistant superintendent and superintendent, I had an ever-present sense of the power of culture on my leadership activities. 3S education would flourish and be sustained only through the creative use of our collective imaginations to recreate a school culture deliberately compatible with the dynamic of 3S education. Fullan (2001) calls this process "reculturing" and regards it as the *sine qua non* of progress. My challenge was to work with others to reculture schools within the wisdom paradigm. In my experience, human beings create their own realities through engagements with others and events. "We inhabit a world that is always subjective and shaped by our interactions with it" (Wheatley, 1994, p. 8). This reculturing was very hopeful because in spite of very difficult political and economic conditions,

I knew that "energy becomes an avenue to attainment" (Wheatley, 1994 pp. 4–5). I felt hopeful that the school environment would be created and invented by our presence in it. This notion gave rise to my work on the development of the *Teacher Leader Endorsement Program (TLEP)*. Fortified with the knowledge that life opens to possibilities through new patterns of connection, teacher leaders discovered new realities and expanding capacities. Our TLEP curriculum fosters energy for teachers to "reach out to grow the world into new possibilities; and reach out to others to create a new being" (Wheatley & Kellner-Rogers, 1996, p. 28). Learning designs created by teacher leaders serve as exemplars of this type of curriculum leadership and are being used in schools today. Additionally, as evidenced so vividly in chapter 9, inspiring currere narratives depicting successful 3S journeys of understandings for students and educators are available. Readers can view these video currere narratives of educators involved in our *Curriculum Leadership Institute* by logging onto http://www.ehhs.kent.edu/cli/.

Navigating obstacles within the school, between the school and the community, with unions and the larger political economy at the levels of local, state, and federal governments was part of my daily work. I made the decision to act as though there were no unaffected outsiders; *all* participated in creating conditions of our interdependence. I borrowed from Wheatley & Kellner-Rogers (1996) and believed that we evoke a potential that is already present; that everything and everybody is in a constant process of discovery and creating; that trial and error should be used to find what works; that any one solution is temporary with no permanently right answers. I operated on the assumption that people are intelligent, creative, adaptive, and meaning seeking. One small change could amplify to create large district changes.

As assistant superintendent, colleagues and I found the wiggle room to transform the grading and reporting practices and infuse authentic performances of understanding through learning designs. The purpose of our 3rd edition of *Transformative Curriculum Leadership* (2007) was to inspire the sustained practice of curriculum judgments attuned to student performances of 3S understanding. I set out to "walk the talk." I knew intuitively that Wiggins and McTighe's (2005) facets of understanding became the toehold teachers needed to make the evolutionary leap from standardized management (SM) to Curriculum Wisdom (CW). Teachers who chose to be involved were provided time for differentiated professional development to build their inquiry and reflective capacities. Not surprisingly under these conditions, the hidden and null curricula surfaced (see Henderson & Gornik, 2007, pp. 47–51). Values and assumptions about race, class, gender, and disability were explored in the classroom as an essential element of the curriculum and democratic morality. The work was challenging and time consuming, but teachers were encouraged and energized by students' life-altering performances of understanding. Both these exhibitions of students' work, as well as their teachers' capacity to evoke such high quality, were sources of inspiration for those teachers who were not quite ready for this high professional challenge.

Reflecting the sentiments of many, one such teacher said, "My second graders are capable of so much more than I realized. The decision to design learning based on deep understanding resulted in amazing discoveries and meaningful learning connections not only about the content, but themselves."

As superintendent, we passed a 7.9 school levy on the first attempt, submitted and were awarded over $3 million in federal, competitive grants for K–12 after-school programming, worked with local parks to revitalize a plot of school land into a preserve now used as a land lab open to school and community, and established a "Positive Energy Committee" comprised of *all* stakeholders committed to the committee's name. Through persistent exercise of wise curriculum judgments, we found people and situations in which 3S education was occurring and did our best to cultivate these practices. I was determined not to confine students, teachers, and parents into narrow roles. Stakeholders choosing to be involved in these projects experienced "freedom to" (Greene, 1988) come together as authentic individuals around 3S projects they could mutually pursue, even though I did not use that vocabulary. Rather than talking about "democratically inspired learning designs," I spoke of "enduring understandings" that would make learning much more meaningful for students. Rather than communicating about "gaining the public trust," we engaged in the "great conversation" (Volmer, 2010), on the community's turf at the community's convenience. People were "free from" (Greene, 1988) limitations and alienation, filled with energy and power, not confined to functions and levels. These manifestations of 3S pedagogy were important signposts-of-the-possible for others in the district who resisted and/or rejected this emerging culture, one in which education is seen not as a circumscribed march to a predetermined end, but as an ongoing, open-ended, recursive journey of understanding for students, teachers, parents, and the community at large. "Consciousness and creativity are inextricably linked in this always discovering world" (Wheatley & Kellner-Rogers, 1996, p. 26), and these powerful dynamics enabled us to take important steps toward building a democratically inspired culture that supported student, faculty, and community growth.

Wen-Ling's R2 Contribution

Tom, thanks for your meaningful thoughts on several of the book's lead learning and cross-paradigm critique themes. I found your ideas on promoting student performance and building public trust worthy of further consideration. However, in the brief space I have, I'd like to focus on the kind of journey of curriculum understanding I believe is necessary for Taiwanese English teachers, if they are to thoughtfully embrace the RCD ideas advanced in this book.

In Taiwan, the Republic of China (R.O.C.), the English language is regarded both as subject matter and as a foreign language taught formally and started in junior high schools. Since the government officially enacted a reform of the

curriculum for grades 1–9, mandating in 2001 that English must be taught beginning in elementary school, the national need for English teachers has increased
considerably. Numerous universities and colleges have offered English teacher
training programs to satisfy market needs. Scholars have published many topics in
the area of the language classroom, primarily in terms of teaching and learning.
However, few scholars have written about EFL (English as foreign language)
teachers themselves, especially concerning teachers' reflective practice on teaching
(Liou, 2000, 2004).

In 1996, the Executive Yuan of Taiwan R. O. C. produced *The General Report
Book of Educational Reform*, suggesting that teachers needed the capacity for curriculum development and design, innovative teaching, action research, and other
professional skills—in short, competence in providing quality education for students in Taiwan. Unfortunately, teachers don't have the background knowledge
in curriculum studies necessary to cultivate the requisite curricular capacities.
As such, one might reasonably ask how a system can expect teachers to achieve
the competences required as curriculum planners if they haven't been taught
how to meet those requirements. Current professional development programs
for English teachers tend to be lectures delivered by experts or workshops sharing experiences. Overall, these experiences are fragmented and unsystematic
(Tsai, 2004). Moreover, the "one-day teacher training" format, in which schools
typically provide on-the-job education for teachers two or three times a year,
is seriously limited because training programs seldom connect with teachers'
professional skills and curriculum knowledge. Tsai (2004) argues that optimal
teacher professional development can't be formulaic or intermittent but rather
must recognize the sustaining need to cultivate educators' resourceful problem
solving capacities through critical reflective inquiry and collegial dialogue on
priority educational aims, supportive institutional policies, and promising pedagogical practices. Such professional development honors teachers' voice, dignity,
and inherent drive to maximize their own and students' growth.

In my mind, the RCD advanced in this book resonates with and systematically extends the critical perspectives advocated by Tsai. As a visiting scholar to
Kent State University during the 2012 academic year, I had the absorbing experience of witnessing Dr. Henderson's embodiment of the study and practice of
3S pedagogy. I felt the inspiration and challenge that comes from dwelling in a
culture and curriculum saturated with trust and holonomy and nurtured through
dynamic processes of deliberation, dialogue, and hermeneutic inquiry. At the time,
I told myself I would apply this approach of curriculum development to design
my own curriculum leadership plan in Taiwan. Pursuing my intention, this semes-
ter I expect to invite five English teachers from different local high schools to join
me in a collegial professional community devoted to exploring the meanings,
processes, and challenges of enacting 3S pedagogy. In my role as lead learner, I
hope to introduce my colleagues to a broad range of study resources, including
Dewey's notion of reflective inquiry, Schwab's concept of deliberative artistry, and

Pinar's concept of complicated conversation. While I believe it will be vital to encourage teachers' pursuit of their own priority educational concerns, within my particular cultural context I also foresee rich emancipating potential in scaffolding issues that juxtapose management and wisdom paradigm perspectives on, for example, authoritarianism and democracy, predetermined and organic activity, positivist and hermeneutic conceptions of knowledge and inquiry. While I anticipate struggles along the way, I'm hopeful that the excitement of discovery, the synergy of collaboration, and the emotional bonds of community make the struggles meaningful and well worth experiencing.

Kauko's R2 Contribution

In Finland, the situation within the curriculum is both interesting and challenging. Reform should be ready in 2016, and this process will keep schooling issues regularly in discussion. Additionally, the last PISA measurement has generated new challenges as Finland's scores went down quite a bit. And although reform pre-information favorably forecasts increased possibilities for integration of different school subjects, one of the current main challenges for Finnish education is that our curriculum is far away from the ideals of a "progressive curriculum in our time" (see Hansen et al., 2008).

Following Rancière's lead (2010), I believe the progressivity of a curriculum is grounded in its commitment to promoting democratic living and being through a dedicated process of constructive, multiperspective engagement with "dissensus." In Finland, a key obstacle to democratic progressivity is the excessively abstract character of the curriculum. As a far cry from the kinds of authentic student performances Tom alludes to in this chapter's Round One introduction, the themes and examples that typify the Finnish curriculum are often remote from students' lived experiences.

How then should educators address this intangibility, this gap of abstraction between the curriculum and the real world? One representative of the Finnish rationale, our famous Hegelian philosopher and educator, J.W. Snellman (1806–1881), showed the way by stating that students should, in conscious, deliberate ways, make clear their relationship to the cultural tradition. They would not passively adapt to the cultural heritage, but instead be active subjects who would 'civilize' themselves in a critical, hermeneutic fashion (Snellman 1840/1982, pp. 161–167). As a representative of the dialectical *Bildung* tradition, Snellman sees, as do Greene (1988), Autio (2009b), and others, that the basis for self-construction resides in a positive concept of freedom. As Greene notes (1988, pp. 46 and 80), the results of these kinds of expansive, freedom-embodying, constructive processes are "to a large degree unpredictable." This existential nature characteristic of positive freedom places a tremendous responsibility on the practical wisdom of progressive educators who are called upon to help students thoughtfully negotiate the conflicting goals and multiple paths potentially available to them.

Finland has, in principle, very good possibilities for developing curricula in a "Snellmanian" progressive direction. Among the positive dimensions in Finnish schooling policy is the autonomous position of teachers. Based on a tradition of now 40 years, Finnish teachers thrive in a culture of public trust that affords them substantial didactical freedom. They can plan their teaching and put it into practice without significant control or interference from external authorities.

The other positive dimension in Finnish schooling policy is the absence of standardized testing, a liberating nonintrusion which helps teachers act creatively when developing their pedagogical ideas. And while Finnish teachers relish the freedom and professional autonomy they possess, I am convinced that they can greatly benefit from the distinct virtues of studying and practicing the kind of 3S pedagogy inherent in this book's vision of RCD. Drawing on my experiences as an elementary teacher and a university scholar, the short list of these RCD virtues that I'd identify are: (a) promoting critical inquiry and collaborative deliberation focused on cultivating democratic capacities and sensibilities amidst inevitable dissensus, (b) designing motivating opportunities for authentic student performances, and (c) expanding meaningful cross-disciplinary curricular integration. Japan's impressive curricular integration work (see Arani, 2008) provides a valuable complement to this book's emphasis on 3S teaching.

In all, I look forward to playing an active role as a lead professional within Finnish education in the promotion of the RCD advanced in this book.

Round Three (R3)

Donna's R3 Contribution

The power that comes from reading everyone's contributions is the reassurance that hope transcends geographical and professional boundaries. I appreciate the messages—sometimes subtle—of optimism throughout the contributions. In an era of standardization where the very word "curriculum" is losing its foothold in many professional conversations, this level of international optimism is critical. As Tero, Aboudou, and Rosie note, education is political. This is undeniable. As such, we could get lost in the frustration of those in power controlling what happens in schools, but instead we look to democratic ideals. From these images, we are able to forge our hope for a curriculum that supports 3S pedagogy. As Rosie notes in her references to reculturing and her account of reculturing schools as both an assistant superintendent and superintendent, we must reculture our field. To do this, we must acknowledge, as Rosie does, that there are no unaffected outsiders. While we recognize how our work is connected globally, we must simultaneously recognize the gaps in what is and what can be. Kauko notes this gap and challenges us to explore how to connect our ideals with our current realities. With this in mind, I agree with Rosie that we create our own realities. I would add that we create those realities within the confines designed and sustained by those in power. As such, the realities we create are approximations of our ideals. To achieve these approximations, we need principled guidance: key bases from which we work within the messiness of today's schools—guidance offered by RCD and 3S pedagogy.

Rosie's R3 Contribution

Imagine … imagine … imagine if all seven of us could participate with a cadre of Finnish, Malian, American, and Taiwanese educators in a Malian "tea group." The inviting nature of "tea groups" in Aboudou's description convinces me that this would be a great way to "start conversations and share joys and sorrows." The spirit of these conversations gets at the heart of practical wisdom and "the capacity to judge rightly in matters relating to life and conduct," as defined in the *Oxford English Dictionary*. *Imagine* if we could agree to use each other as "critical friends" (Barth 2001), to collaboratively study and examine our practice "moving beyond congenial interactions to collegiality and deep deliberations" (Henderson & Gornik, 2007, p. 206), to embrace Donna's challenge to "reconcile the promise of 3S pedagogy with the current reality of the Common Core" in the United States. *Imagine* the interplay: the Finnish with strict opposition to any efforts to narrow the curriculum or privatize education; the Malians and Americans who variously struggle to resist cultural deference to elders, union leaders, change, and the appeal of standardization; the five Taiwanese English teachers being newly introduced to reflective inquiry, deliberative dialogue, and complicated conversations. The energy in the room would be palpable. *Imagine* if we continued the conversations with these questions: What do you wonder about in your teaching practice and why? Why is this issue important to you? What experiences and perspectives brought you to ask this question? Who would benefit from addressing this question? (Samaras, 2011). *Imagine* if we used these tensions to examine our "lived practice" (Samaras, 2011, p. 10) and our own professional growth and learning. *Imagine* if we could move the conversation to position the teacher as the center of "flows of knowledge," in Tero's words, which may "foster the extended professional competence of teachers and provide them with the knowledge and skills needed in negotiations for their public recognition and appreciation as professionals and intellectuals." *Imagine.*

Aboudou's R3 Contribution

Chapter 11 colleagues, it was a true joy reading your remarkable Round Two responses. I was enticed by your eloquence and by the thought-provoking, relevant themes each of you discussed. Again, given space limitations, I'd like to discuss certain insights I pondered as I was reading your contributions. Specifically, I'll discuss Rosie's exemplary leadlearning and Tom's insights about encouraging voice, caring, trust, and belonging within our schools.

Rosie's superintendent leadership much appealed to me. She not only encouraged coworkers and teachers to embody caring pedagogical artistry, but also sought capacity-building opportunities for teachers to undertake 3S pedagogy in their classes. I believe her inspirational contribution will serve as fruitful food for thought in activating similar commitments in other administrators.

I support Tom's advocacy of critical democratic pedagogy. Too often in schools, students are considered immature and unable to make wise decisions. When educators perceive and treat students in this demeaning fashion, I fear they perpetuate a vicious, self-fulfilling prophecy. If we consider them as irresponsible and incapable, they'll behave accordingly. How can they develop their best 'selves' without recognizing these best selves in what they are learning? How can they develop a sense of belonging and trust, care, and problem-solving competence if they do not experience these dynamics in classrooms? Even more, how can teachers positively transform their classrooms if they are not regularly treated with these qualities by their hierarchical superiors?

Barth (2010) noted that "Few schools operate democratically. ... Through what we teach in the 'hidden curriculum' we succeed in conveying to students that democracy is a fraud" (p. 12). Under leadership like Rosie's, democracy can be a lived experience where students are center-stage and where teachers *and* students are seen as partners, not merely targets in the change process (Hargreaves and Shirley, 2009).

To conclude, I believe in the need and potential feasibility of RCD anywhere in the world. While immense challenges exist, advocates of RCD need to act as if RCD can be feasible, if introduced with clarity, fair-minded respect for the local culture, humility, self-critique, and a sustaining commitment to constructive cross-paradigm dialogue and negotiation. Administrators, teachers, and stakeholders need to be willing to undergo their own journeys of 3S understanding. I believe inspired examples and negotiation that embody the above qualities can stimulate that willingness. Then, once teachers embody RCD, they can actually feel it as their responsibility to facilitate their students' journey. After all, if teachers do not accept to go on their own journey of understanding, how can they help their students to do so (Henderson & Gornik, 2007)?

Wen-Ling's R3 Contribution

Hi, chapter 11 colleagues! Your insights and democratic commitments definitely inspire my forthcoming efforts with the five English teachers to whom I alluded in Round Two. Thanks so much for these gifts. Here I'd like to direct my comments to Kauko. Teacher status and curriculum in your country definitely interest me. Teachers are trusted by the public and have autonomy and academic freedom. You note, however, that an obstacle to democratic progressivism is the abstract character of the curriculum resulting in coursework that is too distant from students' lived experiences. In fact, teachers in Taiwan face the same situation. Even though a number of universities have created graduate schools of curriculum and instruction, few know what curriculum construction actually entails.

The Ministry of Education of R.O.C. (Taiwan) established 12-Year Compulsory Education to increase national and international competitiveness and prepare students for twenty-first-century living (2011). It emphasized multifaceted, vivid, active teaching. The MOE provided substantial grants to promote teacher mastery in subject areas; moreover, many teachers have been recruited and coached to train others. Obviously, the MOE is very concerned about educational policy and reform. In order to promote student performance, the MOE has held numerous symposia and workshops to foster teachers' curricular capacities.

In Taiwan, teachers also have some freedom depending on their school level. They can decide what they want to teach using materials given by schools or chosen by them, but can teachers answer the following curriculum questions: "What knowledge is most worthwhile? Why is it worthwhile? How is it acquired or created?" (Schubert, 1986, p. 1). I quoted Schubert's words because "(w)ithout direct consideration of *what* is worthwhile to know and its correlates of *why* and *how*, [all curriculum] activities are devoid of defensible meaning, purpose, and direction" (1986 p. 1, author emphasis).

Truly, the Grades 1–9 Curriculum Reform emphasized "school-based curriculum, cooperative instruction, and professional autonomy" and aimed at cultivating students': (a) basic English skills, (b) interest in learning English, and (c) understanding of native and foreign customs. This reform failed because the MOE did not prepare teachers well in curriculum knowledge and curriculum integration.

As a participant in Kent State's Curriculum Leadership Institute and an observer in its Teacher Leader Endorsement Program, I believe that the RCD content and process are valuable because they: (a) help teachers engage in curriculum study and practice to develop their own grasp of teaching for 3S understanding; (b) cultivate teachers' capacities for reflective inquiry through deliberative conversation; (c) lead teachers to undertake a journey of self-understanding so as to become democratic historical agents; and then (d) facilitate their students' personalized journeys of understanding.

It is my fond hope that, in networking with you, our fellow book colleagues, and innumerable other educators, the compelling ideas exemplified in this book can stimulate effective RCD initiatives in Finland, Taiwan, Mali, the United States, and throughout our highly interdependent world. I am convinced that our world could become a more safe, sustainable, democratically enriched and mature global community, were such initiatives to potently proliferate.

Kauko's R3 Contribution

My first comment applauds Aboudou for highlighting Noddings's priority emphasis on the importance of aims talking. I do so because the insight "aims-talk is to education what freedom is to democracy" could—and should—be one of the main guidelines in Finnish contemporary curriculum reform. Unfortunately, during the curriculum reform period from 1992 to 1994, Finnish teachers had aims-talks for only 20 minutes and, given this restricted time allotment, those talks couldn't adequately address fundamental values. Essentially, the same constricted model continued during the reform of our university policy from 2007 to 2010, one where planned, deliberate, collaborative discussions of central guiding values were nearly nonexistent. While we have commendably resisted standardization and high-stakes testing, experiencing this patterned drift toward "neoliberal" education policy in Finland has me feeling considerably concerned.

So, after seeing this kind of "development" for over 20 years, it was refreshing to read Donna's optimistic thoughts of *hope*, which I agree we do need within curriculum studies, research, and reforms. Hope and certainly affirmation of teachers were also encouragingly evident in the perspectives of all of my chapter 11 colleagues, each in her/his own way indicating that one of the key constructive catalysts when moving away from a market-driven school system to a democratic one is teachers' greater professional autonomy. This culture of professional autonomy is a preeminent value that Finnish teachers substantially experience. Hopefully, it is one that they will steadfastly preserve in the future.

Grounded in this Culture of Trust, it should be quite possible to endorse Dewey's deep faith in human beings: by using our nearly infinite potential we can flourish individually, and by working together we can add progressivity in our increasingly interdependent lives.

Tero's R3 Contribution

I will try to briefly summarize my impressions about the RCD project and how I see its significance through my North European and Finnish-Estonian eyes.

I received my education through the Finnish curricula that are affected in quite a unique way by both Anglo-American and North European *Bildung/Didaktik* traditions. These two traditions are considered "very different intellectual systems" (Westbury, 2000). In fact, the present state of curriculum design in Finland could be arguably described as a state of intellectual and terminological confusion. On the one hand, *Didaktik* ("didaktiikka" in Finnish) still exists in teacher education programs and, to a lesser extent, in official documents. Crucially, it has helped foster a certain vital immunity against standardization, rigid accountability, and privatization, not so much among the Finnish state and education stakeholders, but particularly among Finnish teachers and teacher educators. On the other hand, however, especially prominent in the current moment is the domination of the Anglophone neoliberal curriculum with its demands of standardized performativity. Increasingly, Finnish curriculum is being colonized by Anglophone rhetoric of learning, skills, and competences.

In my view, the most serious theoretical dilemma in the curriculum tradition before the reconceptualization initiative spearheaded by Bill Pinar and others is the void of any convincing account of human mind, psyche, subjectivity, agency and their relations to culture, society, and the world. The whole theory parade from behaviorism to its more cognitive cousins arguably shares the same mechanistic logic where the assumed progressive shift from "behavior" to "cognition" is just the internalized repetition of external behavior schemes. This cavernous void of subjectivity foregrounds an emphasis on asubjective performance, outcome-oriented education policy, and curriculum designs that give that distinctive mechanistic, commodity flavor to the whole enterprise of neoliberal education.

By significant contrast, *Bildung* and *Didaktik* theories, more prominent in the pre–World War II era, echo Immanuel Kant's (1724–1804) Copernican revolution of mind. In these theories, mind is not the "mirror of nature." Rather, we humans are meaning-making creatures who, in principle, are capable of cutting the chain of habitual propensities in our actions. This insight was instrumental to Kant's moral philosophy, the quintessence of which is the *freedom* to choose and to make subjective judgments amidst the determinations of reality. This moral sphere makes education educative, as students and teachers engage in ongoing judgment of what knowledge is of most worth, when, and why. I appreciate Wen-Ling's emphasis on these central curricular questions. A classic statement that symbolizes this intimate link between the pedagogic and the moral is: "Scratch a good teacher and you will find a moral purpose." At its best, an emphasis on the moral shifts teaching from transmission to transformation, as the curriculum is no longer test preparation but a complicated conversation where all participants at every level think about the basic curriculum questions regarding the worth of and interconnections between the subject matter and the related subjective and social dynamics (see Autio, 2014).

To its significant credit, this book's RCD project vitally recognizes distinct, distasteful dimensions of the neoliberal agenda and seeks, through probing study and fair-minded cross-paradigm critique and negotiation, to address these problematic dimensions in the process of judiciously pursuing practices that aspire to both cultivate and balance individual flourishing and democratic community. In all, I sincerely believe that the RCD inquiries, deliberations, and actions reflected in this book will have much to offer by way of stimulating thoughtful work in curriculum and pedagogy, in Finland and around the world.

Round Four (R4)

Certainty lost. Freedom: Chilling … and thrilling. (Tom Kelly, responding to an Oprah Magazine challenge to describe one's life in 6 words)

Peace cannot exist without equality. (Edward Said, *Humanism and Democratic Criticism*)

If you want to make peace with your enemy, you have to work with your enemy. Then he becomes your partner. (Nelson Mandela, *Long Walk to Freedom*)

What a pleasure to read the enlightening perspectives of my chapter 11 colleagues. In concert with earlier chapters, they help inspire my concluding Round Four commentary. My ideas here are meant to resonate with this book's liberating assessment of the Tyler rationale and with its bulls-eye recognition of: (1) the intimate interdependence of the individual and the community; and (2) the primacy of educators enacting a holistic, 3S pedagogy conducive to fulfilling their supreme professional calling: educating persons and shaping culture for flourishing democratic living. While space limitations restrict extensive elaboration of my ideas, these restrictions can affirm one of the book's central developmental themes: there is always more to study, to unpack, to integrate, to transact, to transform.

Responsible Guidance Demands Orderly Designing of the Curriculum

Educational leaders are legitimately expected to provide a responsible, orderly designing of the curriculum so that those in their charge can journey through an optimal course of study. Like parents, educators come to realize that fulfilling this curricular and pedagogic responsibility entails striking a shifting and paradoxical balance between planting roots and cultivating wings, between knowing when to hold on and when to let go. Because the balance is elusive, it is common to err by providing too little and/or too much responsibility and order. How should conscientious educators of any ideological persuasion seek to navigate these difficult straits between the Scylla of insufficient guidance and the Charybdis of excessive control? Reflecting the book's central themes, I share particular problem-solving perspectives in the overlapping sections below.

Life's Unpredictability and Interdependence Compel Evidence-Informed, Artistic, Authentic, and Collaborative Revisioning

There's little doubt that educational research has made important pedagogic advances in a number of significant areas, e.g., in reading, motivation, inquiry, conceptual understanding and cooperative learning. These and other "scientifically based best practices" offer promising protocols and provide potentially important references as educators conscientiously design and implement the curriculum.

There's also little doubt to those with classroom experience that a torrent of confluent factors needs to be judiciously channeled in order for optimal learning to flow. Among the many potent streams in play are the historical, cultural, conceptual, motivational, and maturational forces within each student *and* teacher that continuously swirl in the dynamic vortex of group and institutional setting, all bubbling in variable densities of stability, transience, and immediacy.

This ceaselessly fluid, interpenetrating quality of life supports the strong hypothesis that boundaries and relationships between phenomena (e.g., the conscious and unconscious, the personal and social, the past, present, and future, mind and body, text and context, objective and subjective) are permeable, interconnected, reciprocally influencing, and mutually constitutive. From this hyphenating perspective, one can perhaps sense why certain advocates might feel strongly about the imperative of adopting a holistic 3S pedagogy.

Amid this voluminous complexity, it is also understandable that policy makers, technocrats, external curricular "experts," and various teachers, seeking solid ground, might feel a desperate, preemptive compulsion to funnel this comingling flood of variables into highly prefabricated, sealed, and measurable containers. In this context, we might recall Aboudou's allusion to the comforting appeal of top-down mandates that some teachers experience, and Kauko's citing Maxine Greene's observation about the existential anxieties inherent in the unpredictability associated with human freedom.

The fixating dream of creating "foolproof," "scientifically based" curriculum and pedagogy is nightmarish to this book's contributors and to many others who find it difficult not viewing this dream as delusional, as fundamentally representing both a futile, trust-corroding misunderstanding of the adaptive artistry essential to successful teaching and a lamentable misuse of precious professional development resources. Reflecting on administrative overreach, Hargreaves and Shirley (2009) offer this critical observation:

> Mandated targets, endless testing, scripted programs, a tsunami of spreadsheets, profusions of standards, banks of rubrics, and overwhelming emphases on basics—these are the things that drive teachers to distraction. (p 87)

A disturbing distraction generated by this mandating regime is the ironic undermining of responsible authentic assessment.[2] Authentic assessment seeks to evaluate the actual or expressive (Eisner, 1994), not only the predetermined, targeted outcomes of experiences. Given realities of unpredictability and interdependence, educational outcomes inevitably include both the hidden curriculum—that which is different from what curriculum and teacher explicitly intend—and the null curriculum—connections and perspectives overlooked, undermined, mystified. An important conclusion to be drawn here is this: expressive outcomes are inherent in teaching. Categorically ignoring them and exclusively focusing on evaluating predetermined targets constitute failing to account for and to be sufficiently accountable to what actually transpires in schools.

Hargreaves and Shirley (2009) note a further distraction generated by the outsized imposition of external mandates. Distinguishing evidence-informed accountability from data-driven standardizing accountability, and portraying the former as a responsible conscience and the latter as an overregulating Grand Inquisitor, they criticize autocratic and technocratic proponents of the latter for having "little time for artistry" (p. 29) and for undervaluing and overlooking a key source of authentic educative assessment, the goldmine of instructive data that is students' voice. Based on extensive research conducted by Ron Ferguson (tripodproject.org), educators can now act on well-supported findings that student perceptions of their teachers' instructional performance represent valid perspectives that can narrate connections between teacher pedagogy, student engagement, academic achievement, and whole school climate. As Aboudou noted, Hargreaves and Shirley frame this consultative teacher-student relationship in terms of viewing students as active partners in the change process.

To summarize this section, given the irrepressibly fluid transactions across multiple spheres of life and their resultant unpredictability and complexity, it is inevitable that educators will continually need to check their compasses and stay attuned with students about how the curricular journey is proceeding. Unanticipated construction and needed detours plus educative sidetracks and promising redirections will generate ongoing, on-the-ground revisions of original plans. This adaptive orienteering, productively and flexibly mapped in this book, becomes a defining characteristic of effective teacher education and enlightening curriculum development.

But the need for *revisions* presumes the presence of original visions. I take up this matter of aims talking in the next section.

Becoming Critical Friends of Each Other's Mind: Responsible Guidance Requires Holonomy-Enhancing, Inherently Pragmatic, "Strong Democratic" Aims-Talking

Aims talking is vital philosophical talk that is also immensely practical. It allows educators to provide helpful 'directions' toward an illuminated, desired end. Yet, for a host of reasons, it is typically overlooked or seen as an afterthought: (a) it tends to be time-consuming, conceptually difficult, and inconclusive; (b) it's a moot topic because predetermined standards are seen to incontestably dictate the curriculum; (c) it palpably pales when counterposed to the urgent needs of practical daily lesson planning. Underdevelopment of teachers' aims-talking potencies appears to be a transoceanic phenomenon, as Aboudou, Kauko, Tero, and Win-Ling all note insufficient time given to such communicative capacity building.

Given perpetual restrictions in time and resources, why should we invest in expanding the sophistication of teachers' aims talking? With multiple audiences in mind, I offer six interrelated reasons. Each represents foregrounding a different feature of what is, essentially, one mosaic.

1. To be better able to offer calm, clear, well-considered, and compelling responses to the inevitable student inquiry—"why are we doing (studying) this?"
2. To support the democratic principle that the 'governed' deserve sound reasons from authorities as an informed basis when the former are expected to give their consent to the latter.

3. To better 'psychologize' the curriculum and hence to enhance the engagement, achievement, and institutional loyalty that such motivated participation typically advances.
4. To better embody a MB and MD[3] educative process of discussing across contentious value positions[4] (a) competing curricular priorities and (b) the credibility, possible conflation, and often overlooked multiplicity of means-ends relationships.
5. To help oneself, one's students, colleagues, or other stakeholders determine when to advocate for constructive change and how best to do so, strategically, ethically, and prudently.[5]
6. To help catalyze, at an identity level, a liberating, non-ideological, paradigm-crossing belief in oneself as a public intellectual[6] and ecological cosmopolitan.[7]

The salutary implications of educators developing these aims-talking capacities could be monumental. In comfortably acknowledging the core reality of dissensus (Ranciere, 2010), educators' "strong democratic talk" (Barber, 1984)—generous and respectfully critical toward one's own and others' perspectives—sets a potently felicitous tone to explore, indeed to create, common ground in the process of expanding constructive problem solving across differences. Threading this book is the conviction that in classrooms and other public forums, including inviting places comparable to the Malian tea group setting of which Aboudou speaks, teachers as democratic lead learners should facilitate the examination of culture-shaping and contested paradigmatic ideas and values.

Furthermore, strong aims-talking teachers walk the talk of the American Constitution. They seek to transform hierarchical relations into ones more egalitarian and collectively self-governing; they embrace the community organizer's core rule of never doing for others what they can do for themselves; and they guide student relationships with teachers away from an "I obey" subservience toward more motivational, internally owned stances of "I agree," "We agree," "We decide." In short, they transform the rhetoric of democracy into a non-fraudulent, lived reality.

Responsible Guidance toward Thriving Democratic Practice Compels Thoughtful Reculturing

The reconceptualizing of teaching artistry, leadership, and curriculum central to this book is, and must be, part of a larger effort to reculture education. As Rosie, referencing Fullan (2001), observed in her Round Two commentary, "Research indicates that no matter how far-reaching the vision or brilliant the strategy, neither would be realized if not supported by the culture."

The reculturing task before us is formidable. Despite whatever noble intentions exist, the current conditions of autocracy and technocracy tend to metastasize "trickery and treachery" in oversight and data reporting (Hargreaves and Shirley, 2009, p. 39) and function to commit the capital crime of undermining the kind of synergistic trust that Confucius determined is the signature social bond without which a government and its representatives cannot legitimately stand (O'Neill, 2002, p. 3).

Given these systemic forces and the cynicism they can breed, compounded by a Manichean political culture wherein superficial sound bites and ad hominem barbs assault conceptual depth and corrode civil community, are there any non-Pollyannaish bases to hope that matters can substantially improve? Hargreaves and Shirley certainly think so. Drawing on extensive research, their book, *The Fourth Way*, illuminates multiple promising paths toward constructive reform, guided by what they identify as various horizons of hope, pillars of purpose, principles of professionalism, and catalysts of coherence. Importantly, while their focus is not at the crucial level of curriculum development and personal narrative characterizing this book, essentially all the ideas they advocate support the curriculum wisdom paradigm being advanced here.[8]

Zeroing in on matters more specifically curricular, Donna's Round Two and Three contributions inspire me because I intuit her as consciously *choosing* to snatch hope from its often fragile perch. Donna instructively points us to features of the Common Core curriculum that, in its current infancy, gurgle with democratic potential. These include its emphasis on critical thinking skills, close reading of texts, more depth and less coverage, and career and college readiness. Donna's faith in the power of the possible mobilizes me to ponder what priority ideas and connections we educators should seek to probe and *uncover* and how we can help to optimally shape the transition into new territory richly hospitable to all citizens.[9]

There are definitely additional encouraging signs. For example, we know that successful activism becomes even more possible when backed by powerful business interests. Google undoubtedly deserves such a designation and, in a *New York Times* column (Friedman, 2014), Google's VP in charge of hiring is quoted as saying "test scores are worthless ... We found that they don't predict anything." With near absolute absence of facetiousness, I'd say that what Google is looking for are graduates of the curriculum perspectives portrayed in this book.[10] They're looking for individuals who have "the ability to process on the fly ... to pull together disparate bits of information." That is, to make wise, integrating judgments that "see things together." Additionally vital are qualities the VP labels "emergent leadership" (the confident ability to take initiative in a group problem-solving context as well as the selfless recognition to know when to step back and let others take charge). The VP captured this balanced blend of assertiveness and ownership, humility and open-mindedness as follows:

> The people ... who we want to hire will have a fierce position. They'll argue like hell. They'll be zealots about their point of view. But then you say, 'Here's a new fact,' and they'll go, 'Oh, well, that changes things; you're right.'"

Friedman puts the presence of these countervailing forces this way: "You need a big ego and a small ego in the same person at the same time."

This dynamic duality seems muscular in its enlightening and emancipating implications for cultural critique and for curriculum and professional development. In general, the reconciling coexistence of big and small ego disrupts the dominant dichotomizing contention that passionate advocacy precludes honest examination and self-critical acknowledgment of the legitimacy of disconfirming data and associated alternative viewpoints. To advance these dimensions of emergent leadership, reconceptualized curricular efforts might seek to encourage important developmental moments in democratic dialogue, suggestively represented in such expressions as "I strongly believe this," "Oh, I wasn't aware of that," "I'm now not sure," "Maybe I'm wrong," "You could be right," "I need to study this more and talk to different people," "I want to be informed, fair-minded, and proud in the conclusions I draw and the actions I take."

That powerful corporate forces find the leadership capacities of RCD graduates attractive doesn't mean they'll embrace another corollary that seems to follow, i.e., the decoupling of teacher advocacy from reflexive charges of indoctrination and from alleged violations of "needlessly neutered" notions of neutrality (Said, 2004, p. 140), accusations that can function to de-intellectualize and silence teachers' critical public voice, intimidating them into "gracious submission."[11] Subordination to the will of the powerful is antithetical to the defining characteristics of a public intellectual—illuminating and challenging the demystifications and exploitations of power, with courage and intellectual integrity (Said, 2004). Such expectations for teachers to be public intellectual leaders represent a tall order, demanding a dramatic cultural shift in the current education landscape. Yet as this book's critically pragmatic approach to transformation advises, small-scale beginnings can ripple throughout a system into powerful multiplier effects.

Rosie's contributions entrancingly echo this transformative perspective. Her sophisticated change initiatives were directed at democratic capacity and culture-building aims that transcended technical and ideological preoccupations and synergized into programs big and small, institutionalized and individualized, holistic and holonomy-heightening. Particularly inspirational to me are Rosie's (a) astute attention to the power of accessible language,[12] evidenced in her avoidance of academic jargon and her evocative "Positive Energy Committee," (b) her foundational affirmation of the individual's immanence as a perpetual shaper of culture, not merely its bearer, and (c) her optimistic embrace of the provisional, the emergent, the "always discovering." These encouraging sensibilities intertwine in her twin synergizing beliefs regarding the perpetual presence of a transcendent potential and the culture-transforming potential of small changes.

Concluding Remarks for This Moment: Seeing Together in 4D

Intending to resonate with my fellow book contributors, I conclude this temporary culmination of my own long journey of understanding with these hopefully opening, closing words. In very broad terms, to fulfill its aim of providing responsible guidance to all in addressing the challenges and possibilities that life presents, the curriculum universally needs to help us understand and thrive amidst these irrepressible forces: the irreducible interdependence of ideas and people, life's unpredictability and diversity, and the complexity and existential freedom that inexorably inheres in our very being in the world. In various ways awaiting our best collaborative deconstructive and reconstructive efforts, these forces appear as insistent fact, consistent obligation, and persistent opportunity. In multiple senses, we need to develop our capacities to see together with extraordinary, 4D vision, 360 in its horizontal and vertical integration. We need *disciplined study* that vigilantly holds our own confirmation biases in check and draws on the ever-evolving insights that intelligent method, social/scientific research, and philosophical and artistic expression richly afford us. However, we also need critically pragmatic *discretionary* judgment to problem solve decisions that educators and other professionals clairvoyantly know cannot be impeccably scripted/forecasted, despite sophisticated technology, advanced algorithms, and other means for attempting to tame the nature of our world.

And despite the anxious, if understandable, concerted efforts of some of our fellow humans to preserve what is seen as special territory, and thus, from the perspective of the whole, to try to go it alone, we all need much *dialogue* across *differences*, if we are to understand the signature forces cited above and thus to strengthen our freedom and security in the context of our collective destiny. The book's authors believe that the reculturing, recursive dialogue to which we are called is dichotomy-disrupting, justice-seeking, linguistically sensitive, synergistically generous, and respectfully critical in the unifying spirit of cross-paradigm study and strong democratic talk. By contrast, we do not believe we are being narrowly ideological, self-serving, nor Don Quixote-like. So, while we soulfully see RCD and 3S pedagogy as providing responsible curricular guidance in engaging the challenges our world faces, it is in the emergent leadership spirit of humility, heft, and hope that we invite ongoing dialogue with you. We have all diligently sought to make our invitations to join this complicated conversation appealing ones. As we doggedly continue our inclusionary efforts to expand the vibrancy of democratic living, we enthusiastically welcome your unique and value-adding participation.

Endnotes

1   Holonomy is a concept permeating this book. It conveys the notion of autonomy and wholeness coexisting within a context of interdependence and community support.

2 See my Round One commentary on authenticity.

3 MB and MD refer to Methodological Believing and Methodological Doubting. See Round One and chapter 5.

4 Haidt's (2012) research on ideologies offers a generative focus for the strong democratic talk discussed in this section.

5 Confronting power and perceived injustice is a pressing challenge. Advocacy of disruptive refusal to submit to practices judged harming to students and professional integrity is portrayed by several chapter authors.

6 Ball (2013) describes how Foucault sought to challenge his own presumptions, perpetually refusing the calcification of his ideas or himself.

7 See chapter 7.

8 See chapters 3 and 4.

9 Donna's CC skepticism is also instructive. See Karp's (2013–2014) perceptive CC critique.

10 See Beth's chapter 7 concurring views.

11 See Dan's chapter 2 discussion of Pinar's concept of gracious submission.

12 Citing Dr. Johnson's 'corrective' dialogue, Said (2004) urges the creation of non-mystifying commentary crafted as if the person being discussed were "reading you in your presence" (143). On language and culture, it is noteworthy that there is no indigenous Finnish word for accountability (Hargreaves and Shirley, 2009, p. 54).

ABOUT THE BOOK'S COLLABORATIVE TEAM

Tero Autio is Professor of Curriculum Theory at the School of Doctoral Studies, Institute of Education, Tallinn University, Estonia. He is vice-president for the European Association of Curriculum Studies. His scholarship covers curriculum theories in the Americas, Europe, and Asia; theories of subjectivity, culture, and politics; and trans/inter/national education policies.

Aboudou Hamidou Berthé is Fulbright Scholar from Mali, pursuing a Master's of Education in Curriculum and Instruction with Curriculum and Teaching Studies as specialization, at Kent State University. Back home, he was a high school English teacher. He is honored to be on the book team.

Beth A. Bilek-Golias studied undergraduate music, graduate architecture, and doctoral curriculum and instruction. She is a daughter of educators; a musician and artist; registered architect; assistant professor; and Outreach and Service Coordinator for the College of Architecture and Environmental Design at Kent State University. Beth is married and a proud mother of four.

Donna Adair Breault is a Department Head at Missouri State University. She is the author of five books and has articles published in a number of journals including *Teaching and Teacher Education*, *Educational Theory*, and the *International Journal of Leadership in Education*.

Daniel J. Castner teaches kindergarten and is a doctoral candidate at Kent State University. His dissertation study examines public school early childhood educators' ethical commitments as they are enacted with and against their dominant cultures of curriculum. Dan's scholarly interests include curriculum studies, early childhood education, and Alain Badiou's philosophical project.

Christine Fishman is an elementary and graduate school teacher in Ohio. She strives to contribute in the project of remaking education in humane, equitable ways. Chris studies the art of teaching and is eager to further develop aesthetic dimension and wisdom-loving orientation in her pedagogy.

Rosemary Gornik is Assistant Professor at Kent State University in educational administration. She began her elementary teaching career in 1973, and served as principal, assistant superintendent, and superintendent from 1985 to 2013. Rosemary earned her doctorate in Curriculum and Instruction from Kent State University in 2003. Her research interest focuses on teacher leadership.

Jen Griest has 15 years experience in special education, and currently teaches students in grades K–4. Her lead-learning initiative of bringing yoga to schools has formed into a small business doing educational consulting and yoga instruction. Afterlight Fitness and the Yoga 4 Classrooms program will continue helping Jen pursue Ghandi's mantra, "being the change."

Catherine E. Hackney is Associate Dean of Administrative Affairs and Graduate Education in the College of Education, Health, and Human Services at Kent State University. Her scholarship has centered on exploring contemporary notions of leadership informed by feminist theory and democratic living. She is presently writing a book exploring feminist leadership.

James G. Henderson is Professor of Curriculum Studies at Kent State University, where he coordinates the C&I M.Ed. and Ph.D. programs. His scholarship addresses the arts of democratic curriculum leadership. He has served as co-editor of the *Journal of Curriculum and Pedagogy* and as chair of the Professors of Curriculum.

Thomas E. Kelly is Associate Professor of Education at John Carroll University, where he coordinates the Middle Childhood and Adolescent and Young Adult Teacher Licensure programs. His scholarly interests focus primarily on the meaning, promise, and challenge of critical democratic pedagogy.

Kauko Komulainen is University Lecturer in the Department of Teacher Education at the University of Helsinki. He has also been a University Lecturer in Drama Education in the Department of Teacher Education at the University of Oulu. His research interests include curriculum studies, integration and unification, drama education, and Finnish literature.

Wen-Ling Lou is Assistant Professor in the Department of Applied Foreign Languages at Aletheia University, R.O.C. (Taiwan). Her Ph.D. is in Curriculum and Instruction with a major in foreign language education from Kent State

University. Her scholarly interests include curriculum leadership, teacher professional development, and second-language teaching and learning.

Petra Pienkosky Moran is a doctoral student at Kent State University. Petra taught for 11 years in K–12 settings and has been involved with the National Writing Project at Kent State University for 12 years. Writing has always helped her make sense of her educational journey and connect with others.

Wendy Samford has 13 years of administrative and central office experience. She finished her Ph.D. at Kent State University recently and continues her lead-learning journey by reading constantly and teaching at the college level. She is happily married and proudly recognizes the individual accomplishments of her four children.

Jennifer L. Schneider is a doctoral candidate in Curriculum and Instruction at Kent State University. She has an academic and teaching background in art education, art history, and English education. Her scholarly interests dwell at the intersections of art, experience, memory, and place.

Susan School is a kindergarten teacher and has taught in the public school system for 19 years. She has completed the Kent State Teacher Leader Endorsement Program and holds a Master Teacher certification and a Lead Professional Educator license. Susan holds various leadership positions in her school district.

Konni Stagliano is a third-grade teacher and is currently in her twelfth year of teaching. She completed the Kent State Teacher Leader Endorsement Program in 2013 and holds a Master Teacher certification and a Lead Professional Educator license.

Boni Wozolek is a doctoral candidate in the School of Teaching, Learning and Curriculum Studies at Kent State University. Her work focuses on questions of social justice, qualitative research methods, and teaching practice. In addition to her work as a scholar, Boni teaches world languages to high school students.

REFERENCES

Abeles, V., & Congdon, J. (Co-Directors). (2009). *Race to nowhere* [Documentary]. United States: Reel Link Films.

Ahmed, S. (2010). Happy objects. In M. Gregg & G. J. Seigworth (Eds.), *The affect theory reader* (pp. 29–51). Durham, NC: Duke University Press.

Airton, L. (2013). Leave "those kids" alone: On the conflation of school homophobia and suffering queers. *Curriculum Inquiry, 43*(5), 532–562.

Allington, R. L. (2012). Every child, every day. *Educational Leadership, 69*(6), 10–15.

Allington, R. L., & Nowak, R. (2004). "Proven programs" and other unscientific ideas. In D. Lapp, C. C. Block, E. J. Cooper, J. Flood, N. Roser, & J. Tinajero (Eds.), *Teaching all the children: Strategies for developing literacy in an urban setting* (pp. 93–102). New York, NY: Guilford Press.

Anthony, K. (2012). Studio culture and student life. In J. A. Ockman & R. Williamson (Eds.), *Architecture school: Three centuries of educating architects in North America* (pp. 396–401). Cambridge, MA: MIT Press.

Aoki, T. (2005). *Curriculum in a new key: The collected works of Ted T. Aoki* (W. F. Pinar & R. L. Irwin, Eds.). Mahwah, NJ: Lawrence Erlbaum Associates.

Appiah, A. (2006). *Cosmopolitanism: Ethics in a world of strangers.* New York, NY: W. W. Norton & Company.

Apple, M. W. (2001). *Educating the "Right" way: Markets, standards, God, and inequality.* New York, NY: Routledge.

Apple, M. W. (2005). Education, markets, and an audit culture. *Critical Quarterly, 47*(1–2), 11–29.

Apple, M. W. (2006). *Educating the "right" way: Markets, standards, God, and inequality.* (2nd ed.). New York, NY: Routledge.

Apple, M. W. (2009). Controlling the work of teacher. In D. J. Flinders & S. J. Thornton (Eds.), *The curriculum studies reader* (3rd ed., pp. 199–213). New York, NY: Routledge. (Original work published 1986)

Arani, M. (2008). *Japan's national curriculum reforms: Focus on integrated curriculum approach.* Retrieved from http://www.eric.ed.gov/PDFS/ED505389.pdf

Arendt, H. (1958). *Human condition.* Chicago, IL: University of Chicago Press.

Aristotle. (2011). *Aristotle's Nicomachean ethics* (R. C. Bartlett & S. D. Collins, Trans.). Chicago, IL: The University of Chicago Press.

Armstrong, T. (2006). *The best school: How human development research should inform educational practice*. Alexandria, VA: Association for Supervision and Curriculum Development [ASCD].

Arum, R., & Roksa, J. (2011). *Academically adrift*. Chicago, IL: University of Chicago Press.

Association of American Colleges and Universities. (2013). *What is a 21st century liberal education*. Retrieved from http://www.aacu.org/leap/what_is_liberal_education.cfm

Au, K., & Jordan, C. (1981). Teaching reading to Hawaiian children: Finding a culturally appropriate solution. In H. T. Trueba, G. P. Guthrie, & K. Au (Eds.), *Culture and the bilingual classroom: Studies in classroom ethnography* (pp. 139–152). Rowley, MA: Newbury.

Autio, T. (2006). *Subjectivity, curriculum, and society*. New York, NY: Routledge.

Autio, T. (2009a). From Gnosticism to globalization: Rationality, trans-Atlantic curriculum discourse, and the problem of instrumentalism. In B. Baker (Ed.), *New curriculum history* (pp. 69–95). Rotterdam, Netherlands: Sense Publishers.

Autio, T. (2009b). Globalization, curriculum, and new belongings of subjectivity: Beyond the nexus between psychology (curriculum) and the nation-state (Didaktik). In E. Ropo & T. Autio (Eds.), *International conversations on curriculum studies* (pp. 1–20). Rotterdam, Netherlands: Sense Publishers.

Autio, T. (2014). The internationalization of curriculum research. In W. F. Pinar (Ed.), *The international handbook of curriculum research* (2nd ed., pp. 17–31). New York, NY: Routledge.

Ayers, W. (1993). *To teach: The journey of a teacher*. New York, NY: Teachers College Press.

Ayers, W. (2013). Education for a changing world. In D. Breault & R. Breault (Eds.), *Experiencing Dewey: Insights for today's classroom* (2nd ed., pp. 119–122). New York, NY: Routledge.

Ayers, W. C. (2010). The standards fraud. In A. S. Canestrari & B. A. Marlowe (Eds.), *Educational foundations: An anthology of critical readings* (2nd ed., pp. 183–186). Los Angeles, CA: Sage Publications. (Original work published 2000)

Ayers, W. C. (2012, November 6). *An open letter to President Obama from Bill Ayers*. Retrieved from http://www.good.is/posts/an-open-letter-to-president-obama-from-bill-ayers

Ayers, W. C., Quinn, T., & Stovall, D. (Eds.). (2009). *Handbook of social justice in education*. New York, NY: Routledge.

Badiou, A. (2001). *Ethics: An essay on the understanding of evil* (P. Hallward, Trans.). London, UK: Verso.

Badiou, A. (2005a). *Infinite thought: Truth and the return to philosophy* (O. Feltham & J. Clemens, Trans. & Eds.). London: Continuum.

Badiou, A. (2005b). *Being and event* (O. Feltham, Trans.). New York: Continuum. (Original work published 1988)

Badiou, A. (2012). *Philosophy for militants* (B. Borsteels, Trans.). Brooklyn, NY: Verso.

Baker, B. (2009). Borders, belonging, beyond: New curriculum history. In B. Baker (Ed.), *New curriculum history* (pp. ix–xxxv). Rotterdam, Netherlands: Sense Publishers.

Baldacchino, J. (2009). *Education beyond education: Self and the imaginary in Maxine Greene's philosophy*. New York, NY: Peter Lang Publishing.

Ball, S. J. (2013). *Foucault, power and education*. New York, NY: Routledge.

Banchero, S. (2011, December 1). Teacher faction expands to L.A. *The Wall Street Journal*, 258(129), p. A6.

Barber, B. (1984). *Strong democracy: Participatory politics for a new age*. Berkeley, CA: University of California Press.

Barone, T. (2001). *Touching eternity: The enduring outcomes of teaching*. New York, NY: Teachers College Press.

Barth, R. S. (2001). Teacher leader. *Phi Delta Kappan*. 82(6), 443–449.

Barth, R. S. (2008). Foreword. In G. A. Donaldson, *How leaders learn: Cultivating capacities for school improvement* (pp. ix–xi). New York, NY: Teachers College Press.

Bartunek, J. M., & Moch, M. K. (1987). First-order, second-order, and third-order change and organization development interventions: A cognitive approach. *The Journal of Applied Behavioral Science*, 23(4), 483–500.

Behm, N., Rankins-Robertson, S., & Roen, D. (2014, January/February). The case for academics as public intellectuals. *Academe*, 100(1). Retrieved from http:www.aaup.org/article/case-academics-public-intellectuals

Belenky, M. F., Clinchy, B. M., & Goldberger, N. R. (1986). *Women's ways of knowing: The development of self, voice, and mind*. New York, NY: Basic Books.

Bennett, J. (2011). *Vibrant matter: A political ecology of things*. Burham, NC: Duke University Press.

Berliner, D. C., & Biddle, B. J. (1995). *The manufactured crisis: Myths, fraud, and the attack on America's public schools*. Cambridge, MA: Perseus.

Bielskis, A. (2011). Alasdair MacIntyre and the Lithuanian new left. In P. Blackledge & K. Knight (Eds.), *Virtue and politics: Alasdair MacIntyre's revolutionary Aristotelianism* (pp. 290–306). Notre Dame, IN: University of Notre Dame Press.

Bilek-Golias, B. A. (2012). *An ethnographic inquiry into a curriculum culture: Studying how a liberal arts approach and leadership studies may be embodied and enacted in the design studio within an architectural professional education*. (Unpublished doctoral dissertation). Kent State University, Kent, Ohio.

Blackledge, P., & Knight, K. (2011). Introduction: Toward a virtuous politics. In P. Blackledge & K. Knight (Eds.), *Virtue and politics: Alasdair MacIntyre's revolutionary Aristotelianism* (pp. 1–10). Notre Dame, IN: University of Notre Dame Press.

Blankstein, A. M. (2004). *Failure is not an option: Six principles that guide student achievement in high-performing schools*. Thousand Oaks, CA: Corwin Press.

Block, A. A. (2004). *Talmud, curriculum, and the practical: Joseph Schwab and the Rabbis*. New York, NY: Peter Lang.

Bloom, H. (1998). *Shakespeare: The invention of the human*. New York, NY: Riverhead Books.

Blumenfeld-Jones, D. S. (2012). *Curriculum and the aesthetic life: Hermeneutics, body, democracy, and ethics in curriculum theory and practice*. New York, NY: Peter Lang.

Bobbitt, F. (1918). *The curriculum*. New York, NY: Houghton Mifflin.

Bourdieu, P. (1993). *The field of cultural production*. Cambridge, UK: Polity Press.

Bowers, C. A. (1987). *Elements of a post-liberal theory of education*. New York, NY: Teachers College Press.

Boyer, E., & Mitgang, L. (1996). *Building community: A new future for architecture education and practice*. Princeton, NJ: The Carnegie Foundation for the Advancement of Teaching.

Bresler, L. (Ed.). (2004). *Knowing bodies, moving minds: Toward embodied teaching and learning*. Boston, MA: Kluwer Academic Publishers.

Brighouse, H. (2004). *Justice*. Malden, MA: Polity Press.

Brookfield, S. (1990). *The skillful teacher*. San Francisco, CA: Jossey-Bass.

Brown, K. D., & Brown, A. L. (2010). Silenced memories: An examination of the socio-cultural knowledge on race and racial violence in official school curriculum. *Equity & Excellence in Education*, 42(2), 139–154.

Bruner, J. (1986). *Actual minds, possible worlds*. Cambridge, MA: Harvard University Press.

Buckingham, M., & Coffman, C. (1999). *First, break all the rules*. New York, NY: Simon & Schuster.

Burke, T. (1994). *Dewey's new logic: A reply to Russell.* Chicago, IL: The University of Chicago Press.

Burton, N., & Purdy C. (2013, November 19). *Oxford Dictionaries word of the year 2013: Selfie.* Retrieved from http://blog.oxforddictionaries.com/press-releases/oxford-dictionaries-word-of-the-year-2013/

Bush, G. (2007). President Bush congratulates presidential scholars, discusses NCLB reauthorization. Message posted to http://www.whitehouse.gov/news/releases/2007/06/20070625.-7.html

Caine, R. N., & Caine, G. (1997). *Education on the edge of possibility.* Alexandria, VA: ASCD.

Callinicos, A. (2011). Two cheers for enlightenment universalism. Or, why it's hard to be an Aristotelian revolutionary. In P. Blackledge & K. Knight (Eds.), *Virtue and politics: Alasdair MacIntyre's revolutionary Aristotelianism* (pp. 54–78). Notre Dame, IN: University of Notre Dame Press.

Calvino, I. (1988). *Six memos for the next millennium.* Cambridge, MA: Harvard University Press.

Carr, J. F., & Harris, D. E. (2001). *Succeeding with standards.* Alexandria, VA: ASCD.

Chambers, I. (2001). *Culture after humanism: History, culture, subjectivity.* New York, NY: Routledge.

Cherryholmes, C. H. (1988). *Power and criticism: Poststructural investigations in education.* New York, NY: Teachers College Press.

Cherryholmes, C. H. (1999). *Reading pragmatism.* New York, NY: Teachers College Press.

Christodoulou, N. (2010). Embodied curriculum. In C. Kridel (Ed.), *Encyclopedia of curriculum studies* (Vol. 1, pp. 331–332). Los Angeles, CA: Sage Publications.

Cochran-Smith, M., & Lytle, S. L. (2009). *Inquiry as stance: Practitioner research in the next generation.* New York, NY: Teachers College Press.

Coleman, N. (2010). The limits of professional architectural education. *International Journal of Art & Design Education, 29,* 200–212. doi: 10.1111/j.1476-8070.2010.01643.x

Collins, J. (2001). *Good to great.* New York, NY: Harper Collins Publishers.

Cooper, A. J. (1892). *A voice from the South, by a black woman from the South.* Retrieved from http://docsouth.unc.edu/church/cooper/cooper.html

Copple, C., & Bredekamp, S. (2009). (Eds.). *Developmentally appropriate practice in early childhood programs: Serving children from birth through age 8* (3rd ed.). Washington DC: NAEYC.

Countryman, J. (1992). *Writing to learn mathematics.* Portsmouth, NH: Heinemann.

Cremin, L. A. (1961). *The transformation of the school.* New York, NY: Knopf.

Cremin, L. A. (1965). *The genius of American education.* New York, NY: Vintage.

Cuban, L. (2003). *Why is it so hard to get good schools?* New York, NY: Teachers College Press.

Cuff, D. (1991). *Architecture: The story of practice.* Cambridge, MA: MIT Press.

Danielson, C. (2007). *Enhancing professional practice: A framework for teaching* (2nd ed.). Alexandria, VA: ASCD.

Deleuze, G. (1990). *Expressionism in philosophy: Spinoza.* New York, NY: Zone Books.

Deleuze, G. (1994). *Difference and repetition* (P. Patton, Trans.). New York, NY: Columbia University Press.

Deleuze, G., & Guattari, F. (1987). *A thousand plateaus: Capitalism and schizophrenia* (B. Massumi, Trans.). Minneapolis, MN: University of Minnesota Press.

Delpit, L. (1995). *Other people's children: Cultural conflict in the classroom.* New York, NY: The New Press.

den Heyer, K. (2003). Between every "now" and "then": A role for the study of historical agency in history and citizenship education. *Theory & Research in Social Education, 31*(4), 411–434.

den Heyer, K. (2010). (Ed.). *Thinking education through Alain Badiou*. Malden, MA: Wiley-Blackwell.

den Heyer, K. (2014, March). *Unpacking aims talk: An exploration of the educational 'event' in education*. Paper presented at the Canadian Society for the Study of Education, May 25th, 2014, Brock University, Ontario.

Department of the Interior, Bureau of Education (1918). *Cardinal principles of secondary education* (Bulletin No. 35). Washington, DC: Government Printing Office.

Deutsch, D. (2011). *The beginning of infinity: Explanations that transform the world*. New York, NY: Viking.

Dewey, J. (1916). *Democracy and education*. New York, NY: Macmillan.

Dewey, J. (1920). *Reconstruction in philosophy*. New York, NY: Henry Holt and Company.

Dewey, J. (1933). *How we think: A restatement of the relation of reflective thinking to the educative process*. Boston, MA: D.C. Heath & Company. (Original work published 1910)

Dewey, J. (1934). *A common faith*. New Haven, CT: Yale University Press.

Dewey, J. (1938a). *Logic: The theory of inquiry*. New York, NY: Henry Holt & Company.

Dewey, J. (1938b/1998). *Experience and education*. New York, NY: Touchstone.

Dewey, J. (1984). *Individualism old and new*. Amherst, NY: Prometheus Books. (Original work published 1930)

Dewey, J. (1989). *Freedom and culture*. Buffalo, NY: Prometheus. (Original work published 1939)

Dewey, J. (1997). I believe. In L. Menard (Ed.), *Pragmatism: A reader* (pp. 265–271). New York, NY: Vintage Books. (Original work published 1939)

Dewey, J. (2013a). For the creation of a democratic society. In D. Tanner (Ed.), *The sources of a science of education by John Dewey* (pp. 83–84). New York, NY: Liveright. (Original work published 1952)

Dewey, J. (2013b). My pedagogic creed. In D. J. Flinders & S. J. Thornton (Eds.), *The curriculum studies reader* (4th ed., pp. 33–40). New York, NY: Routledge. (Original work published 1897)

Dewey, J., & Bentley, A. F. (1949). *Knowing and the known*. Boston, MA: The Beacon Press.

Dillon, S. (2010, September 28). 4100 Massachusetts students prove small isn't always better. *The New York Times*, 159(55, 177), pp. A1, A18.

Dirkx, J. M. (2008). Care of the self: Mythopoetic dimensions of professional preparation and development. In T. Leonard & P. Willis (Eds.), *Pedagogies of the imagination* (pp. 65–82). New York, NY: Springer Science + Business Media B.V.

Doll, M. A. (2000). *Like letters in running water: A mythopoetics of curriculum*. Mahwah, NJ: Lawrence Erlbaum Associates.

Doll, W. E., Jr. (2006). The culture of method. In W. E. Doll, M. J. Fleener, D. Trueit, & J. St. Julien (Eds.), *Chaos, complexity, curriculum, and culture* (pp. 21–76). New York, NY: Peter Lang.

Doll, W. E., Jr. (2013). The four R's—An alternative to the Tyler rationale. In D. J. Flinders & S. J. Thornton (Eds.), *The curriculum studies reader* (4th ed., pp. 215–222). New York, NY: Routledge.

Donaldson, G. A. (2008). *How leaders learn*. New York, NY: Teachers College Press.

DuBois, W. E. B. (1898). The study of the Negro problems. *The Annals of the American Academy of Political and Social Science*, 11, 1–23.

DuBois, W. E. B. (1903). *The souls of black folk*. Chicago, IL: McClurgand Co.

DuBois, W. E. B. (1926). Criteria of Negro art. *The Crisis*, 32, 290–297.

DuFour, R. (2004). What is a "professional learning community"? *Educational Leadership*, 61(8), 6–11.

Edwards, T. G., & Hensien, S. M. (1999). Changing instructional practice through action research. *Journal of Mathematics Teacher Education*, 2, 187.

Eisner, E. W. (1976). Educational connoisseurship and educational criticism: Their form and functions in education evaluation. *Journal of Aesthetic Education*, 10(3–4), 135–150.

Eisner, E. W. (1994). *The educational imagination: On the design and evaluation of school programs* (3rd ed.). New York, NY: Macmillan.

Eisner, E. W. (1998). Does experience in the arts boost academic achievement? *Journal of Art and Design Education*, 12(1), 51–60.

Eisner, E. W. (2001). What does it mean to say a school is doing well? *Phi Delta Kappa*, 82(2), 367–372.

Eisner, E. W. (2005a). *Reimagining schools*. New York, NY: Routledge.

Eisner, E. W. (2005b, September). Back to whole. *The Whole Child*, 63(1), 14–18. Retrieved from http://www.ascd.org/publications/educational-leadership/sept05/vol63/num01/Back-to-Whole.aspx

Elbow, P. (1986). *Embracing contraries: Explorations in learning and teaching*. New York, NY: Oxford University Press.

Elmore, R., & Skyes, G. (1992). Curriculum policy. In P. Jackson (Ed.), *Handbook of research on curriculum* (pp. 185–215). New York, NY: Macmillian.

Erickson, H. L. (2007). *Concept-based curriculum and instruction for the thinking classroom*. Thousand Oaks, CA: Corwin Press.

Executive, Y. (1996). *The general report book of educational reform*. Retrieved from http://blog.roodo.com/floratien/0b7ed745.pdf

Feiman-Nemser, S. (2001). From preparation to practice: Designing a continuum to strengthen and sustain teaching. *Teachers College Record*, 103(6), 1013–1055.

Fisher, R., Ury, W., & Patton, B. (2011). *Getting to yes: Negotiating agreement without giving in*. New York, NY: Penguin Group.

Fisher, T. (2012). Ethics. In A. Ockman & R. Williamson (Eds.), *Architecture school: Three centuries of educating architects in North America* (pp. 313–315). Cambridge, MA: MIT Press.

Fishman, S. M. (2013). Foundations of Deweyan democracy: Human nature, intelligence, and cooperative inquiry. In D. A. Breault & R. Breault (Eds.). *Experiencing Dewey: Insights for today's classroom* (2nd ed., pp. 151–154). New York, NY: Routledge.

Flew, A. (1984). *A dictionary of philosophy* (2nd ed.). New York, NY: St. Martin's Press.

Foucault, M. (1978). *The history of sexuality: An introduction.* (Vol. 1). New York, NY: Random House Publishers.

Foster, W. (1986). *Paradigms and promises: New approaches to educational administration*. Amherst, NY: Prometheus Books.

Fowler, L. G. (2006). *A curriculum of difficulty: Narrative research in education and the practice of teachings*. New York, NY: Peter Lang.

Freire, P. (1997). *Pedagogy of the oppressed.* (20th anniversary ed.). New York, NY: Routledge.

Freire, P. (2003). *Pedagogy of the oppressed*. New York, NY: Continuum Publishing Group.

Friedman, T. (2014, February 22). How to get a job at Google. *The New York Times*, p. SR11.

Frost, R. (1920). *Mountain interval*. New York, NY: Henry Holt & Company.

Fullan, M. (2001). *Leading in a culture of change*. San Francisco, CA: Jossey-Bass.

Fullan, M. (2007). *The new meaning of educational change.* (4th ed.). New York, NY: Teachers College Press.

Fuller, S. (2002). *Social epistemology* (2nd ed.). Bloomington, IN: Indiana University Press

Gabriel, R., & Allington, R. L. (2012). The met project: The wrong $45 million dollar question. *Educational Leadership*, 70(3), 44–49.

Gadamer, H. G. (1975). *Truth and method* (G. Barden & J. Cumming, Eds. & Trans.). New York, NY: Seabury.

Gardiner, J. R. (1980). *Stone fox.* New York, NY: HarperCollins.

Garrison, J. (1997). *Dewey and eros: Wisdom and desire in the art of teaching.* New York, NY: Teachers College Press.

Gemignani, M. (2011). Between researcher and researched: An introduction to counter-transference in qualitative inquiry. *Qualitative Inquiry,* 17(8), 701–708.

Gershon, W. S. (2012). Teacher leadership: Leading for social justice in teacher education. In C. Boske & S. Diem (Eds.), *Global leadership for social justice: Taking it from the field to practice* (pp. 139–157). Bingley: UK: Emerald Publishing Limited.

Gershon, W. S. (2013). Resonance, affect, and ways of being: Implications of sensual curriculum for educational theory and urban first graders' literacy practices. *The Journal of School and Society,* 1(1). Retrieved from http://jds.wabash.edu/jds/journal/

Giroux, H., & Penna, A. (1983). Social education in the classroom: The dynamics of the hidden curriculum. In H. Giroux, A. Penna, & D. Purpel (Eds.), *The hidden curriculum and moral education* (pp. 100–121). Berkeley, CA: McCutchan Publishing Corporation.

Greiner, R. (1909). The introduction of the word 'empathy' into English. *BRANCH: Britain Representation and Nineteenth Century History.* In Felluga, D. F. (Ed.), *Extension of Romanticism and Victorianism.* Retrieved from http://www.branchcollective.org

Gombrowicz, W. (2005). *Cosmos* (D. Borchardt, Trans.). New Haven, CT: Yale University Press.

Gottfried, H. (1990, November). *The liberal education of architects: A reflection. A liberal education of architects: A symposium.* Lawrence, KS: University of Kansas. Retrieved from the ERIC database (ED350246)

Grant, C. A. (2009). Bottom-up struggle for social justice: Where are the teachers? In W. C. Ayers, T. Quinn, & D. Stovall (Eds.), *Handbook of social justice in education* (pp. 654–656). New York, NY: Routledge.

Green, J. M. (1999). *Deep democracy: Community, diversity, and transformation.* Lanham, MD: Rowman & Littlefield.

Greene, H. (2013, August 25). Teacher: It's not enough to 'just' teach anymore. In Strauss, V. *The Washington Post.* Retrieved from http://www.washingtonpost.com/blogs/answer-sheet/wp/2013/08/25/teacher-its-not-enough-to-just-teach-anymore/

Greene, M. (1988). *The dialectic of freedom.* New York, NY: Teachers College Press.

Greene, M. (1995). *Releasing the imagination: Essays on education, the arts, and social change.* San Francisco, CA: Jossey-Bass.

Greene, M. (1998). Toward beginnings. In W. F. Pinar (Ed.), *The passionate mind of Maxine Greene: 'I am…not yet.'* (pp. 256–257). London, UK: Falmer Press.

Greene, M. (2001). *Variations on the blue guitar: The Lincoln Center Institutes lectures on aesthetic education.* New York, NY: Teachers College Press.

Greene, M. (2010). Wide-awakeness. In C. Kridel (Ed.), *Encyclopedia of curriculum studies* (Vol. 2, pp. 944–945). Los Angeles, CA: Sage Publication.

Gregg, M., & Seigworth, G. J. (Eds.). (2010). An inventory of shimmers. In M. Gregg & G. J. Seigworth (Eds.), *The affect theory reader* (pp. 1–29). Durham, NC: Duke University Press.

Griffiths, M. (2005, September). A feminist perspective on communities of practice. *Socio-cultural Theory in Educational Research and Practice.* Retrieved from http://www.morwennagriffiths.pwp.blueyonder.co.uk/Philosophy.htm

Grimmett, P. P., & Halvorson, M. (2010). From understanding curriculum to creating curriculum: The case for the co-evolution of re-conceptualized design with re-conceptualized curriculum. *Curriculum Inquiry,* 40(2), 241–262.

Grumet, M. (1988). *Bitter milk: Women and teaching.* Amherst, MA: University of Massachusetts Press.

Guggenheim, D. (2010). *Waiting for superman.* [Documentary]. United States: Walden Media.

Gupta, A., & Ferguson, J. (1997). *Culture, power, place: Explorations in critical anthropology.* Durham, NC: Duke University Press.

Hackney, C. E., & Henderson, J. G. (2014). Develop the instructional leadership capacity of staff. In R. M. Ylimaki (Ed.), *The new instructional leadership: ISLLC standard two* (pp. 107–123). New York, NY: Routledge.

Haddock, A., Millar, A., & Pritchard, D. (Eds.) (2010). *Social epistemology.* Oxford, UK: Oxford University Press.

Haggerson, N. (1971). *To dance with joy.* Jericho, NY: Exposition Press.

Haggerson, N. (2010). Mythopoetics. In C. Kridel (Ed.), *Encyclopedia of curriculum studies* (Vol. 2, pp. 594–595). Thousand Oaks, CA: Sage Publications.

Haidt, J. (2006). *The happiness hypothesis: Finding modern truth in ancient wisdom.* New York, NY: Basic Books.

Haidt, J. (2012). *The righteous mind: Why good people are divided by politics and religion.* New York, NY: Pantheon Books.

Hansen, D. T. (2001). *Exploring the moral heart of teaching: Toward a teacher's creed.* New York, NY: Teachers College Press.

Hansen, D. T., Anderson, R., Frank, J., & Nieuwejaar, K. (2008). Reenvisioning the progressive tradition in curriculum. In F. M. Connelly, M. Fang He, & J. Phillion (Eds.), *The Sage handbook of curriculum & instruction* (pp. 440–459). Los Angeles, CA: Sage Publications.

Hargreaves, A. (2000). Four ages of professionalism and professional learning. *Teachers and Teaching, 6*(2), 151–182.

Hargreaves, A. (2001). Emotional geographies of teaching. *Teachers College Record, 103*(6), 1056–1087.

Hargreaves, A., & Shirley, D. (2009). *The fourth way: The inspiring future for educational change.* Thousand Oaks, CA: Corwin.

Harris, P. (2006). Writing boosts learning in science, math and social studies. *Council Chronicle, 16*(1), Retrieved from http://www.ncte.org/magazine/archives/writingboosts

Hawken, P. (2010). *The ecology of commerce: A declaration of sustainability* (2nd ed.). New York, NY: Harper Collins.

Helfenbein, R. J., & Huddleston, G. (2013). Youth, space, cities: Toward the concrete. *Taboo,* 5–10.

Henderson, J. G. (2010a). *The path less taken: Immanent critique in curriculum and pedagogy.* (J. L. Schneider, Ed.). New York, NY: Educator's International Press.

Henderson, J. G. (2010b). Transformative curriculum leadership. In C. Kridel (Ed.), *Encyclopedia of curriculum studies* (Vol. 2, p. 891). Los Angeles, CA: Sage Publications.

Henderson, J. G. (2012). Thanks for your support, modeling and scholarship. In R. Lake (Ed.), *Dear Nel: Opening the circles of care letters to Nel Noddings* (pp. 109–111). New York, NY: Teacher College Press.

Henderson, J. G., & Gornik, R. (2007). *Transformative curriculum leadership* (3rd ed.). Upper Saddle River, NJ: Merrill Prentice Hall.

Henderson, J. G., Hutchison, J., & Newman, C. (1998). Maxine Greene and the current/future democratization of curriculum studies. In W. F. Pinar (Ed.), *The passionate mind of Maxine Greene* (pp. 190–212). London, UK: Falmer Press.

Henderson, J. G., & Kesson, K. R. (1999). *Understanding democratic curriculum leadership.* New York, NY: Teachers College Press.

Henderson, J. G., & Kesson, K. R. (2001). Curriculum work as public intellectual leadership. In K. Sloan & J. Sears (Eds.), *Democratic curriculum theory and practice: Retrieving public spaces* (pp. 1–23). Troy, NY: Educator's International Press.

Henderson, J. G., & Kesson, K. R. (2004). *Curriculum wisdom: Educational decisions in democratic societies*. Upper Saddle River, NJ: Merrill/Prentice Hall.

Henderson, J. G., & Slattery, P. (2008). Evaluating a pragmatic understanding of artistry, development, and leadership. *Journal of Curriculum & Pedagogy*, 5(2), 1–9.

Hendry, P. M. (2011). *Engendering curriculum history*. New York, NY: Routledge.

Henning, K. N. (2012). Criminalizing normal adolescent behavior in communities of color: The role of prosecutors in juvenile justice reform. *Cornell Law Review*, 98, 383–462.

Hill, J. (2005). Criticism by design: Drawing, wearing, weathering. *The Journal of Architecture*, 10(3), 285–293. doi: 10.1080/13602360500162386

Hirsch, E. D. (1988). *Cultural literacy: What every American needs to know*. New York, NY: Random House.

Hlebowitsh, P. (1993). *Radical curriculum theory reconsidered: A historical approach*. New York, NY: Teachers College Press.

Hlebowitsh, P. (2004). *Designing the school curriculum*. Upper Saddle River, NJ: Pearson.

Hlebowitsh, P. (2010). Curriculum development. In C. Kridel (Ed.), *Encyclopedia of curriculum studies* (Vol. 1, pp. 202–205). Los Angeles, CA: Sage Publications.

Honan, W. H. (1995, December 9). Ernest Boyer, National leader in education, dies at 67. *The New York Times*. Retrieved from http://www.aacu.org/leap/what_is_liberal_education.cfm

hooks, b. (1994). *Teaching to transgress: Education as the practice of freedom*. New York, NY: Routledge.

Huang, X. M. (2005). A study of English teacher professional development in elementary school. *Guidance of Elementary Education Bimonthly*, 44(5), 39–42.

Hudak, G. (2010). The miracle of authorship as a moment of truth: A letter to Maxine Greene. In R. Lake (Ed.), *Dear Maxine: Letters from the unfinished conversation with Maxine Greene* (pp. 48–51). New York, NY: Teachers College Press.

Huebner, D. E. (1999). *The lure of the transcendent: Collected essays by Dwayne E. Huebner*. (V. Hillis, Ed.) Mahwah, NJ: Lawrence Erhlbaum Associates.

Jackson, P. W. (1986). *Life in classrooms*. New York, NY: Holt, Rinehart & Winston.

Jacob, M. (2013, July). AIA perspective: Engaging the public in new ways. *ARCHITECT*. Washington, DC: Hanley Wood.

Jardine, D. W. (1998). *To dwell with a boundless heart: Essays in curriculum theory, hermeneutics, and the ecological imagination*. New York, NY: Peter Lang.

Jenkins, K. (2004). Ethical responsibility and the historian: On the possible end of a history "of a certain kind." *History and Theory, Theme Issue 43*, 43–60.

Jenlink, P. M. (2010). Leadership education priorities for a democratic society. *Scholar-Practitioner Quarterly*, 4(4), 306–308.

Johnson, M. (2002). Embodied knowledge. In D. Scott (Ed.), *Curriculum studies: Major themes in education* (Vol. 1, pp. 338–354). New York, NY: Routledge.

Joseph, P. B. (2010). Holistic curriculum. In C. Kridel (Ed.), *Encyclopedia of curriculum studies* (Vol. 1, p. 446–448). Los Angeles, CA: Sage Publications.

Joseph, P. B. (2011). (Ed.). *Cultures of curriculum* (2nd ed.). New York, NY: Routledge.

Jupp, J. C. (2014, February 7). Basic principles of curriculum and instruction (Review of the book *Basic principles of curriculum and instruction*). *Teachers College Record*. Retrieved from http://www.tcrecord.org/Content.asp?ContentID=17409

Kane, J. (1994). Knowing and being. *Holistic Education Review*, 7(2), 2–4.

Karp, S. (2013–14, Winter). The problems with the Common Core. *Rethinking Schools, 28*(2), 10–17.

Kegan, R. (1982). *The evolving self: Problem and process in human development*. Cambridge, MA: Harvard University Press.

Kegan, R. (1994). *In over our heads: The mental demands of modern life*. Cambridge, MA: Harvard University Press.

Kegan, R., & Laskow-Lahey, L. (2009). *Immunity to change: How to overcome it and unlock the potential in yourself and your organization*. Boston, MA: Harvard Business School Publishing.

Kekes, J. (1995). *Moral wisdom and good lives*. Ithaca, NY: Cornell University Press.

Kelly, J. (2014, January/February). Only human. *The University of Chicago Magazine*. Retrieved from http://mag.uchicago.edu/science-medicine/only-human

Kelly, T. (2010). Engaging dissensus: Selected principles and reflections. In Henderson, J. G., *The path less taken: Immanent critique in curriculum and pedagogy* (J. L. Schneider, Ed., pp. 91–96). Troy, NY: Educator's International Press.

Kessler, S., & Swadener, B. B. (1992). (Eds.). *Reconceptualizing the early childhood curriculum: Beginning the dialogue*. New York, NY: Teachers College Press.

Kesson, K. R., & Henderson, J. G. (2010). Reconceptualizing professional development for curriculum leadership: Inspired by John Dewey and informed by Alain Badiou. In K. den Heyer (Ed.), *Thinking education through Alain Badiou* (pp. 62–77). West Sussex, UK: Wiley-Blackwell.

Kincheloe, J. L. (2001). Describing the bricolage: Conceptualizing a new rigor in qualitative research. *Qualitative Inquiry, 7*(6), 676–692.

Kincheloe, J. L. (2005). On to the next level: Continuing the conceptualization of the bricolage. *Qualitative Inquiry, 11*(3), 323–350. doi: 10.1177/1077800405275056

Kincheloe, J., & Pinar, W. (Eds.). (1994). *Curriculum as social psychoanalysis: The significance of place*. Albany, NY: SUNY Press.

Kliebard, H. M. (1970). Reappraisal: The Tyler rationale. *School Review, 78*(2) 259–272.

Kliebard, H. M. (1987). *The struggle for the American curriculum 1893–1958*. New York, NY: Routledge.

Kliebard, H. M. (1992). *Forging the American curriculum: Essays in curriculum history and theory*. New York, NY: Routledge.

Kliebard, H. M. (2013). The rise of scientific curriculum-making and its aftermath. In D. J. Flinders & S. J. Thornton (Eds.), *The curriculum studies reader* (4th ed., pp. 69–78). New York, NY: Routledge.

Klimek, K. J., Ritzehein, E., & Sullivan, K. D. (2008). *Generative leadership: Shaping new futures for today's schools*. Thousand Oaks, CA: Corwin Press.

Korman, G. (2002). *No more dead dogs*. New York, NY: Hyperion Books.

Kouzes, J. M., & Pousner, B. Z. (2007). *The leadership challenge* (4th ed.). San Francisco, CA: Jossey-Bass.

Kreisberg, S. (1992). *Transforming power: Domination, empowerment, and education*. Albany, NY: State University of New York Press.

Kristof, N. (2014, February 16). Smart minds, slim impact. *The New York Times*, p. 11.

Kuklick, H. (2002). Professional status and the moral order. In A. Anderson & J. Valente (Eds.), *Disciplinarity at the fin de siècle* (pp. 126–152). Princeton, NJ: Princeton University Press.

Kumar, A. (2013). *Curriculum as meditative inquiry*. New York, NY: Palgrave Macmillan.

Kumashiro, K. K. (2002). *Troubling education: Queer activism and anti-oppressive pedagogy*. New York, NY: Routledge.

Ladson-Billings, G. (1995). But that's just good teaching! The case for culturally relevant pedagogy. *Theory into Practice*, 34(3), 159–165.

Langer, E. J. (1997). *The power of mindful learning*. Reading, MA: Addison-Wesley.

Lather, P. (2007). *Getting lost: Feminist efforts toward a double(d) science*. Albany, NY: SUNY Press.

Lave, J., & Wenger, E. (1991). *Situated learning: Legitimate peripheral participation*. New York, NY: Cambridge University Press.

Lee, G. C. (1961). *Crusade against ignorance: Thomas Jefferson on education*. New York, NY: Teachers College Press.

Leistyna, P. (2009). Preparing for public life: Education, critical theory and social justice. In W. C. Ayers, T. Quinn, & D. Stovall (Eds.), *Handbook of social justice in education* (pp. 51–58). New York, NY: Routledge.

Lieberman, A., & Friedrich, L. (2007). Teachers, writers, leaders. *Educational Leadership*, 65(1), 42–47.

Lieberman, A., & Friedrich, L. D. (2010). *How teachers become leaders: Learning from practice and research*. New York, NY: Teachers College Press.

Lieberman, A., & Miller, L. (2004). *Teacher leadership*. San Francisco, CA: Jossey-Bass.

Lieberman, A., & Wood, D. R. (2003). *Inside the national writing project: Connecting network learning and classroom teaching*. New York, NY: Teachers College Press.

Lindle, J. C. (2010). William P. Foster's promises for educational leadership: Critical idealism in an applied field. *Scholar-Practioner Quarterly*, 4(4), 167–174.

Liou, H.-C. (2000). *Reflective practice and English teacher education: Theory, research, and implications*. Taipei, Taiwan: Crane.

Liou, H.-C. (2004). A review of recent language teaching literature in Taiwan. *English Teaching and Learning*, 29(1), 1–21.

Little, J. W. (1982). Norms of collegiality and experimentation: Workplace conditions of school success. *American Educational Research Journal*, 19(3), 325–340.

Little, J. W. (1990). The persistence of privacy: Autonomy and initiative in teachers' professional relations. *Teachers College Record*, 91(4), 509–536.

Los Angeles Times. (2012, January 13). Study: Test scores can identity effective teachers. *The Bellingham Herald*, p. 1.

Luxon, N. (2013). *Crisis of authority, politics, trust, and truth-telling in Freud and Foucault*. Cambridge, MA: Cambridge University Press.

Macdonald, E., & Shirley, D. (2009). *The mindful teacher*. New York, NY: Teachers College Press.

Macdonald, J. B. (1995). *Theory as a prayerful act: The collected essays of James B. Macdonald* (B. J. Macdonald, Ed.). New York, NY: Peter Lang.

Macdonald, J. B., & Purpel, D. E. (1987). Curriculum and planning: Visions and metaphors. *Journal of Curriculum and Supervision*, 2(2), 178–192.

MacLeod, J. (2008). *Ain't no makin' it: Aspirations and attainment in a low-income neighborhood* (3rd ed.). Boulder, CO: Westview Press.

Malewski, E. (2010). Introduction: Proliferating curriculum. In E. Malewski (Ed.), *Curriculum studies handbook: The next moment* (pp. 1–39). New York, NY: Routledge.

Malone, H. J. (2013). *Leading educational change: Global issues, challenges and lessons on whole-system reform*. New York, NY: Teachers College Press.

March, J. K., & Peters, K. H. (2008). *Designing instruction: Making best practices work in standards-based classrooms*. Thousand Oaks, CA: Corwin Press.

Marshall, J. D., Sears, J. T., & Schubert, W. H. (2000). *Turning points in curriculum: A contemporary American memoir*. Upper Saddle River, NJ: Prentice Hall.

Marzano, R. J. (2004). *Building background knowledge*. Alexandria, VA: ASCD.

Massumi, B. (2002). *Parables for the virtual: Movement, affect, sensation*. Durham, NC: Duke University Press.

Massumi, B. (2010). The future birth of the affective fact: The political ontology of threat. In M. Gregg & G. J. Seigworth (Eds.), *The affect theory reader* (pp. 52–71), Durham, NC: Duke University Press.

Massumi, B. (2011). *Semblance and event: Activist philosophy and the occurrent arts*. Cambridge, MA: MIT Press.

Maxcy, S. J. (1995). Beyond leadership frameworks. *Educational Administration Quarterly*, 31, 473–483.

May, T. (2005). *Gilles Deleuze: An introduction*. New York, NY: Cambridge University Press.

McClintock, R. (1971). Toward a place for study in a world of instruction. *Teachers College Record*, 73(2), 161–205.

McCracken, N. M., & McCracken, H. T. (2001). Teaching in the time of testing: What have you lost? *The English Journal*, 91(1), 30–35.

McDonough, W., & Braungart, M. (2009). *Cradle to cradle: Remaking the way we make things*. London, UK: Vintage.

McElfresh-Spehler, R., & Slattery, P. (1999). Voices of imagination: The artist as prophet in the process of social change. *International Journal of Leadership in Education*, 2(1), 1–12.

McLeod, D. B. (2008). Research on affect in mathematics education: A reconceptualization. In D. A. Grouws (Ed.), *Handbook of research on mathematics teaching* (pp. 575–596). New York, NY: MacMillan.

Meier, D. (2002). *In schools we trust: Creating communities of learning in an era of testing and standardization*. Boston, MA: Beacon Press.

Meier, D., Sizer, T. R., & Sizer, N. F. (2004). *Keeping school: Letters to families from principals of two small schools*. Boston, MA: Beacon Press.

Mejias, U. A. (2013). *Off the network: Disrupting the digital world*. Minneapolis, MN: University of Minnesota Press.

Melton, G. (2014, January 30). Share this with all the schools, please. Retrieved from http://momastery.com/blog/2014/01/30/share-schools/

Miller, A. (2007). Rhetoric, paideia and the old idea of a liberal education. *Journal of Philosophy of Education*, 41(2), 183–206.

Miller, J. L. (1990). *Creating spaces and finding voices: Teachers collaborating for empowerment*. Albany, NY: State University of New York Press.

Miller, J. L. (2005). *Sounds of silence breaking: Women, autobiography, curriculum*. New York, NY: Peter Lang.

Mills, C. W. (1998). *Blackness visible: Essays on philosophy and race*. New York, NY: Cornell University Press.

Ministry of Education. (2011). *12-Year Compulsory Education*. Retrieved from http://english.moe.gov.tw/ct.asp?xItem=7084&ctNode=784&mp=1

Murcutt, G. (2009, May 9). AIA Honor Awards 2009: Gold Medal—Glenn Murcutt. *Architectural Record*, 105–110.

Muschamp, H. (2002, November 10). For all you observers of the urban extravaganza. *The New York Times*, p. 34.

Nancy, J. (2010). *The truth of democracy* (P. Brault & M. Naas, Trans.). France: Fordham United Press.

National Commission on Excellence in Education. (1983). *A nation at risk: The imperative for education reform*. Washington, DC: U.S. Government Printing Office.

National Council of Architectural Registration Boards. (2009). *2009 Conditions for Accreditation*. Washington, DC: Author.

Nespor, J. (1997). *Tangled up in school: Politics, space, bodies and signs in the educational process*. Mahwah, NJ: Lawrence Erlbaum.

Nichols, J. D. (2011). *Teachers as servant leaders*. Lanham, NY: Rowman & Littlefield Publishers.

No Child Left Behind (NCLB) Act of 2001, Pub. L. No. 107-110 115, Stat. 1425 (2002).

Noddings, N. (1984). *Caring: A feminine approach to ethics and moral education*. Berkeley, CA: University of California Press.

Noddings, N. (2003). *Happiness and education*. Cambridge, UK: Cambridge University Press.

Noddings, N. (2005). What does it mean to educate the WHOLE CHILD? *Educational Leadership*, 63(1), 8–13.

Noddings, N. (2006). Educational leaders as caring teachers. *School Leadership & Management*, 26(4), 339–345.

Noddings, N. (2007). *Philosophy of education* (2nd ed.). Boulder, CO: Westview Press.

Noddings, N. (2009a). The aims of education. In D. J. Flinders & S. J. Thorton (Eds.), *The curriculum studies reader* (3rd ed., pp. 245–438). New York, NY: Routledge.

Noddings, N. (2009b). What can teachers learn from research? *Kappa Delta Pi Record*, 46(1), 23–34.

Noddings, N. (2012). *Peace education: How we come to love and hate war*. Cambridge, UK: Cambridge University Press.

Noddings, N. (2013). *Education and democracy in the 21st century*. New York, NY: Teachers College Press.

North, C. (2012). Owning the 'buts': High school students confront history and heterosexism. In S. Hughes & T. R. Berry (Eds.), *The evolving significance of race* (pp. 49–69). New York, NY: Peter Lang.

Null, J. W. (2008). Curriculum development in historical perspective. In F. M. Connelly (Ed.), *The Sage handbook of curriculum & instruction* (pp. 478–490). Los Angeles, CA: Sage Publications.

Null, W. (2011). *Curriculum: From theory to practice*. Lanham, MD: Rowman & Littlefield Publishers.

Nussbaum, M. (1997). *Cultivating humanity: A classical defense of reform in liberal education*. Boston, MA: Harvard University Press.

Nussbaum, M. C. (2010). *Not for profit: Why democracy needs the humanities*. Princeton, NJ: Princeton University Press.

Nussbaum, M. C. (2011). *Creating capabilities: The human development approach*. Cambridge, MA: The Belknap Press.

Ockman, J. A. (2012). Introduction: The turn of education. In J. A. Ockman & R. Williamson (Eds.), *Architecture school: Three centuries of educating architects in North America* (p. 32). Cambridge, MA: MIT Press.

O'Loughlin, M. (2006). *Embodiment and education: Exploring creatural existence*. Dordrecht, Netherlands: Springer.

O'Neill, C. (1995). *Drama worlds: a framework for process drama*. Portsmouth, NH: Heinemann.

O'Neill, O. (2002). *A question of trust: The BBC Reith lectures 2002*. Cambridge, UK: Cambridge University Press.

Orr, D., McAlister, L. L., Kahl, E., & Earle K. (Eds.). (2006). *Belief, bodies and being: Feminist reflections on embodiment*. Washington, D.C.: Bowman & Littlefield Publishers.

Ortner, S. B. (2006). *Anthropology and social theory: Culture, power and the acting subject*. Durham, NC: Duke University Press.

Pascoe, C. J. (2007). *Dude, you're a fag: Masculinity and sexuality in high school.* Los Angeles, CA: University of California Press.

Palmer, P. J. (2007). *The courage to teach: Exploring the inner landscape of a teacher's life.* San Francisco, CA: Jossey-Bass.

Parker, W. (1996). *Educating the democratic mind.* Albany, New York: SUNY Press.

Patterson, C. J. (2013). Schooling, sexual orientation, law, and policy: Making schools safe for all students. *Theory into Practice*, 52(3), 190–195.

Pear, R. (2012, December 27). Doctors warned on "divided loyalty." *The New York Times*, 162(55, 998), p. A16.

Pearson, P. D., & Hoffman, J. V. (2011). Principles of practice for the teaching of reading. In T. Rasinski (Ed.), *Rebuilding the foundation: Principles of practice for the teaching of reading* (pp. 9–38). Bloomington, IN: Solution Tree Press.

Perez-Gomez, A. (2007). Ethics and poetics in architectural education. In G. Caicco (Ed.), *Architecture, ethics, and the personhood of place* (pp. 119–133). Lebanon, NH: University Press of New England.

Phillips, C. (2007). *Socrates in love: Philosophy for a passionate heart.* New York, NY: W. W. Norton & Co.

Piercy, M. (1973). *To be of use: Poems.* New York, NY: Doubleday.

Pinar, W. F. (Ed.). (1975). *Curriculum theorizing: The reconceptualists.* Berkeley, CA: McCutchan.

Pinar, W. F. (1994). *Autobiography, politics, and sexuality: Essays on curriculum 1972–1992.* New York, NY: Peter Lang.

Pinar, W. F. (Ed.). (1998). *The passionate mind of Maxine Greene: 'I am not yet'.* Bristol, PA: Falmer Press.

Pinar, W. F. (1999a). Foreword. In J. G. Henderson & K. R. Kesson (Eds.), *Understanding democratic curriculum leadership* (pp. vii–xvi). New York, NY: Teachers College Press.

Pinar, W. F. (1999b). Response: Gracious submission. *Educational Researcher*, 28(1), 14–15.

Pinar, W. F. (Ed.). (2000). *Curriculum studies: The reconceptualization.* Troy, NY: Educator's International Press.

Pinar, W. F. (2001). *The gender of racial politics and violence in America: Lynching, prison rape, and the crisis of masculinity.* New York, NY: Peter Lang.

Pinar, W. F. (2004). *What is curriculum theory?* Mahwah, NJ: Lawrence Erlbaum.

Pinar, W. F. (2006). *The synoptic text today and other essays: Curriculum development after the reconceptualization.* New York, NY: Peter Lang.

Pinar, W. F. (2007). *Intellectual advancement through disciplinarity: Verticality and horizontality in curriculum studies.* Rotterdam, Netherlands: Sense Publishers.

Pinar, W. F. (2009). *The worldliness of a cosmopolitan education.* New York, NY: Routledge.

Pinar, W. F. (2011). *The character of curriculum studies: Bildung, currere, and the recurring question of the subject.* New York, NY: Palgrave Macmillan.

Pinar, W. F. (2012). *What is curriculum theory* (2nd ed.). New York, NY: Routledge.

Pinar, W. F. (2013a). Plagiarism and the Tyler rationale. *Journal of the American Association for the Advancement of Curriculum Studies*, 9(1), 1–13.

Pinar, W. F. (2013b). *Curriculum studies in the United States: Present circumstances, intellectual histories.* New York, NY: Palgrave Macmillan.

Pinar, W. F., & Grumet, M. R. (1976). *Toward a poor curriculum.* Dubuque, IA: Kendall-Hunt.

Pinar, W. F., & Irwin, R. L. (Eds.). (2004). *Curriculum in a new key: The collected works of Ted T. Aoki.* Mahwah, NJ: Lawrence Erlbaum.

Pinar, W. F., Reynolds, W. M., Slattery, P., & Taubman, P. M. (1995). *Understanding curriculum: An introduction to the study of historical and contemporary curriculum discourses.* New York, NY: Peter Lang.

Pink, D. H. (2009). *Drive: The surprising truth about what motivates us*. New York, NY: Penguin Group.

Pirsig, R. M. (1974). *Zen and the art of motorcycle maintenance*. New York, NY: Bantam Books.

Potts, M. W. (2002, Feb. 1). Arun Gandhi shares the Mahatma's message. *West-India, 27*(13), 34.

Ralston, S. J. (2013). Taking experiential givenism seriously. *SAGE Open, 3*, 1–9. doi: 10.1177/2158244013497031

Rancière, J. (2010). *Dissensus: On politics and aesthetics* (S. Corcoran, Ed. & Trans.). London, UK: Continuum.

Rathvon, N. (2008). *Effective school interventions: Evidence-based strategies for improving student outcomes* (2nd ed.). New York, NY: The Guilford Press.

Reeves, D. B. (2010). *Transforming professional development into student results*. Alexandria, VA: ASCD.

Rich, M. (2013, May 1). NewSchools fund attracts more capital. *The New York Times, 162*(56, 123), p. A14.

Rietzug, U. C. (2010). Educational leaders or compliant bureaucrats? *Scholar-Practioner Quarterly, 4*(4), 319–322.

Robinson, Sir K. (2011). *Changing educational paradigms* [Video file]. Retrieved from http://sirkenrobinson.com/skr/

Romano, T. (2000). *Blending genre, altering style: Writing multigenre papers*. Portsmouth, NH: Boynton/Cook.

Rosenblatt, L. M. (1994). *The reader, the text, the poem: The transactional theory of the literary work*. Carbondale, IL: Southern Illinois University.

Rutledge, A. (2012, November 8). The case for general education. *DesignIntelligence*. Retrieved from http://www.di.net/articles/the-case-for-general-education/

Ryan, F. X. (2011). *Seeing together: Mind, matter and the experimental outlook of John Dewey and Arthur F. Bentley*. Great Barrington, MA: The American Institute for Economic Research.

Sabini, M. (2011). Wittgenstein's ladder: The non-operational value of history in architecture. *Journal of Architectural Education, 64*(2), 46–58.

Sahlberg, P. (2011). *Finnish lessons: What can the world learn from educational change in Finland?* New York, NY: Teachers College Press.

Said, E. W. (2012). *Humanism and democratic criticism*. New York, NY: Columbia University Press.

Saltman, K. (2012). The rise of venture philanthropy and ongoing neoliberal assault on public education. In W. H. Watkins (Ed.), *The assault on public education: Confronting the politics of corporate school reform* (pp. 55–62). New York, NY: Teachers College Press.

Samaras, A. P. (2011). *Self-study teacher research: Improving your practice through collaborative inquiry*. Thousand Oaks, CA: Sage.

Samaras, A. P., & Freese, A. R. (2006). *Self-study of teaching practices*. New York, NY: Peter Lang Publishing.

Schaar, J. J. (1979). Melville's Benito Cereno. *Theory and Society, 7*, 417–452.

Schleiermacher, F. (1983/1826). *Pädagogische Schriften 1*. Munich, Germany: Klett-Cotta.

Schön, D. (1983). *The reflective practitioner: How professionals think in action*. New York, NY: Basic Books.

Schön, D. (1985). *The design studio*. London, UK: RIBA.

Schön, D. (1990). *Educating the reflective practitioner: Toward a new design for teaching and learning in the professions*. San Francisco, CA: Jossey-Bass.

Schoorman, D., & Bogotch, I. (2010). Moving beyond 'diversity' to 'social justice': The challenge to re-conceptualizing multicultural education. *Intercultural Education*, 21(1), 79–85.

Schubert, W. H. (1986). *Curriculum: Perspective, paradigm, and possibility*. New York, NY: Macmillan.

Schwab, J. J. (1971). The practical: Arts of the eclectic. *School Review*, 79, 493–542.

Schwab, J. J. (1973). The practical 3: Translation into curriculum. *School Review*, 81, 501–522.

Schwab, J. J. (1978). *Science, curriculum, and liberal education*. Chicago, IL: The University of Chicago Press.

Schwab, J. J. (1983). The practical 4: Something for curriculum professors to do. *Curriculum Inquiry*, 13, 239–266.

Schwab, J. J. (2004). The practical: A language for curriculum. In D. J. Flinders & S. J. Thornton (Eds.), *The curriculum studies reader* (2nd ed., pp. 103–117). New York, NY: Routledge. (Original work published 1969)

Schwandt, T. A. (2002). Understandings of evaluation practice. In J. L. Kincheloe & S. R. Steinberg (Eds.), *Evaluation practice reconsidered*. New York, NY: Peter Lang.

Schwartz, B., & Sharpe, K. (2010). *Practical wisdom: The right way to do the right thing*. New York, NY: Riverhead Books.

Sedgwick, E. K. (2003). *Touching feeling: Affect, pedagogy, performance*. Durham, NC: Duke University Press.

Seigfried, C. H. (1996). *Pragmatism and feminism: Reweaving the social fabric*. Chicago, IL: University of Chicago Press.

Seo, M., & Creed, W. E. (2002). Institutional contradictions, praxis, and institutional change: A dialectical perspective. *The Academy of Management Review*, 27(2), 222–247.

Sergiovanni, T. J. (1992). *Moral leadership: Getting to the heart of school improvement*. San Francisco, CA: Jossey-Bass.

Sergiovanni, T. J. (2004). *The principalship: A reflective practice perspective* (5th ed.). Boston, MA: Allyn & Bacon.

Shener, Ö. (2012). *East-West Sufi sayings of love and wisdom*. CreateSpace Publishing.

Sidorkin, A. M. (1999). *Beyond discourse: Education, the self, and dialogue*. Albany, NY: State University of New York Press.

Sirotnik, K. A. (2002). Promoting responsible accountability in schools and education. *Phi Delta Kappan*, 83(9), 662–673.

Slattery, P. (1995). *Curriculum development in the postmodern era*. New York, NY: Garland Publishing.

Sleeter, C. (2011). Introduction. In C. Cleeter & C. Cornbleth (Eds.), *Teaching with vision: Culturally responsive teaching standards-based classrooms* (pp. 1–10). New York, NY: Teachers College Press.

Smith, D. G. (2014). Wisdom responses to globalization. In W. F. Pinar (Ed.), *International handbook of curriculum research* (2nd ed., pp. 45–59). New York, NY: Routledge.

Smith, F. (1988). *Joining the literacy club: Further essays into education*. Portsmouth, NH: Heinemann.

Snellman, J. V. (1982). About Academic Studies. In *Snellman, J. V: Works 1* (pp. 161–189). Jyväskylä, Finland: Gummerus Publishers. (Original work published 1840)

Spillane, J. P. (2006). *Distributed leadership*. San Francisco, CA: Jossey-Bass.

Spillane, J. P., & Diamond, J. B. (2007). *Distributed leadership in practice*. New York, NY: Teachers College Press.

Spinoza, B. (1959). *Ethics: On the correction of understanding* (A. Boyle, Trans.). London, UK: Everyman's Library.

Springgay, S., & Freedman, D. (Eds.). (2007). *Curriculum and the culture of body*. New York, NY: Peter Lang.

Springgay, S., & Freedman, D. (2010). Sleeping with cake and other touchable encounters: Performing a bodied curriculum. In E. Malewski (Ed.), *Curriculum studies handbook: The next movement* (pp. 228–239). New York, NY: Routledge.

Stanley, W. B. (1992). *Curriculum for utopia: Social reconstructionism and critical pedagogy in the postmodern era*. Albany, NY: State University of New York Press.

Stokes, L. Hirabayashi, J., Murray, A., & Senauke, L. (2011). *The enduring quality and value of the National Writing Project's teacher development institutes: Teachers' assessments of NWP contributions to their classroom practice and development as leaders*. Retrieved from: http://www.inverness-research.org/reports/2011-11-Rpt-NWP-NWP-Survey-TeacherInst-Final.pdf

Stuhr, J. J. (1997). *Genealogical pragmatism: Philosophy, experience, and community*. Albany, NY: State University of New York Press.

Tafuri, M. (1976). *Architecture and utopia: Design and capitalist development* (B. L. L. Penta, Trans.). Cambridge MA: The MIT Press.

Tanner, D., & Tanner, L. (2007). *Curriculum development: Theory into practice* (4th ed.). Upper Saddle River, NJ: Merrill/Prentice Hall.

Tanzer, K., & Longoria, R. (Eds.). (2007). *The green braid: Towards an architecture of ecology, economy, and equity*. New York, NY: Routledge.

Tatum, A. (2007). Building the textual lineages of African American male adolescents. In K. Beers, R. Probst, & L. Rief (Eds.), *Adolescent literacy: Turning promise into practice* (pp. 81–85). Portsmouth, NH: Heinemann.

Taubman, P. M. (2009). *Teaching by numbers, deconstructing the discourse of standards and accountability in education*. New York, NY: Routledge.

Torres, C. A. (2010). Struggling for the soul of the nation: Educational policy, democratic leadership, and radical democracy in neoliberal times. *Scholar-Practioner Quarterly*, 4(4), 338–341.

Tsai, P. G. (2004). The implementation dilemma and the way of solution for grade 1–9 English curriculums. In Ministry of Education (Ed.), *Taiwan 1–9 curriculum teaching innovation: A compilation of experience outcome in the field of English language advance training program* (pp. 31–34). Taiwan: Ministry of Education Press.

Tsing, A. L. (2005). *Friction: An ethnography on global connection*. Princeton, NJ: Princeton University Press.

Tuana, N. (1992). *Woman and the history of philosophy*. St. Paul: MN: Paragon House.

Tyler, R. W. (1949). *Basic principles of curriculum and instruction*. Chicago, IL: University of Chicago Press.

van Manen, M. (1980, April). *Pedagogical theorizing*. Paper presented at the annual conference of the American Educational Research Association, Boston, MA.

Varenne, H., & McDermott, R. (1998). *Successful failure: The school America builds*. Boulder, CO: Westview.

Vedder, R. (2011, January 20). Academically adrift: A must-read. *The Chronicle of Higher Education*. Retrieved from http://chronicle.com/blogs/innovations/academically-adrift-a-must-read/28423

Vischer, R., Mallgrave, H. F., & Ikonomou, E. (1994). *Empathy, form, and space: Problems in German aesthetics, 1873–1893*. Santa Monica, CA: Getty Center for the History of Art and the Humanities.

Vollmer, J. (2010). *Schools cannot do it alone: Building public support for America's public schools*. Fairfield, IA: Enlightenment Press.

Waite, D. (2010). Preparing educational leaders to serve a democratic society. *Scholar-Practioner Quarterly*, 4(4), 367–370.

Walker, D. F. (1971, November). The process of curriculum development: A naturalistic model. *School Review*, 80, 51–65.

Walker, D. F. (2003). *Fundamentals of curriculum: Passion and professionalism* (2nd ed.). Mahwah, NJ: Lawrence Erlbaum Associates.

Walker, D. F., & Soltis, J. F. (2009). *Curriculum and aims* (5th ed.). New York, NY: Teachers College Press.

Wang, H. (2014). A nonviolent perspective on internationalizing curriculum studies. In W. F. Pinar (Ed.), *International handbook of curriculum research* (pp. 67–76). New York, NY: Routledge.

Watkins, W. H. (2001). *The white architects of black education: Ideology and power in America 1865–1954*. New York, NY: Teachers College Press.

Watkins, W. H. (2012a). The new social order: An educator looks at economics, politics and race. In W. H. Watkins (Ed.), *The assault on public education: Confronting the politics of corporate school reform* (pp. 7–32). New York, NY: Teachers College Press.

Watkins, W. H. (2012b). Re-imagining public education. In W. H. Watkins (Ed.), *The assault on public education: Confronting the politics of corporate school reform* (pp. 189–192). New York, NY: Teachers College Press.

Wayne, A. (2009). High-stakes testing and curriculum control: A qualitative metasynthesis. In D. J. Flinders & S. J. Thornton (Eds.), *The curriculum studies reader* (3rd ed., pp. 286–302). New York, NY: Routledge.

Weiss, G. (1999). *Body image: Embodiment and intercorporeality*. New York, NY: Routledge.

Weiss, L., & Fine, M. (1992). *Beyond silenced voices: Class, race, and gender in United States schools*. Albany, NY: State University of New York Press.

Westbrook, R. (1993). *John Dewey and American democracy*. Ithaca, NY: Cornell University Press.

Westbury, I. (2000). Teaching as a reflective practice: What might Didaktik teach curriculum? In I. Westbury, S. Hopmann, & K. Riquarts (Eds.), *Teaching as a reflective practice: The German Didaktik tradition* (pp. 15–39). New York, NY: Routledge.

Westbury, I., Hopmann, S., & Riquarts, K. (Eds.). (2000). *Teaching as a reflective practice: The German didaktik tradition*. Mahwah, NJ: Lawrence Erlbaum Associates.

Wheatley, M. J. (1994). *Leadership and the new science*. San Francisco, CA: Berrett-Koehler.

Wheatley, M. J., & Kellner-Rogers, M. (1996). *A simpler way*. San Francisco, CA: Berrett-Koehler.

Whitcomb, D. (2011). Introduction. In A. Goldman & D. Whitcomb (Eds.), *Social epistemology: Essential readings* (pp. 1–11). Oxford, UK: Oxford University Press.

Whitney, A. (2008). Teacher transformation in the National Writing Project. *Research in the Teaching of English*, 43(2), 144–187.

Wiggins, G., & McTighe, J. (2005). *Understanding by design* (2nd ed.). Alexandria, VA: ASCD.

Williamson, B. (2013). *The future of the curriculum: School knowledge in the digital age*. Cambridge, MA: The MIT Press.

Willis, P. (1981). *Learning to labor: How working class kids get working class jobs*. New York, NY: Columbia University Press.

Winfield, A. G. (2007). *Eugenics and education in America: Institutionalized racism and the implication of history, ideology, and memory*. New York, NY: Peter Lang.

Woodson, C. G. (1933). *The mis-education of the Negro*. N.P.

Wraga, W. G. (1999). Extracting sun-beams out of cucumbers: The retreat from practice in reconceptualized curriculum studies. *Educational Researcher*, 28(1), 4–13.

Ylimaki, R. M. (2011). *Critical curriculum leadership: A framework for progressive education.* New York, NY: Routledge.

Zafon, C. R. (2001). *Shadow of the wind.* New York, NY: Penguin Books.

Zeichner, K. M. (1995). Reflections of a teacher educator working for social change. In F. Korthagen & T. Russell (Eds.), *Teachers who teach teachers* (pp. 11–24). London, UK: Falmer Press.

Zemelman, S., Daniels, H., & Hyde, A. (2005). *Best practice: Today's standards for teaching and learning in American schools* (3rd ed.). Portsmouth, NH: Heinemann.

Zhao, Y. (2009). *Catching up or leading the way: American education in the age of globalization.* Alexandria, VA: ASCD.

Zull, J. E. (2002). *The art of changing the brain: Enriching the practice of teaching by exploring the biology of learning.* Sterling, VA: Stylus Publishing.

INDEX

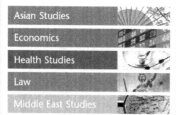